Believable

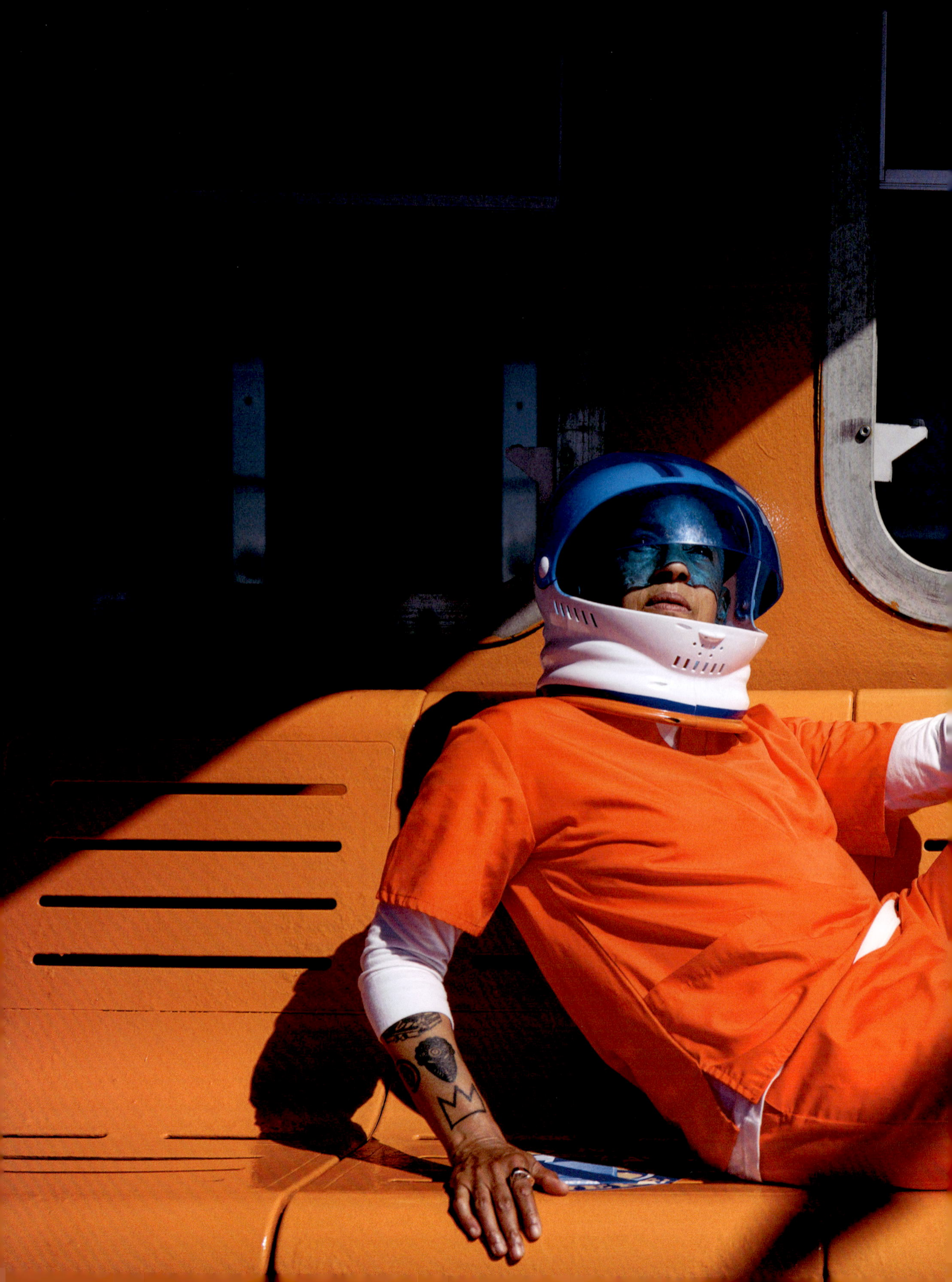

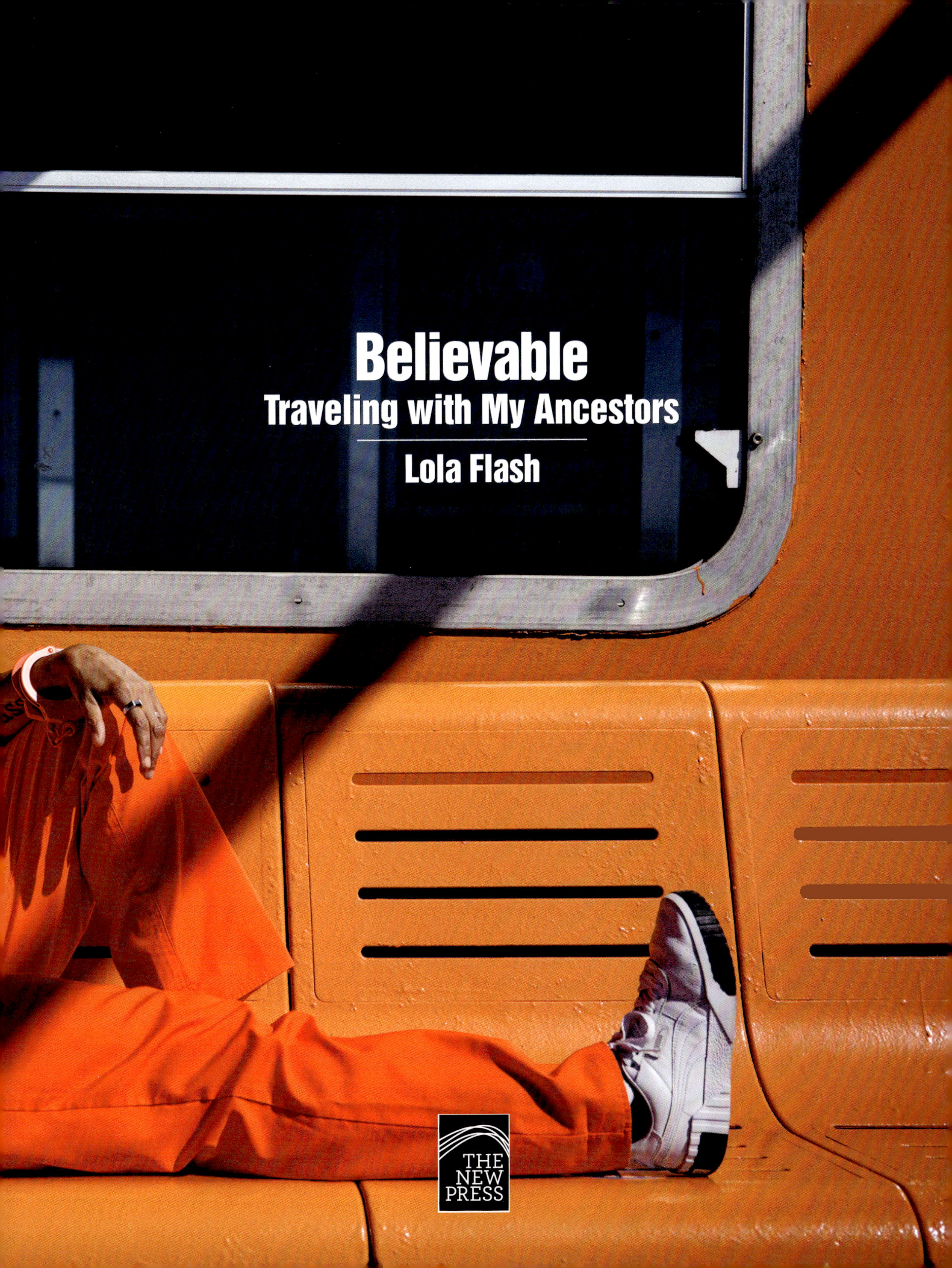

Believable

Traveling with My Ancestors

Lola Flash

THE NEW PRESS

Published in the United States by The New Press, New York, 2023
Distributed by Two Rivers Distribution

ISBN 978-1-62097-753-8 (pb)
ISBN 978-1-62097-769-6 (ebook)
CIP data is available

The New Press publishes books that promote and enrich public discussion and understanding of the issues vital to our democracy and to a more equitable world. These books are made possible by the enthusiasm of our readers; the support of a committed group of donors, large and small; the collaboration of our many partners in the independent media and the not-for-profit sector; booksellers, who often hand-sell New Press books; librarians; and above all by our authors.

www.thenewpress.com

Book design and composition © 2023 by Emerson, Wajdowicz Studios (EWS)
This book was set in FF Meta, Franklin Gothic, Helvetica Inserat, Helvetica Neue, News Gothic, and Zapf Dingbats

Printed in the United States of America

10 9 8 7 6 5 4 3 2 1

Preface

JON STRYKER

The project was born out of conversations that I had with Jurek Wajdowicz. He is an accomplished art photographer and frequent collaborator of mine, and I am a lover of and collector of photography. I owe a great debt to Jurek and his design partner, Lisa LaRochelle, in bringing this book series to life.

Both Jurek and I have been extremely active in social justice causes—I as an activist and philanthropist and he as a creative collaborator with some of the household names in social change. Together we set out with an ambitious goal to explore and illuminate the most intimate and personal dimensions of self, still too often treated as taboo: sexual orientation and gender identity and expression. These books continue to reveal the amazing multiplicity in these core aspects of our being, played out against a vast array of distinct and varied cultures and customs from around the world.

Photography is a powerful medium for communication that can transform our understanding and awareness of the world we live in. We believe the photographs in this series will forever alter our perceptions of the arbitrary boundaries that we draw between others and ourselves and, at the same time, delight us with the broad spectrum of possibility for how we live our lives and love one another.

We are honored to have Lola Flash as a collaborator in *Believable*. Flash, and the other photographers in this ongoing series, are more than craftspeople: they are communicators, translators, and facilitators of the kind of exchange that we hope will eventually allow all the world's people to live in greater harmony. ■

Jon Stryker, philanthropist, architect, and photography devotee, is the founder and board president of the Arcus Foundation, a global foundation promoting respect for diversity among peoples and in nature.

Eyes That Commit II—Doing Their Work[1]

RENÉE MUSSAI

What happens when a visionary, veteran Black lesbian photographer dons an orange prison jumpsuit and astronaut's helmet, and turns their camera on themselves? And they then evocatively title the ensuant artwork(s) in reference to a mythical planetary constellation, an astronomic alignment, or conjunction, of celestial bodies in transit, passing, eclipsing, gravitating? What might we make of this subversive, conjoining gesture—both sartorial and lingual—and all its imbued symbolisms: oxygen, pressure, protection; compression and oppression, liberation and flight; ventilation, vigilation, visitation; voyage, escape, travel . . . color, camouflage, and hypervisibility—*doing time,* figuratively and symbolically?

Summer 2019, pre-pandemic: thinking deeply about embodiment, and the incarceration of Black and Brown people of color in the U.S. penal system, Lola Flash's "afronaut" visual avatar was born, a moment that marked a turning point in their long artistic career and one that spoke palpably to a pervasive social atmosphere suffused with racial injustices, a "total climate"[2] permeated by toxic particles of anti-Black and anti-gay sentiments that make it difficult—and at times fatally impossible—to breathe. And so, at the intersection of fact and fiction, putting *themselves* at the very center of their—our—living and breathing, they created a new photographic narrative imbued with futurity, with a beautiful, potent, diasporic feasibility. *Syzygy* opened a door—a portal—to a new kind of artistic liberation for Flash: an experiential, existential space for inscription—a space of refuge and retreat—of sustained *photographic response-ability*[3] that became, simultaneously, a practice of visual self-care. It conjured a space in which to *imagine otherwise*, for the series continued as an evolving portrait-of-the-self *in motion* throughout the pandemic, when there was little opportunity to make portraits of others. It became a space in which to travel, both literally and metaphorically: here, they practice a kind of performative (queer) Afro-nautic, Afro-futurist, Afro-autographic camouflage of acute in/visibility, a dance of insistence and resistance, of transference and transcendence. To photograph oneself in an orange jumpsuit makes it difficult not to be seen, to be recognized, to be remembered. Like the space helmet, it is a symbol of transition and movement, worn during voyages or while being *transported* or *imprisoned*. One is about freedom, fugitivity, and flight; the other about captivity, capture, and confinement. Between them, an equilibrium is created: a space where all the "isms" of more than forty years of practicing art as activism collide, converge, and commune.

These, and all their bodies of work, serve as testaments to a lifelong commitment working at the forefront—or the frontlines—of genderqueer visual politics, documenting, commemorating, and preserving the legacies of women, LGBTQIA+ constituencies, and communities of color. They not only challenge a myriad of interconnected and intersectional biases and isms—from racism to ageism to classism, homo- and transphobic discriminations—but also incessantly, unapologetically, courageously, collaboratively (re)claim and mine photographic spaces as crucial sites for visual pleasure, as sites for inscription, for representation, for visibility, for difference—racial, sexual, cultural—and for social justice and visual equity. Theirs is a sensorial, sensual, scopic, socio-political aesthetic space where art, life, and advocacy are intimately and profoundly connected—and felt, often forcing our senses into action through violently visual—radical—insurgent imagery of racially ambiguous and gender non-conforming figures, who reside both leisurely and sincerely inside apocalyptic pools that denote liquid states of being: bodies entwined in sexual embrace or defiantly locked in moments of protest, their skin rendered in other-worldly, *cross-colored*, deeply saturated hues. At other times, evocatively lit and photographically elevated (diasporic) figures appear beautifully, self-possessively, *believably* centered—past, present, and future ancestors, perhaps?—visualized, immortalized, and powerfully mediated through Flash's empathetic lens, wherein enigmatic abstractions and assertive realisms do not compete, but complement each other: a mode of "queering" the visual that is at once transgressive and sublime, inclusive and exclusive.

Queerness, in Flash's multiverse, is bathed in color, imbued with love, an embrace: infinitely generous and open. It is a queerness that is not restricted to gender representations or sexual identities, but stretches voluptuously across ages, races, places. These are not "just" images[4] but *just* visions, visibilities, and visualities that are equitable and radically/beautifully different. These just images foreground the political, social, cultural, and aesthetic priorities of women, non-binary figures, and trans people of color—*theirstories, ourstories, herstories*: bold visions that translate as amplification, activation, animation.

One of the things that always strikes me when I think of Flash's work—or witness them *at work*—is the immense generosity and sensitivity in how they allow their participants, muses, and models space to just be, to breathe, to perform, to become, and to reform. They never enforce their vision or their project(s) on others; they simply invite others to step into their world, where they offer space for representation, space for visibility, space for manifestation, space for evocation, space to collectively engage in a mission of continuous world-building, through socially engaged photographic portraitures infused with soothing, restorative, transmural elixirs of visual justice, visual equity, and visual activism. And what is thus made visible is a fluidity, a liquidity—yet infinitely solid, in its corporeal and socio-political *image* matter—a communal consciousness, cosmogenic collectivity and courageous chorality.

And yet visibility is also dangerous. Flash's work becomes even more urgent when we pause for a moment and think transculturally, transracially, and transexually, and consider that while we may enjoy our freedoms here/now/today, others elsewhere are facing situations unfathomable to many of us . . . Colonial anti-homosexuality legislations are not only upheld but updated *and* sharpened by contemporary politicians on the African continent, for example, while myriad legal, social, cultural, economic, and ontological challenges posed by Eurocentric, neoliberal architectures of heteronormativity and patriarch-isms continue to put marginalized communities at risk and must be exposed. Echoing *Black lesbian warrior poet* Audre Lorde who recognized visibility as both our deepest vulnerability and our greatest strength, Flash's visual activism—their ongoing labor—as a self-proclaimed *Black lesbian photographer* continuously reminds us that we must keep *doing the work*, that "our silences will not protect us."[5]

As I reflect, I am reminded of something the late Toni Morrison once expressed, a life-affirming proclamation that writer Akwaeke Emezi credits as having changed their life. They write, in a letter to Morrison: "'I stood at the border, stood at the edge, and claimed it as central,' you said, your voice weighted with intent. 'Claimed it as central, and let the rest of the world move over to where I was.'"[6] It seems poignant to evoke this sentiment here, because Flash has always—resolutely, restlessly, rigorously—occupied their own center: claimed it as central not only for themselves, but for all of us, imbuing its edges and its core *with intent*, for those of us who have for too long been positioned outside of societal "mainstream" narratives or spaces—visual and otherwise—for all of us relegated for too long to designated peripheries, circumscribed temporalities, restricted spatialities, for all of us whose bodies are deemed queer, deviant, different, colored, othered. There is a beautiful profusion of disavowal that continually unfolds in Flash's visual spheres: a disavowal that refuses to shift bodies—their body and the bodies of those they portray—into exogenously defined centers of (hetero)normativity occupied by cultural tyrants, privileged persecutors, or institutional gatekeepers; a disavowal that refuses boundaries and limitations, binaries, and dichotomies of any kind. Their magical center is a gathering, a spell: an amorous acknowledgment, activation, and amplification of presences.

Another thing that strikes me, as I sit here writing these words, quietly reflecting on forty years of praxis and more than twenty years of intimate friendship (and collaboration), is the way Flash's oeuvre is characterized by both this profound sense of refusal—a refusal of all that binds, precludes, prescribes—and a delineating diffusion *and* infusion of an equally strong sense of liberation and realization: a manifestation that propels us forward, into a future—into futures—that holds space for Black and Brown and queer people to breathe, be, and become.

At the center of their practice—a praxis of visual care and visual commitment—are continual acts of envisioning and engendering: an *imag(in)ing* of new futures, birthing new futurities, new possibilities, new potentialities, and new visualities. Yet these are polyvalent, transmuting visions that are always unequivocally grounded in the present—in multiple overlapping and converging presents—while simultaneously acknowledging, honoring, our many concurrent, still breathing, still reverberating, collective and individual pasts. Flash's work is an ongoing visio-conversation conducted in many tenses and in many tongues, all of which are summoned with great attentiveness, and courage.

Over the years, they have forged a visual vernacular that entails a myriad of urgent—critical, crucial, compelling—portraitures, traversing photographic genres in a tentacular modality that is always profoundly moving—affecting and affectual, effectual and effecting—and never static, in neither form nor content: from their explosive early cross-color documentary work to their often larger-than-life honorific portrait series—from *salt* to *surmise* to *[sur]passing* and *LEGENDS*, to name but a few—culminating in the most recent neo-conceptual, auto-performative, Afro-futurist *syzygy*, where they channel themselves as both image-maker and image-traveler.

These are lifelong commitments to being and becoming, prevailing and proclaiming, preserving and propelling: acute visual commitments scripted in an affirmative grammar of generosity and potentiality . . . vital photographic odes to the decolonial/remedial/transvisual "for" that births and sustains life, art, and love, and breath—personal, political, pleasurable.

Recognizable. Breathable. Believable.

Repeat.

[thank you, Lola, for your being and breathing and persevering and believing] ■

---

1 "Eyes That Commit" was first used as a title for my essay in *Lola Flash: 1986 to Present*, an exhibition catalogue published by Pen & Brush (New York, 2018). The expression "eyes that commit" is borrowed from an untitled poem in Nayyirah Waheed's self-published collection *salt*. (2013), p. 98. The subtitle "Doing Their Work" references Audre Lorde: "Because I am woman, because I am Black, because I am lesbian, because I am myself – a Black woman warrior poet doing my work – come to ask you, are you doing yours?" In: Audre Lorde, "The Transformation of Silence into Language and Action," in *Your Silence Will Not Protect You* (London: Silver Press, 2017), p. 3.

2 Christina Sharpe, *In the Wake: On Blackness and Being* (Durham, NC: Duke University Press, 2016), p. 21.

3 The term "response-ability" was coined by Toni Morrison.

4 Inspired by Roland Barthes's notion of "not just an image but a **just** image."

5 Audre Lorde, "The Transformation of Silence into Language and Action," in *Your Silence Will Not Protect You* (London: Silver Press, 2017), pp. 2–3.

6 Akwaeke Emezi, *Dear Senthuran: A Black Spirit Memoir* (London: Faber & Faber Ltd, 2021), p. 77.

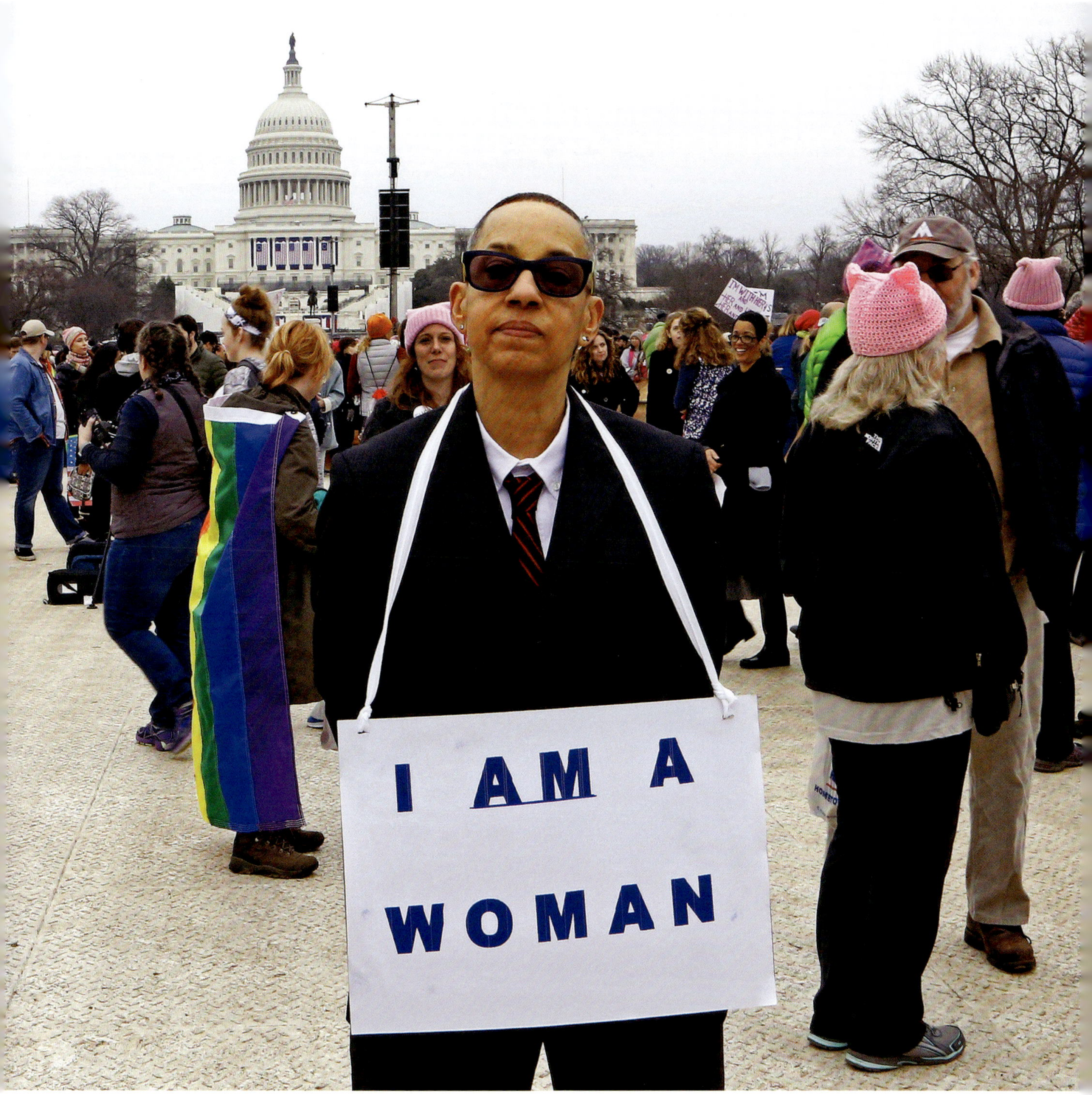
I AM A
WOMAN

Cross Colour

Notable Cross Colour work documenting queer black life during the AIDS crisis as well as moments of LGBTQIA+ joy. Flash gets to the center of militant eroticism, race, and gender within the 1990s queer community.

Self-Portrait, 1991
New York

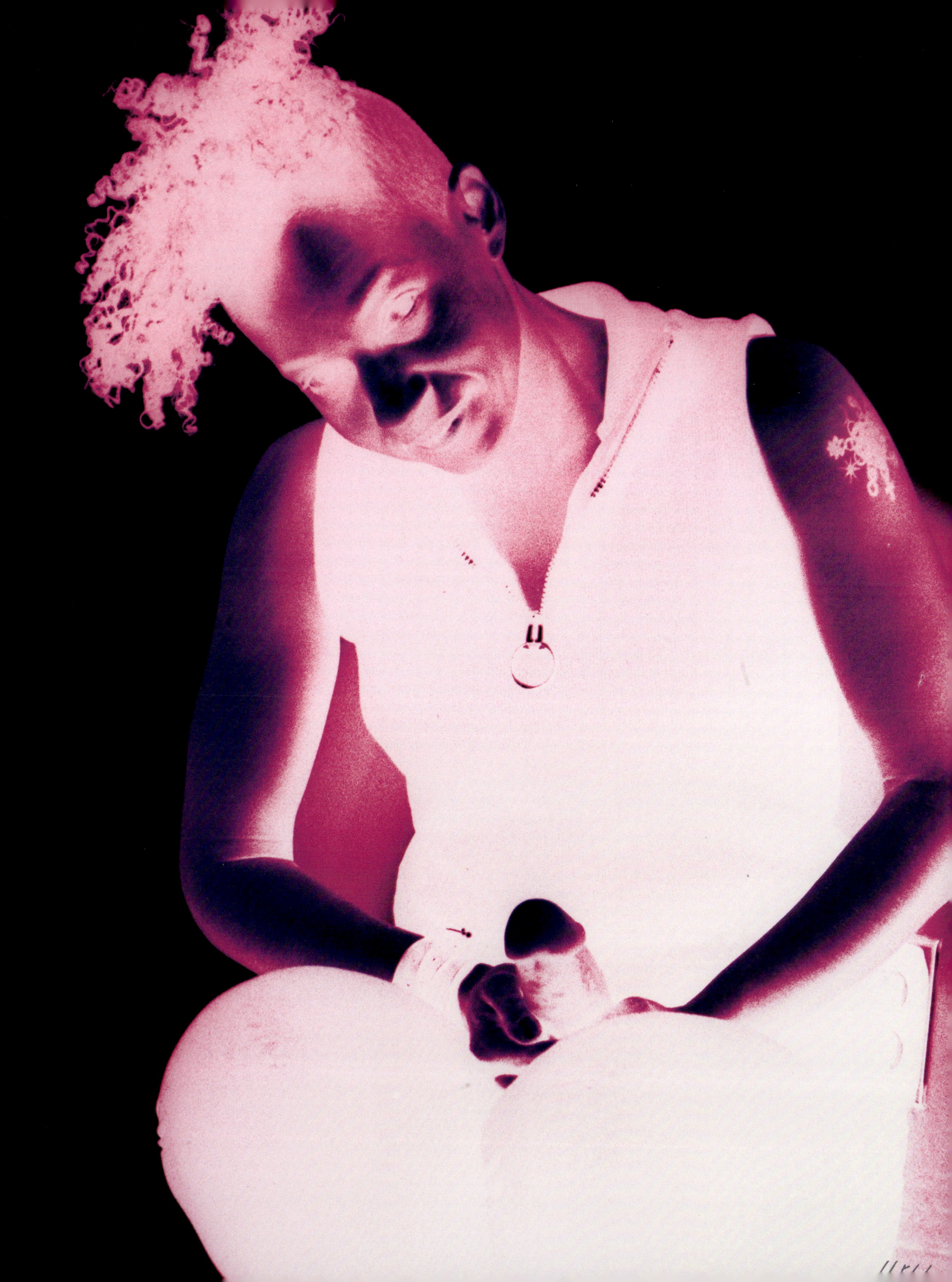

U Is for Upside-down, 1993
New York
Series: Gay to Z

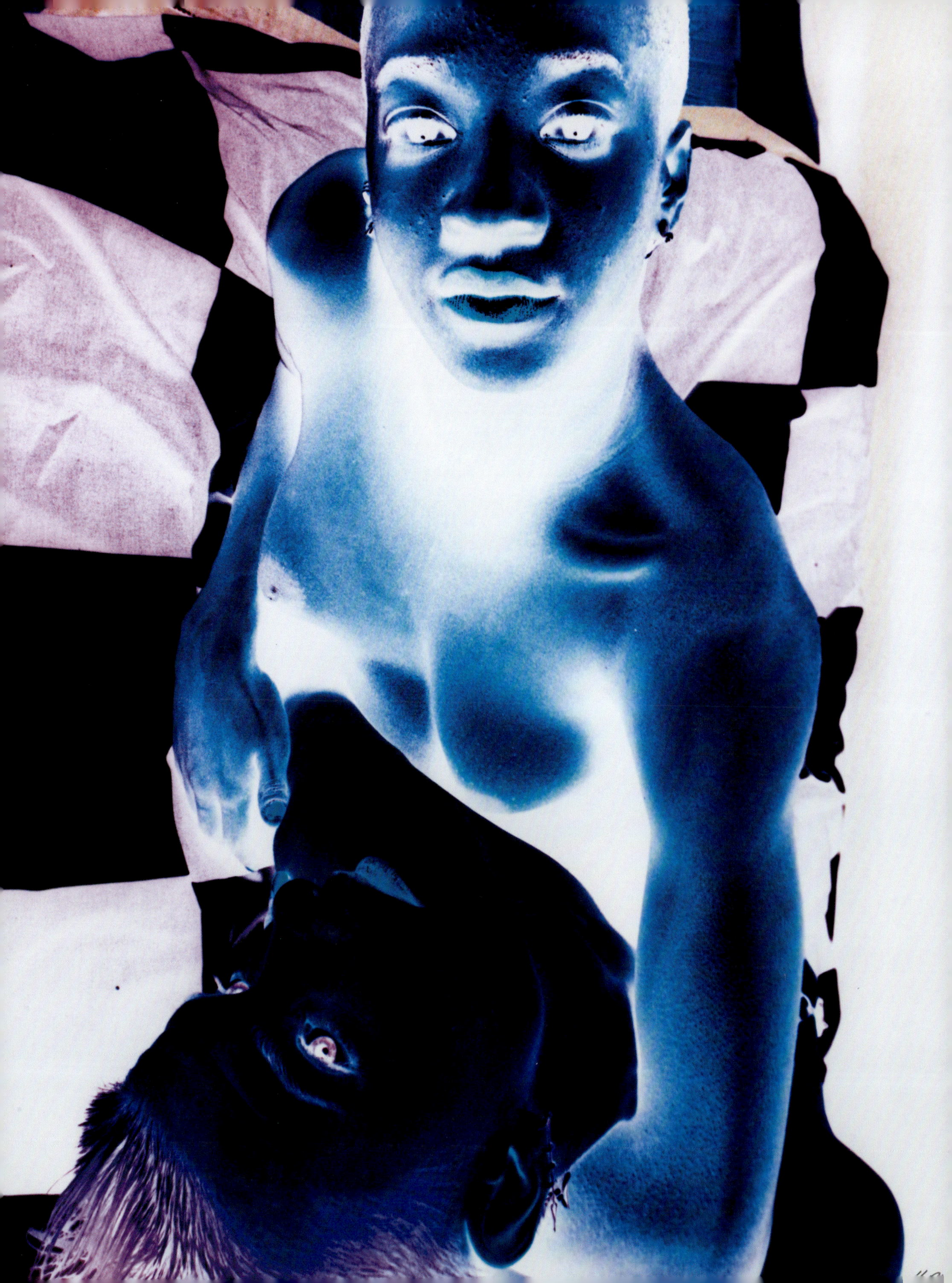

Tit Kiss, circa 1990
New York

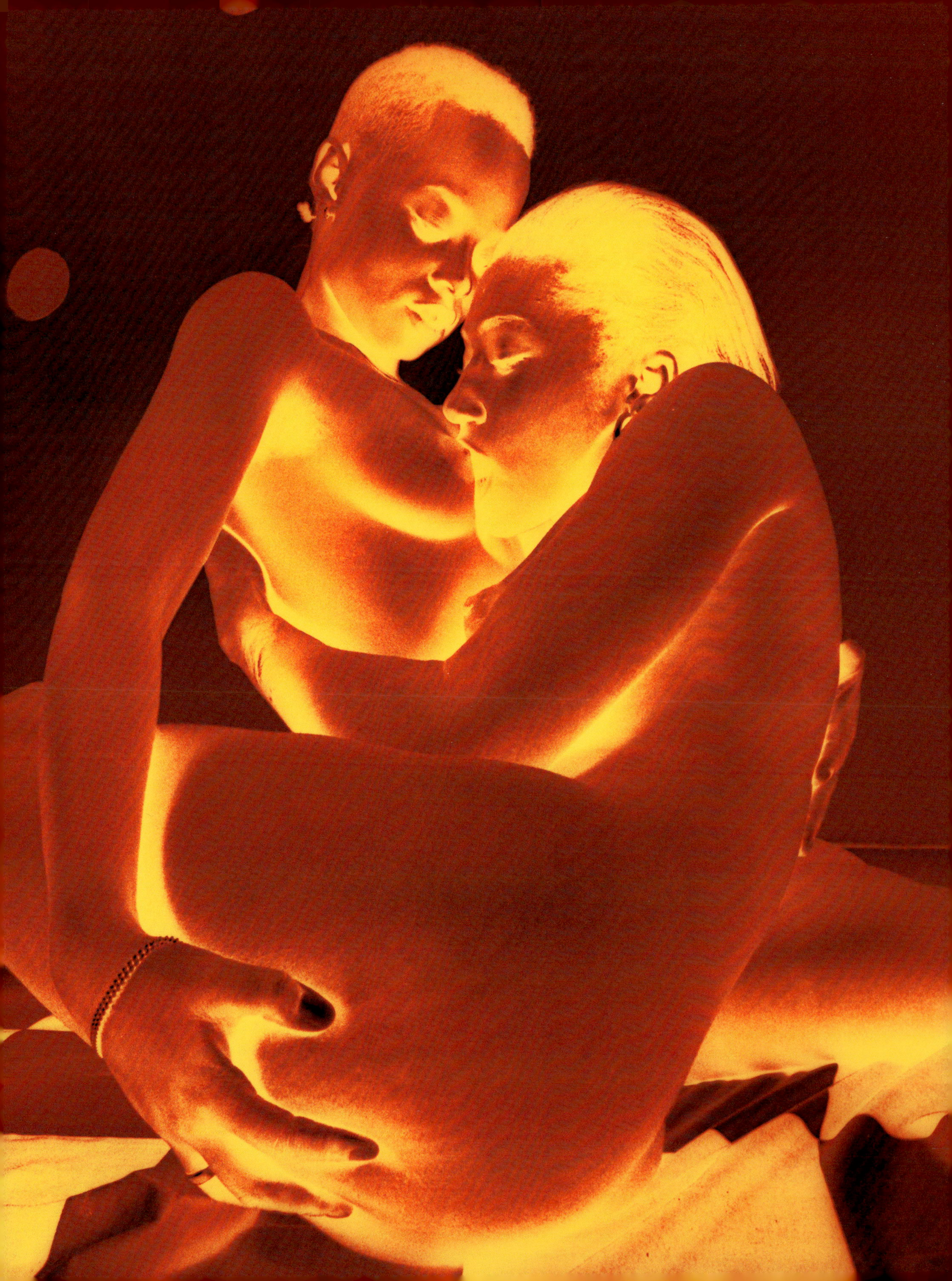

J Is for Judge, 1993
London
Series: Gay to Z

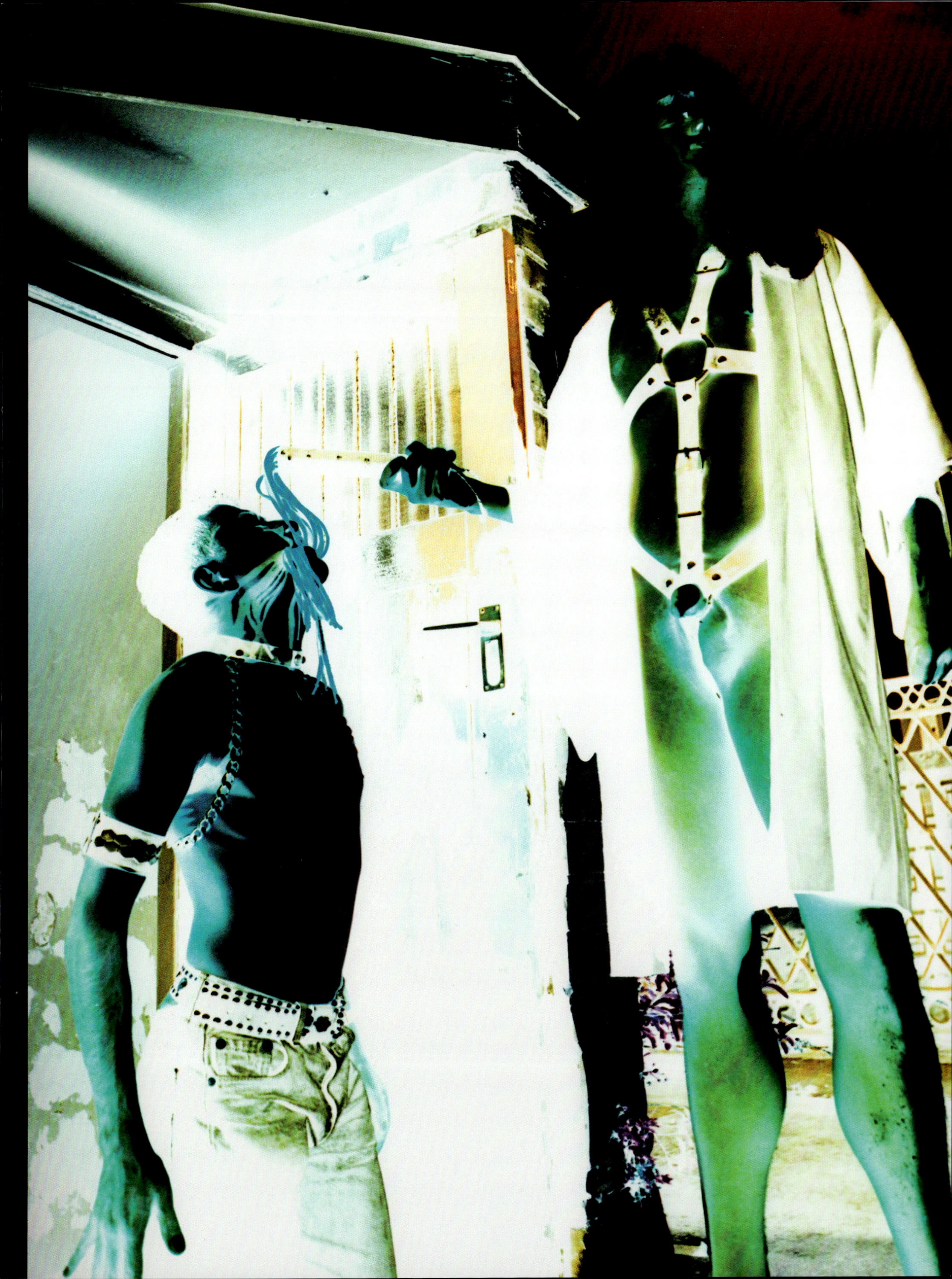

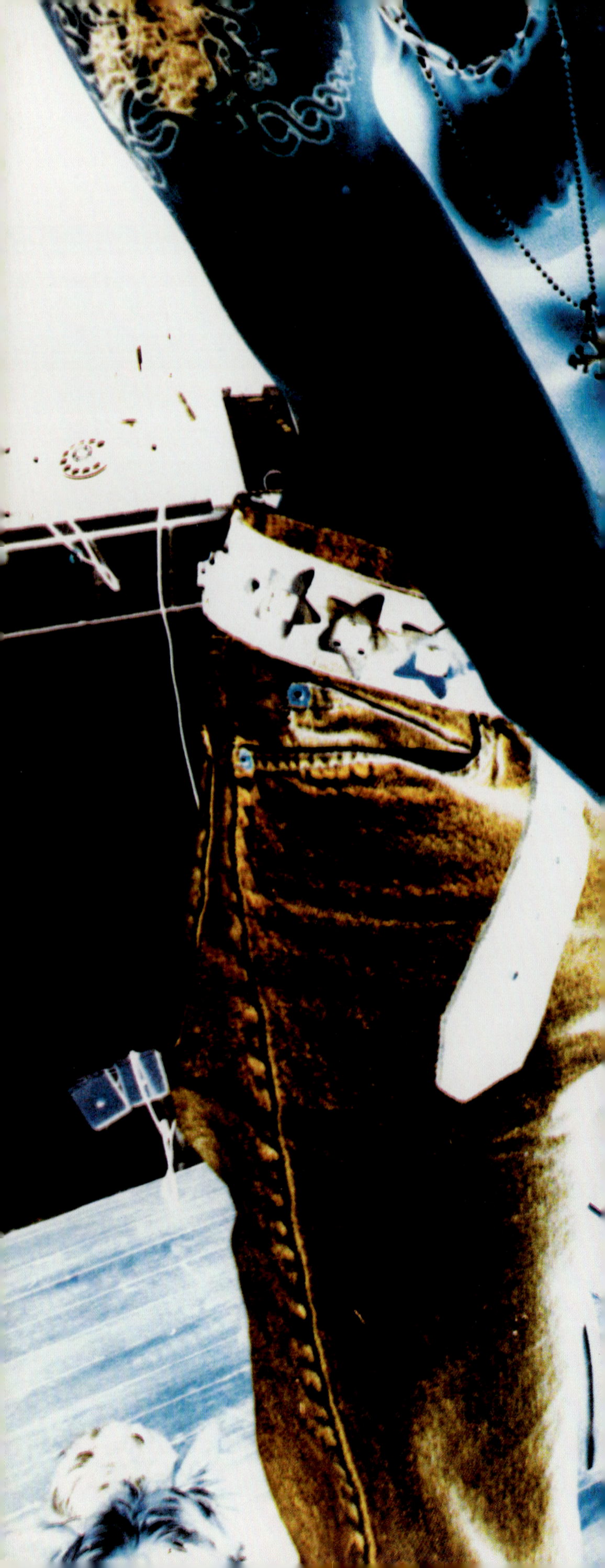

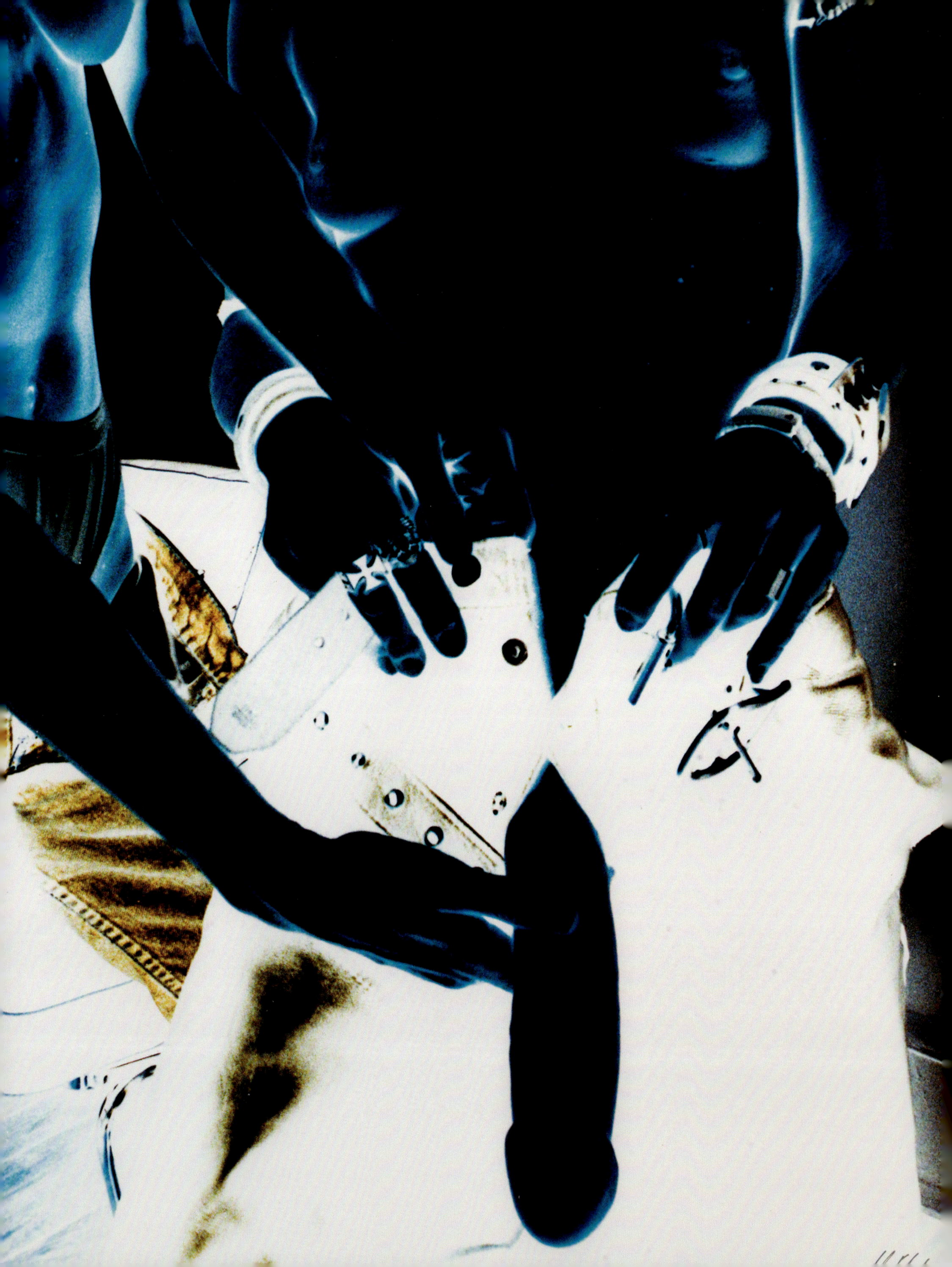

BJ, 1991
London

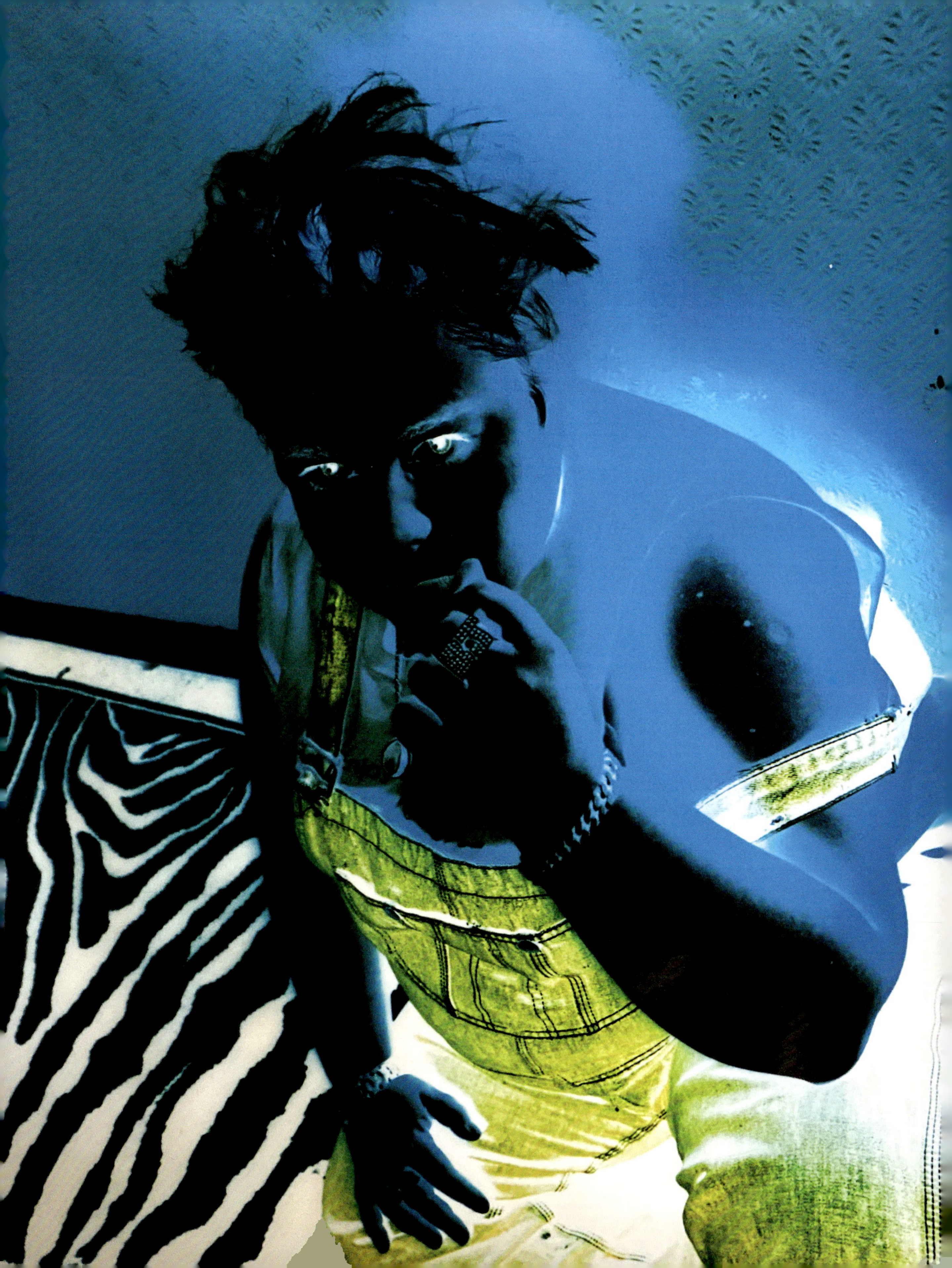

Cow Girl, circa 1994
London

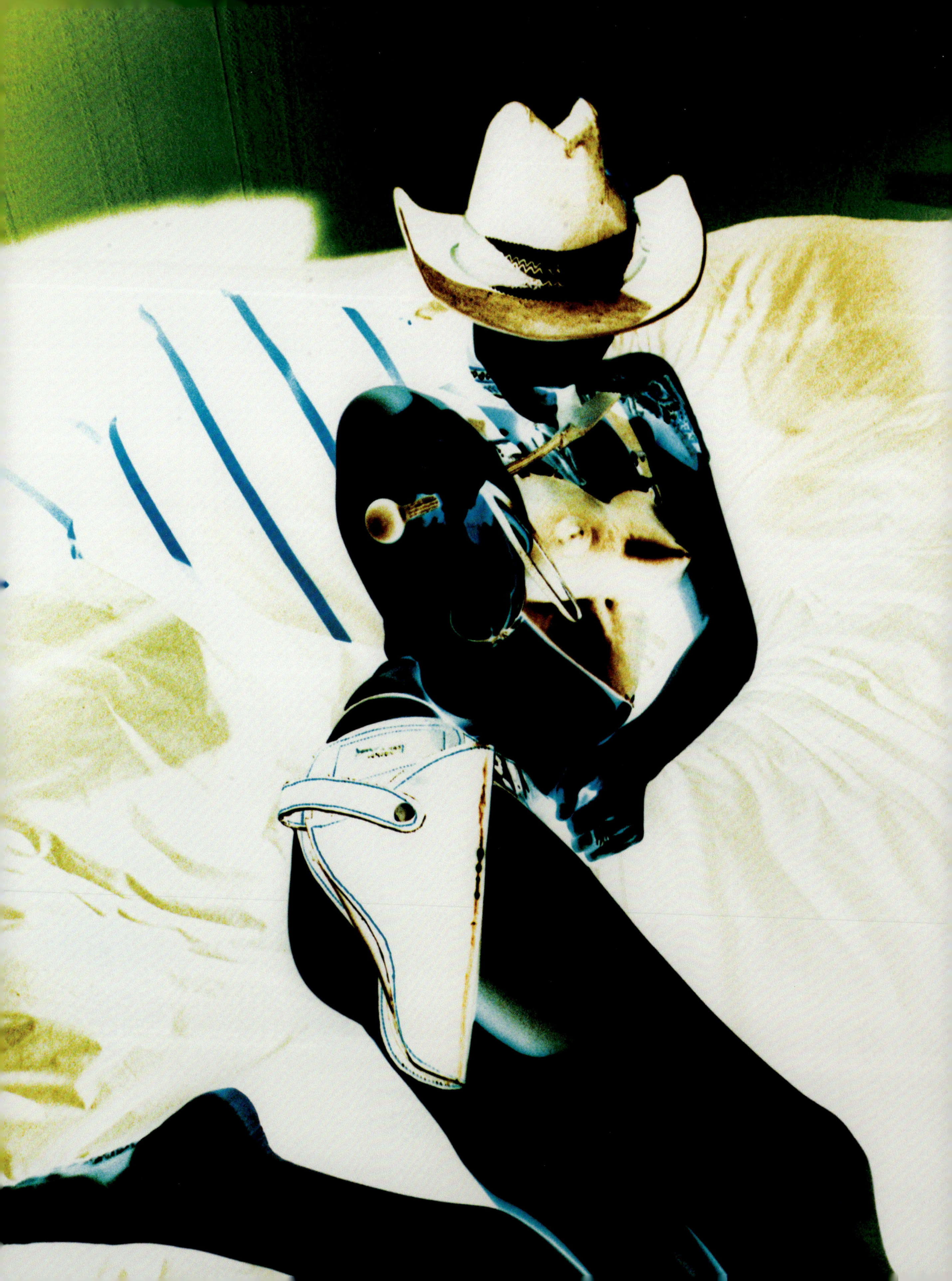

Band Aids, 1987
Provincetown

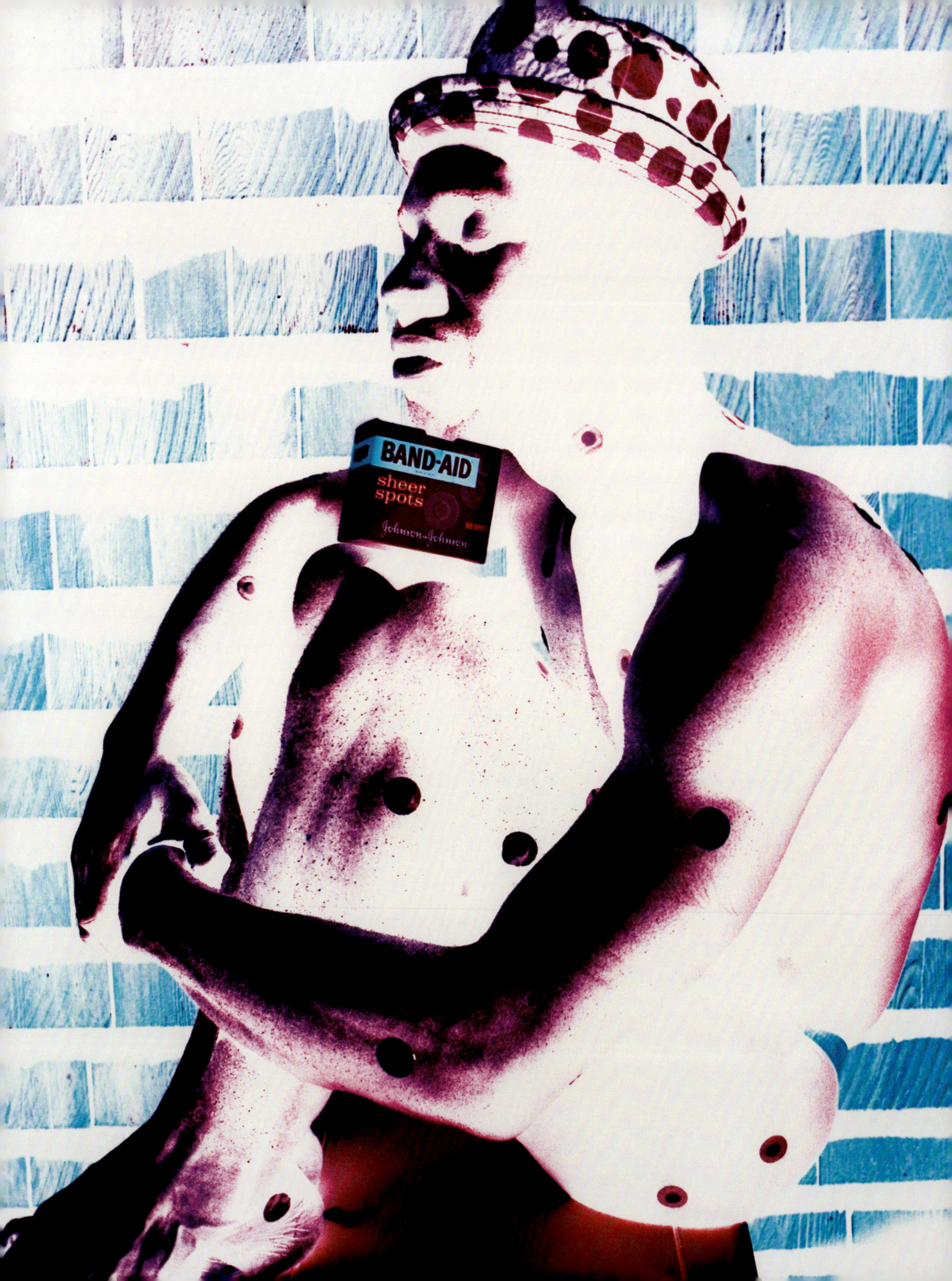
BAND-AID
sheer spots
Johnson & Johnson

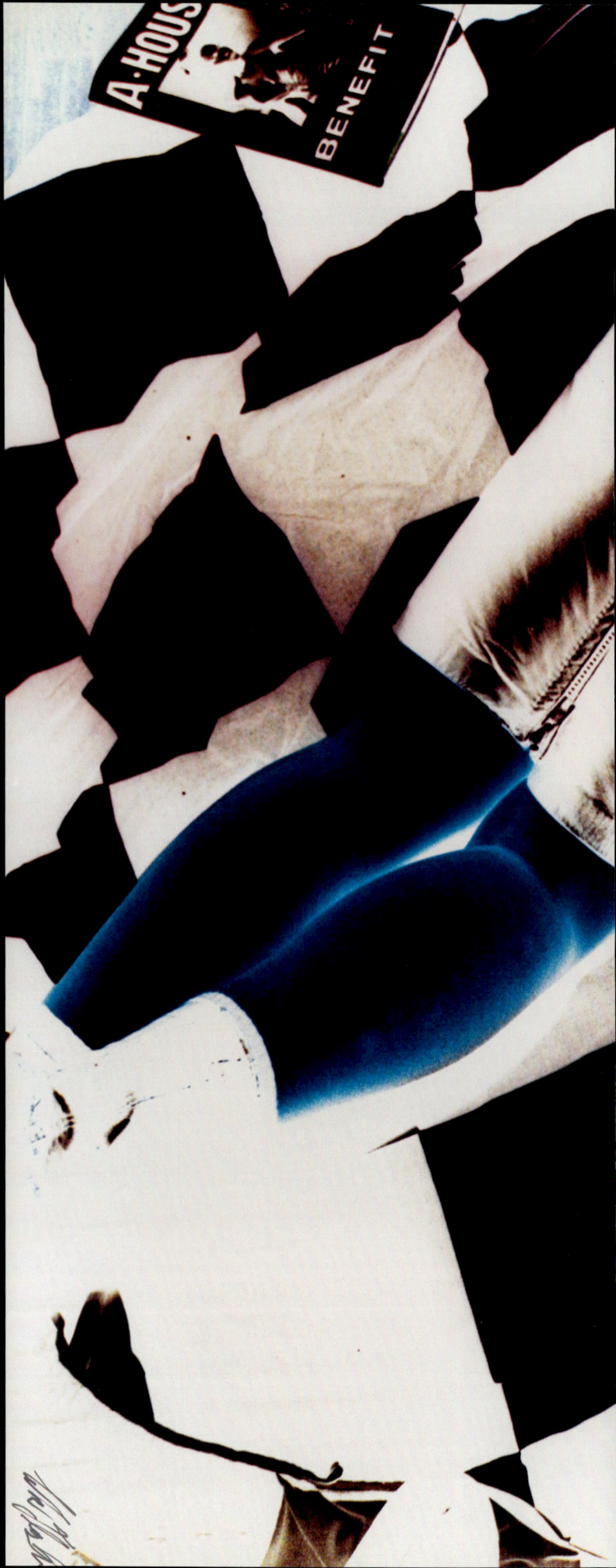

AIDS Is Killing Artists
Self Portrait, 1990
Provincetown

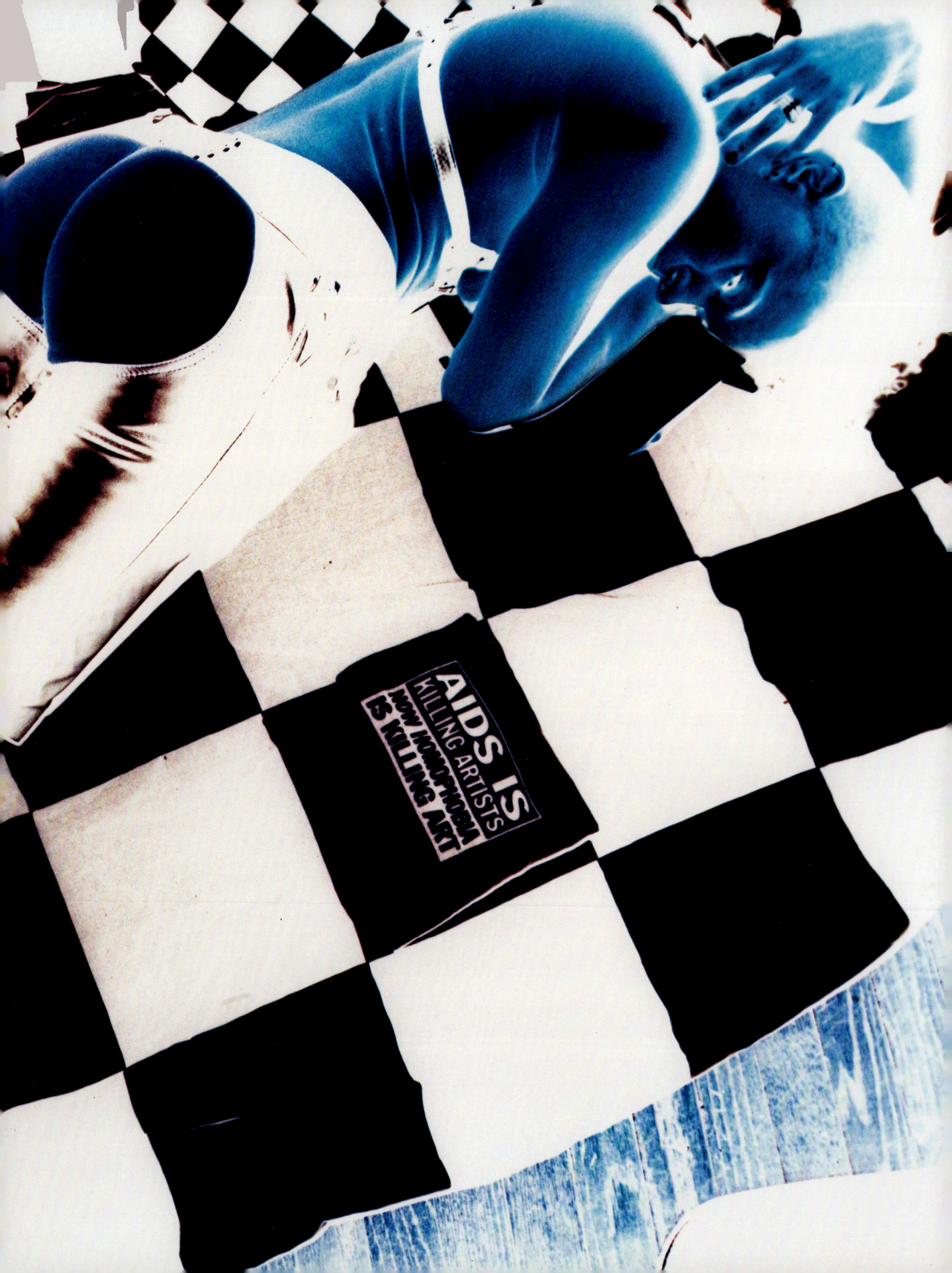
AIDS IS
KILLING ARTISTS
NOW HOMOPHOBIA
IS KILLING ART

Silence = Death, circa 1989
Provincetown

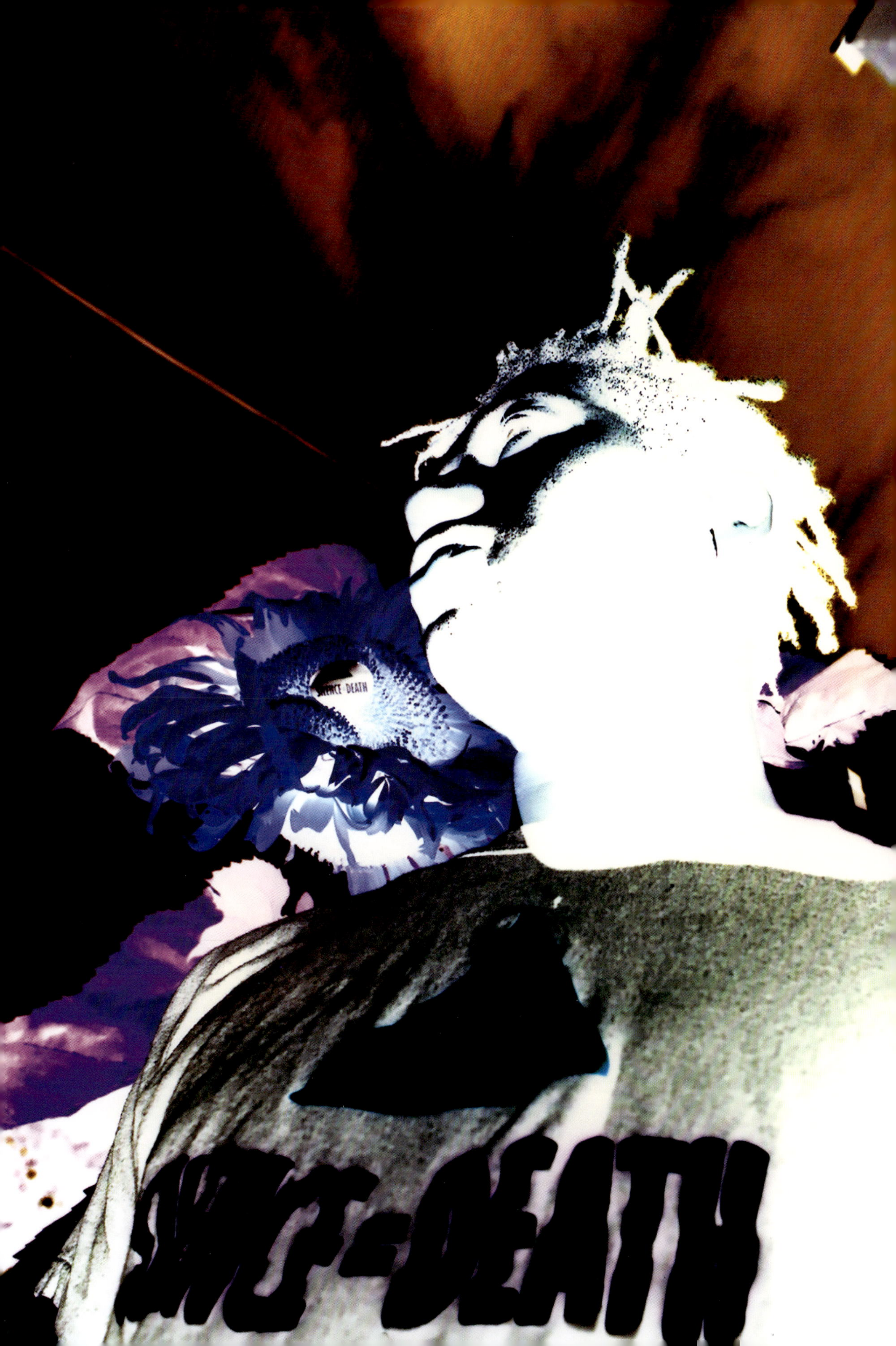
SILENCE = DEATH

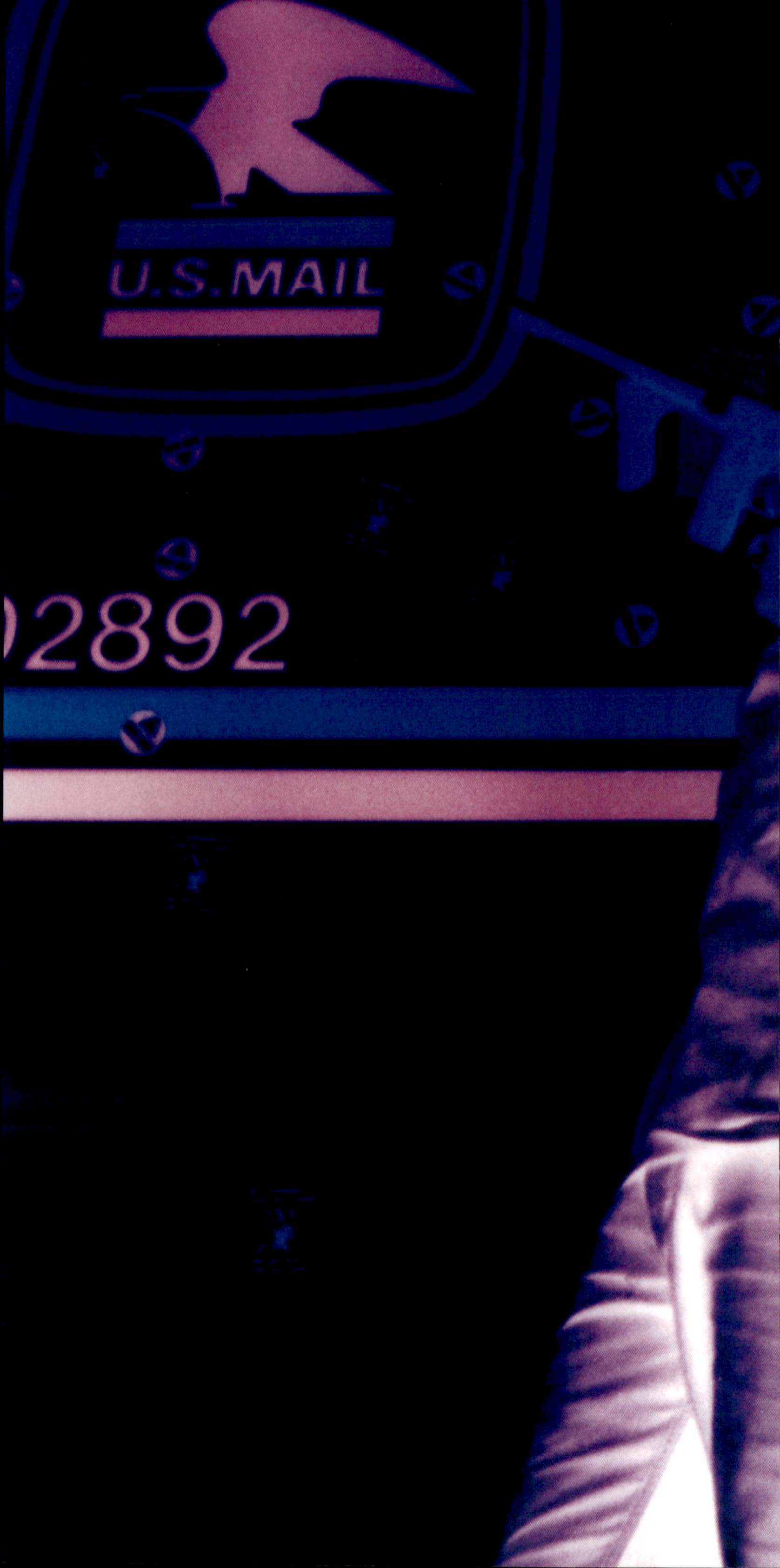

AIDS Warriors, 1988
New York

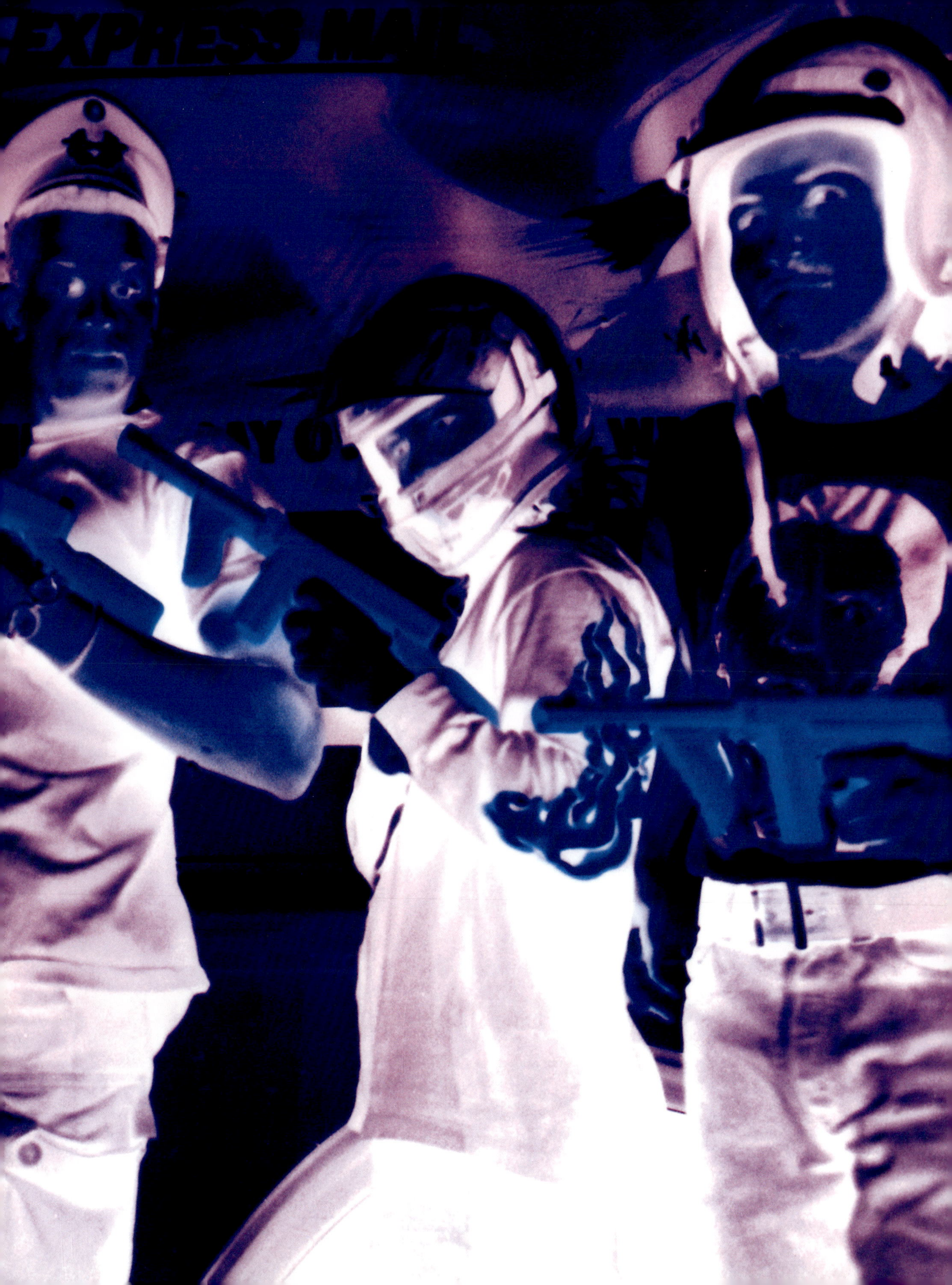
EXPRESS

Boys Kissing, 1988
Provincetown

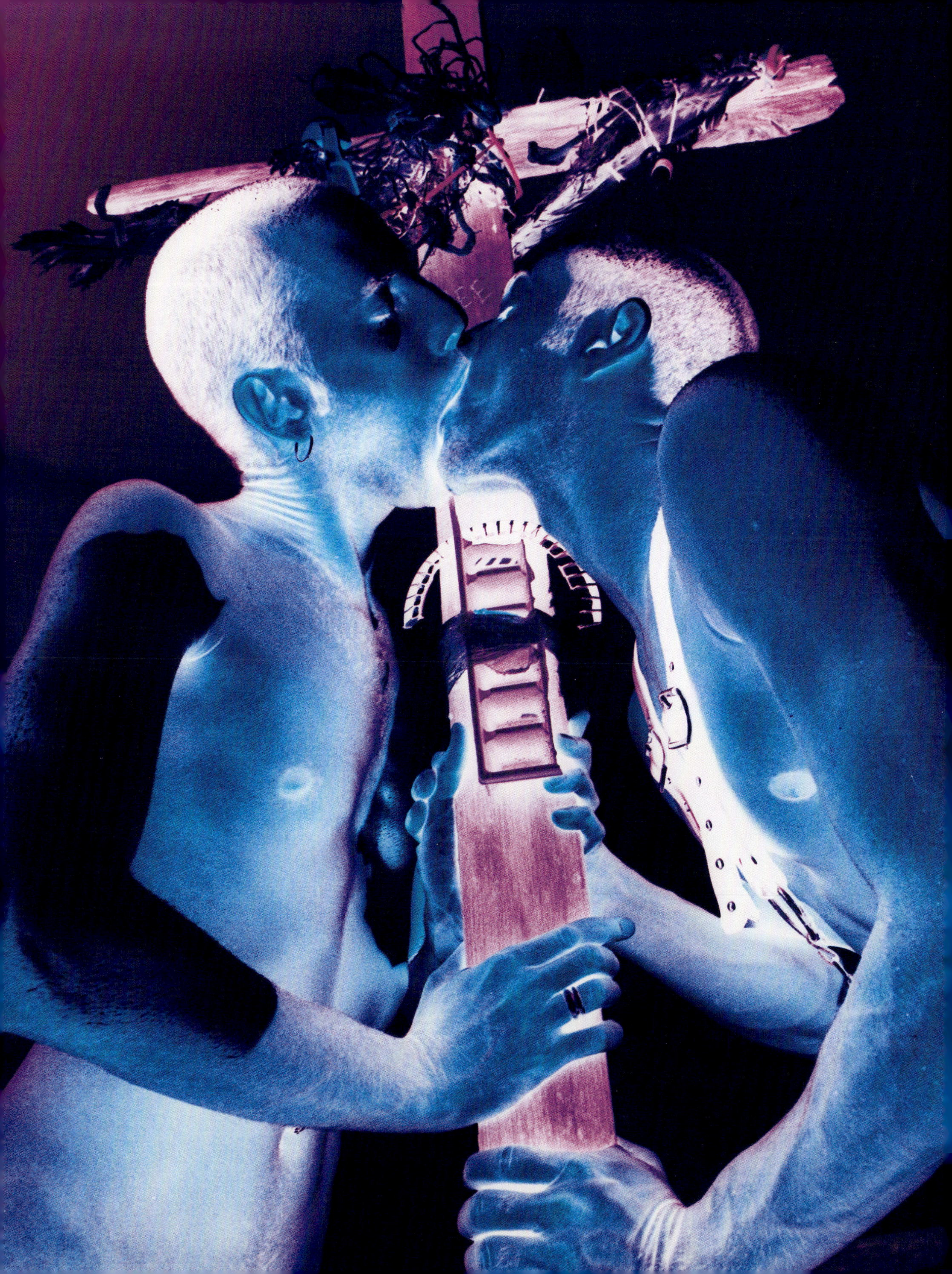

K Is for KKK, 1993
Provincetown

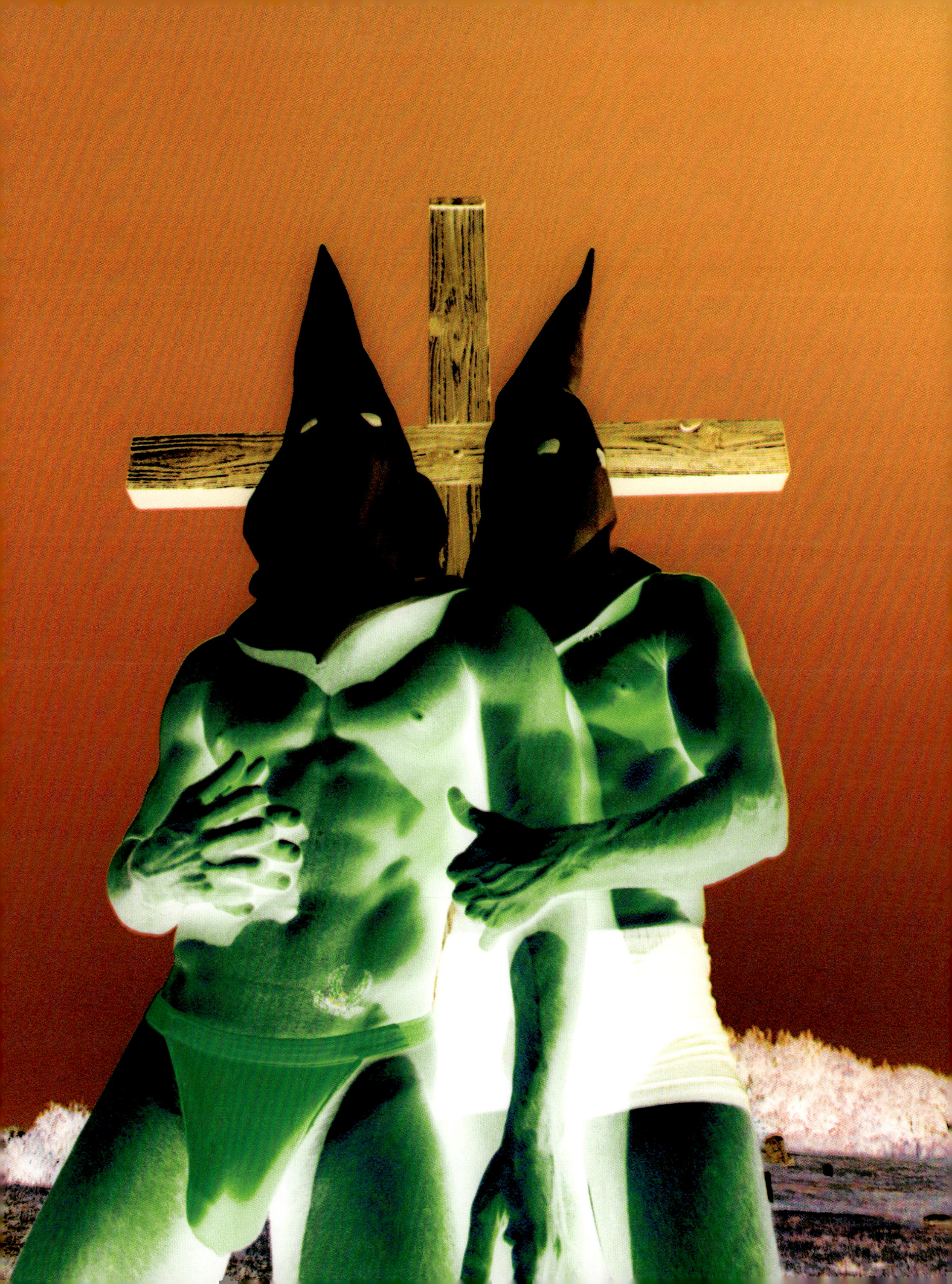

[sur]passing

These selections are part of a work in progress called [sur]passing. It is based on a series of larger than life-size color portraits that probe the impact skin pigmentation plays on Black identity and consciousness. This scandalous and often heart-wrenching story line dates back to colonial America, and it clearly perseveres today.

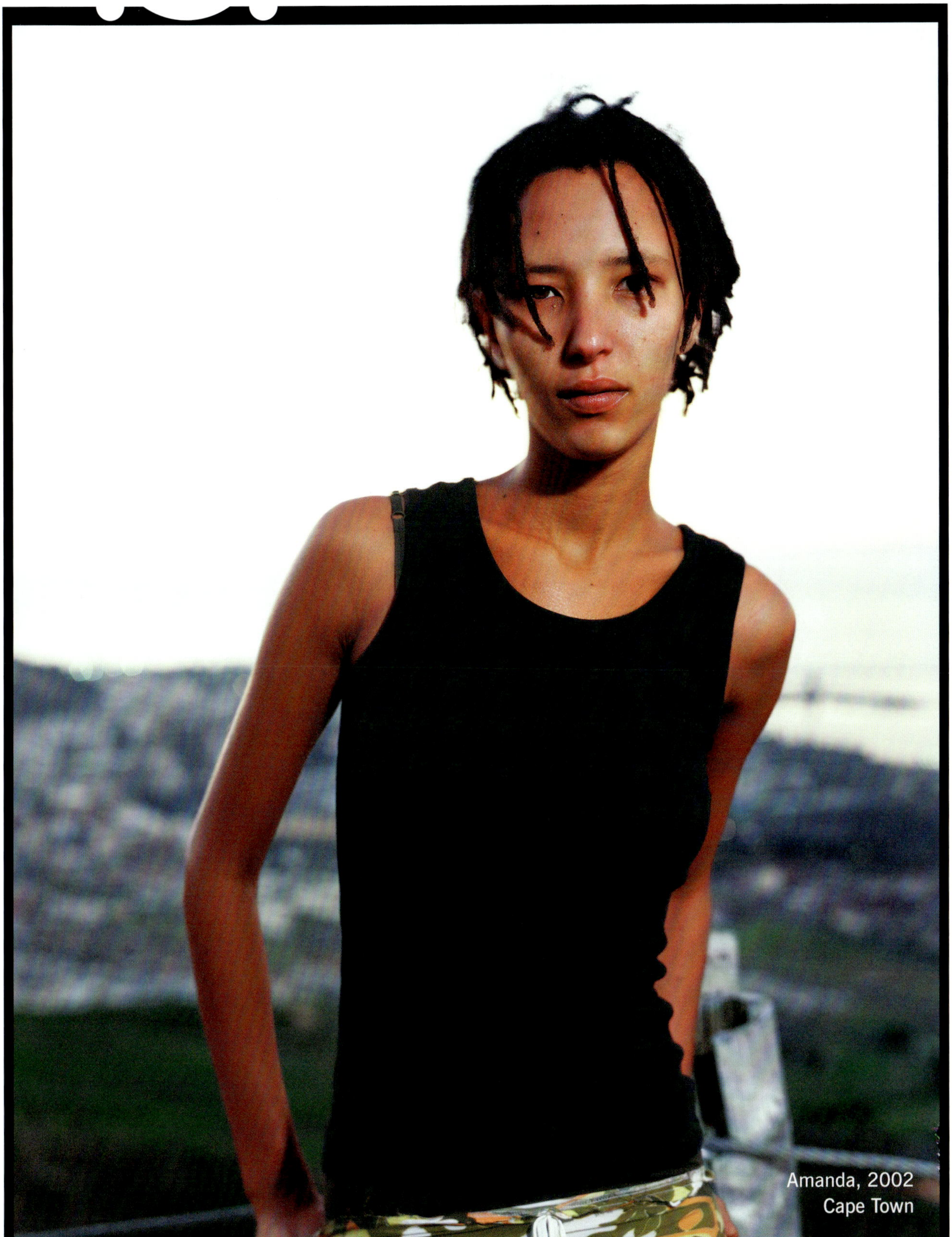

Amanda, 2002
Cape Town

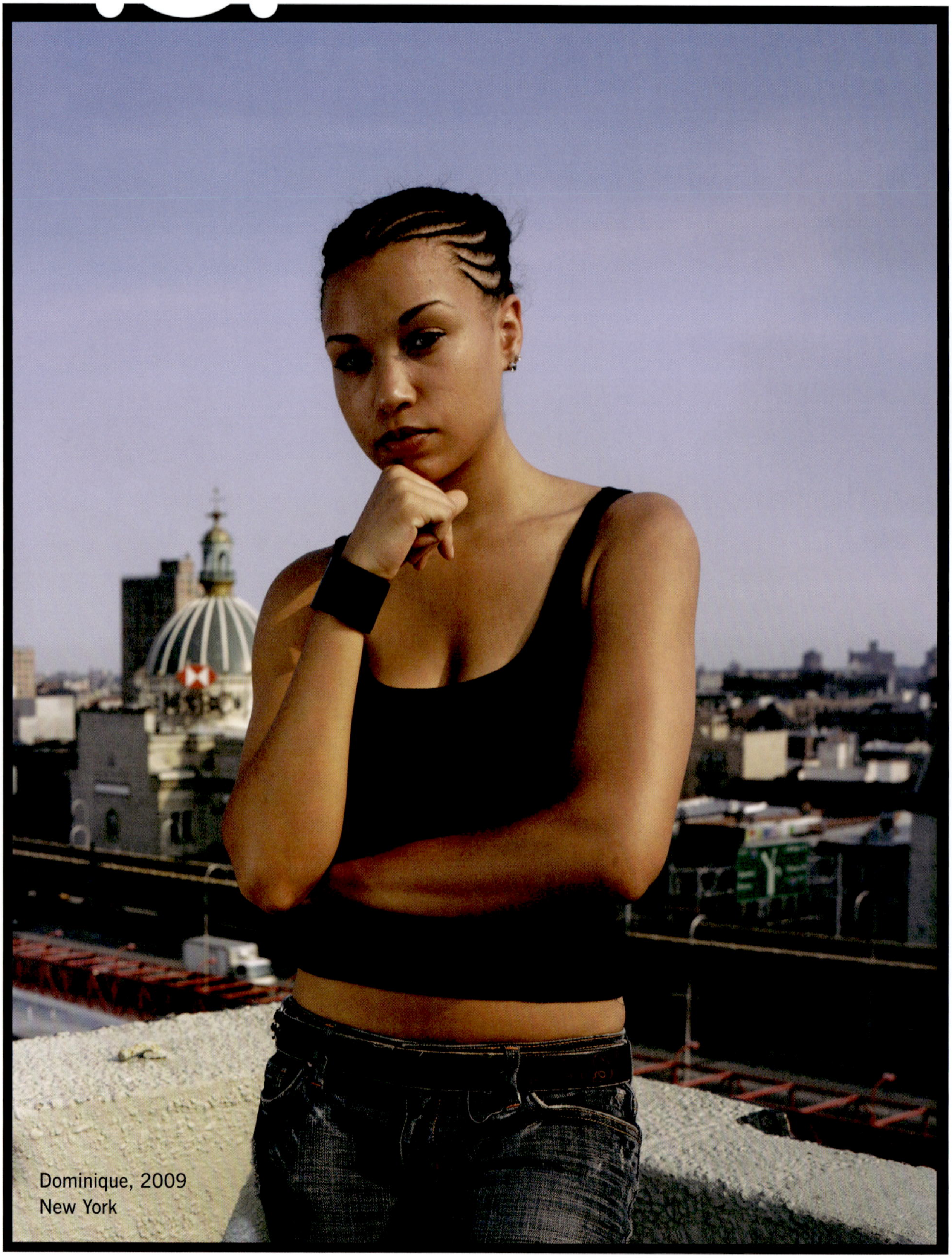

Dominique, 2009
New York

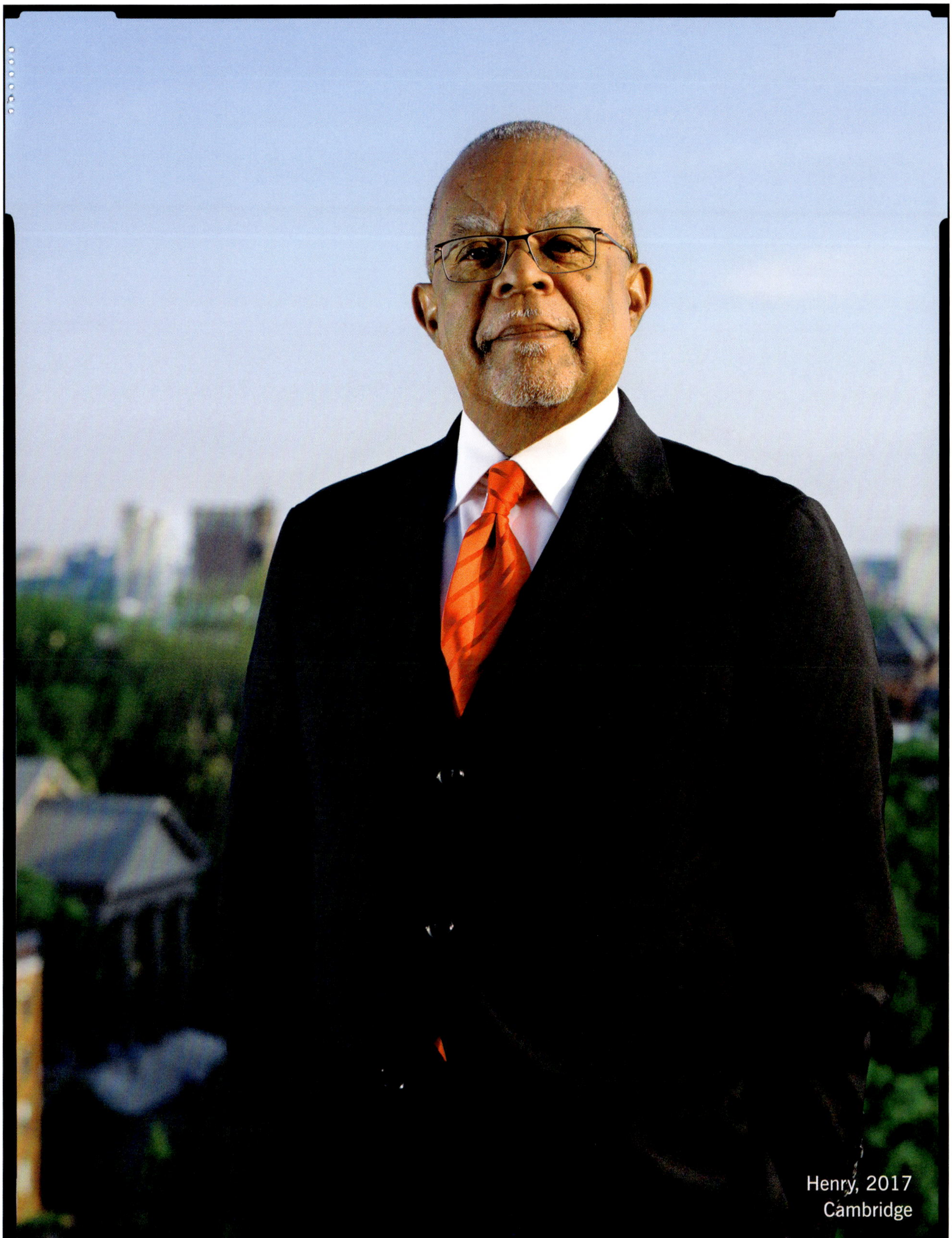

Henry, 2017
Cambridge

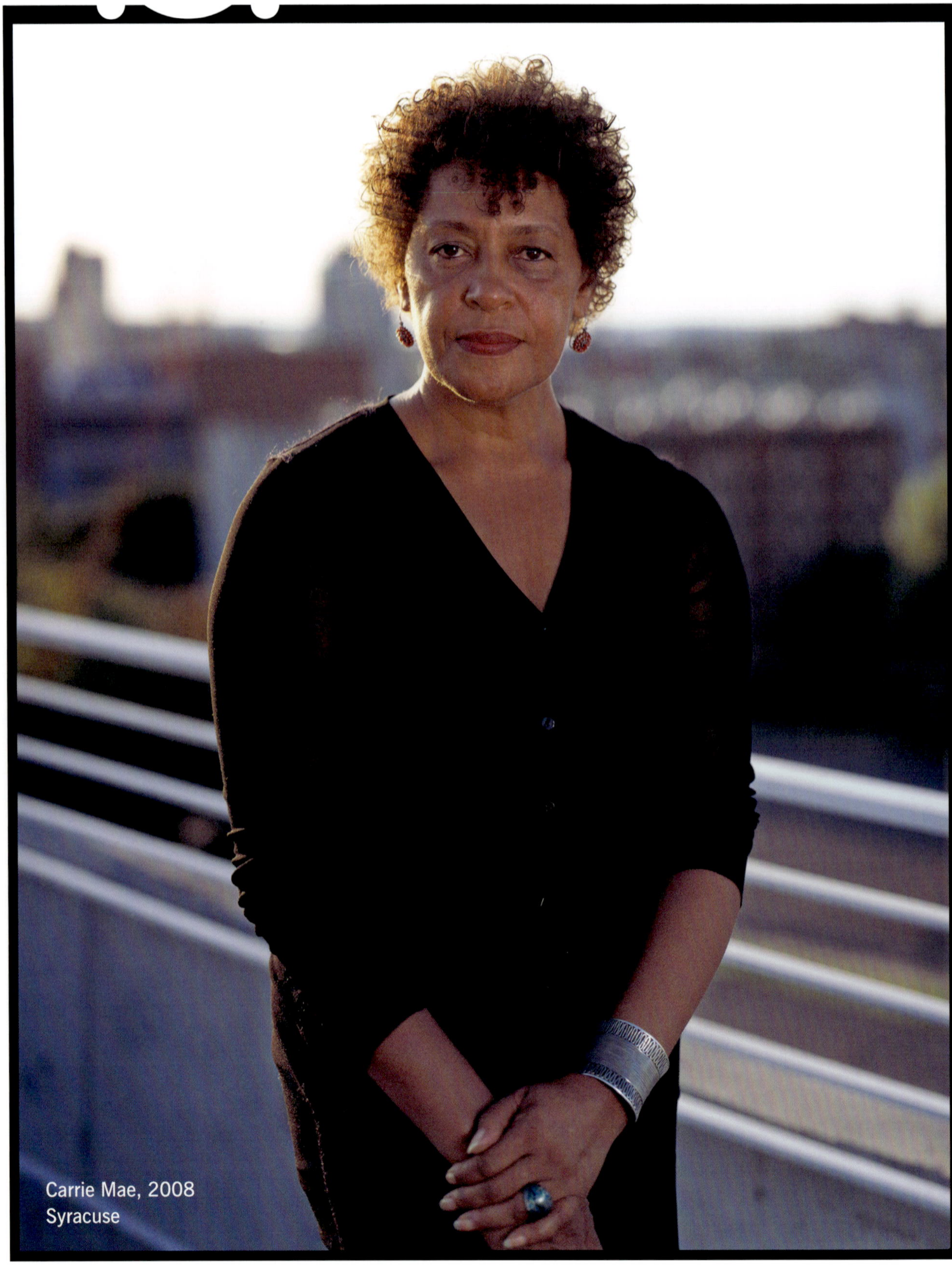

Carrie Mae, 2008
Syracuse

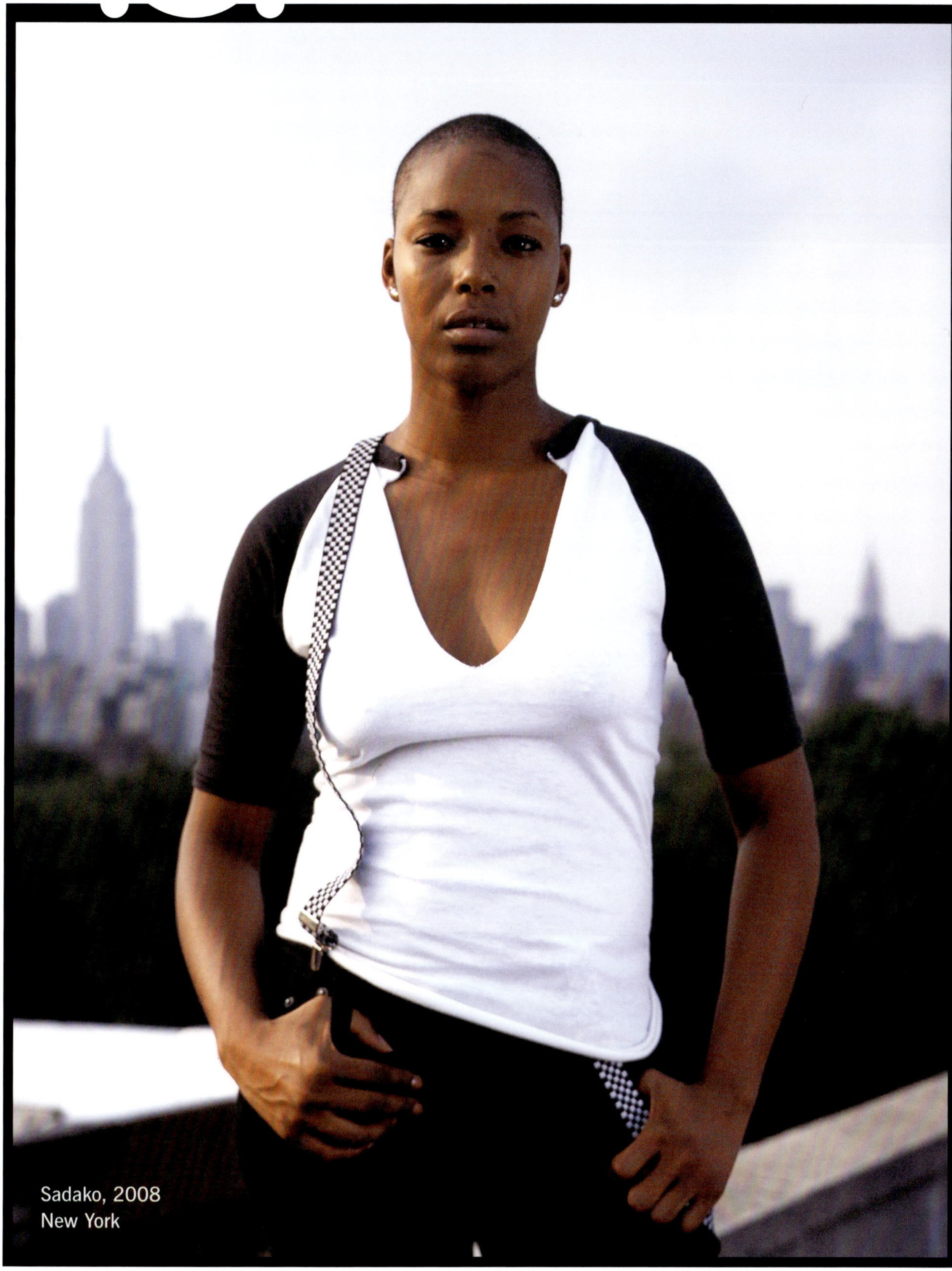

Sadako, 2008
New York

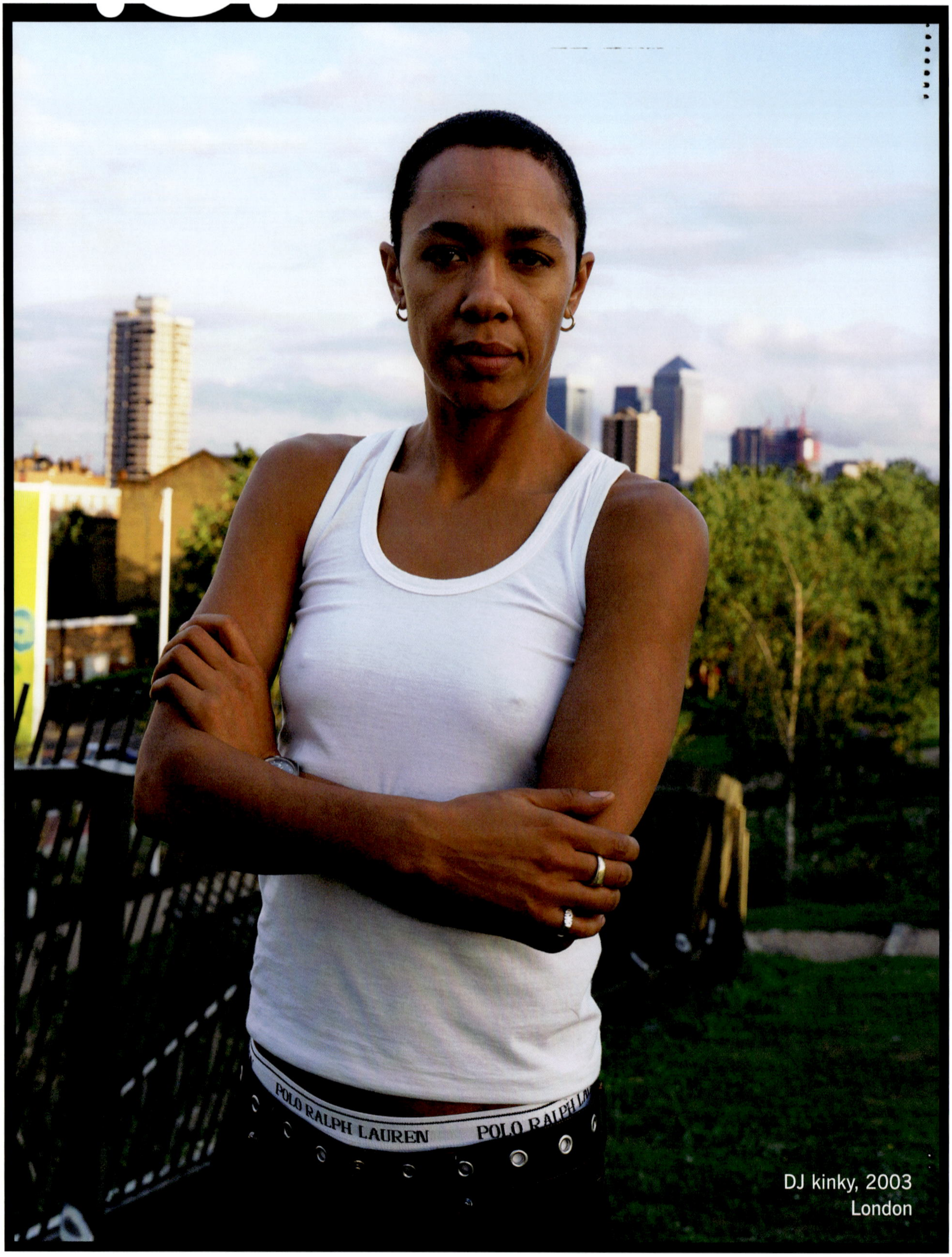

DJ kinky, 2003
London

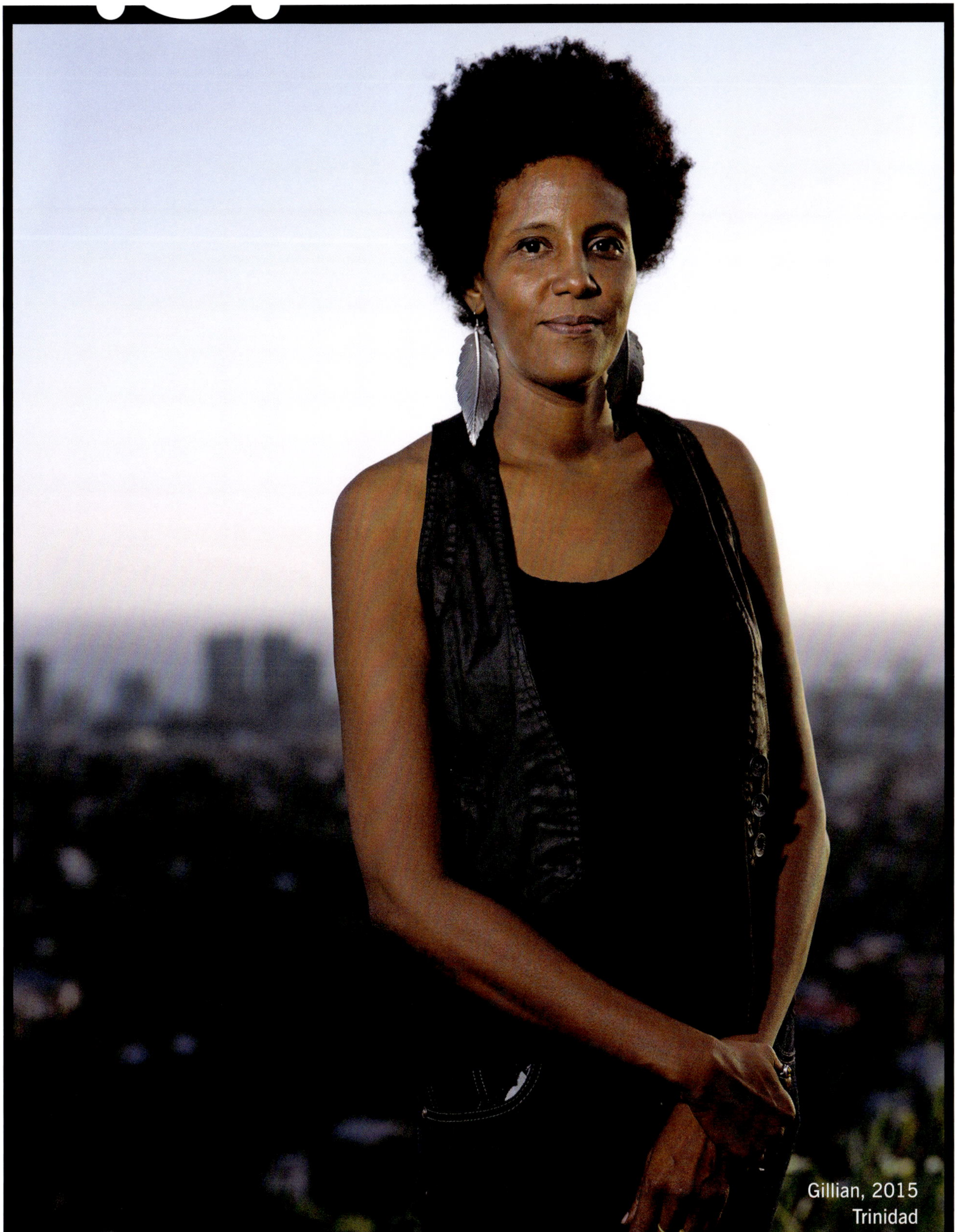

Gillian, 2015
Trinidad

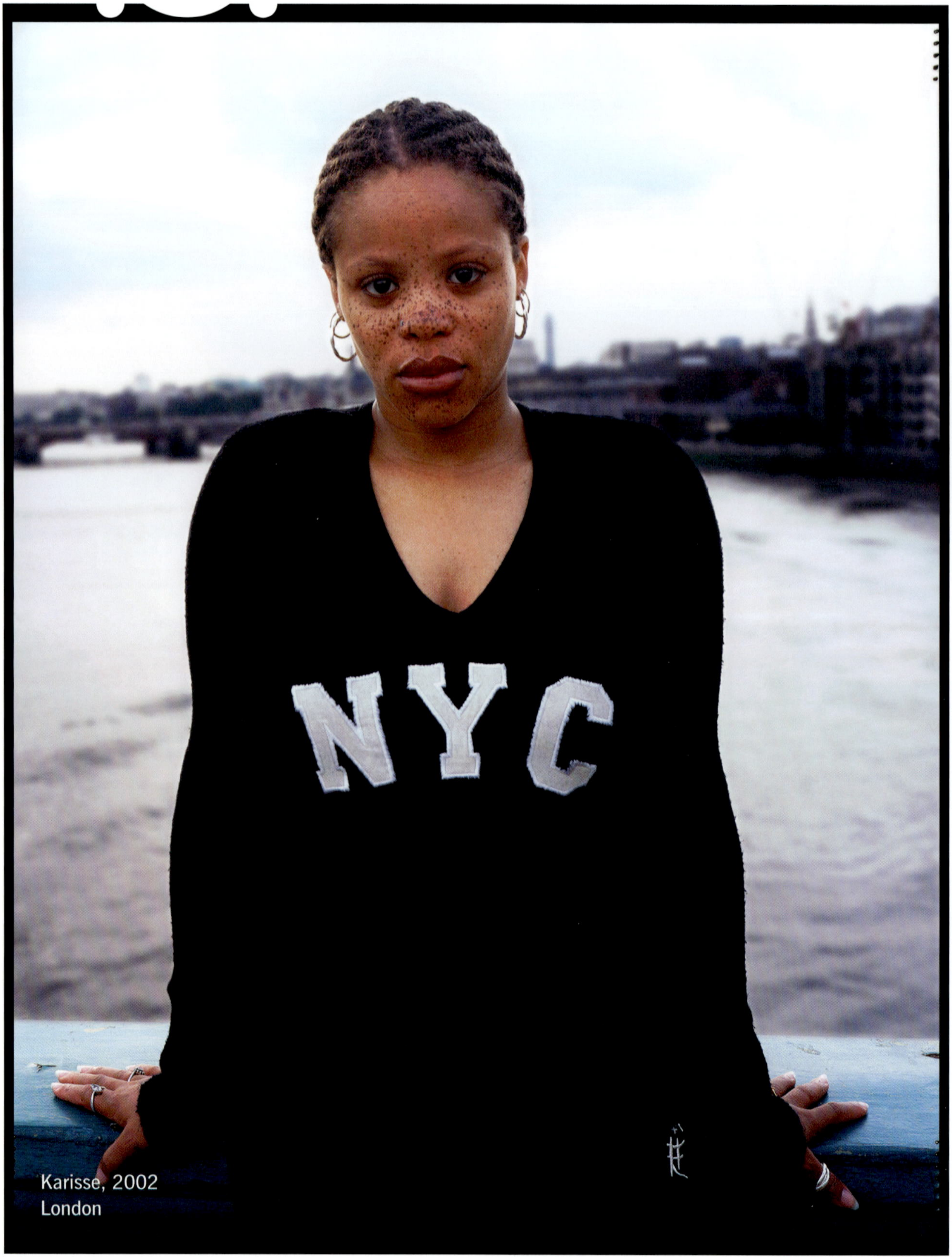

Karisse, 2002
London

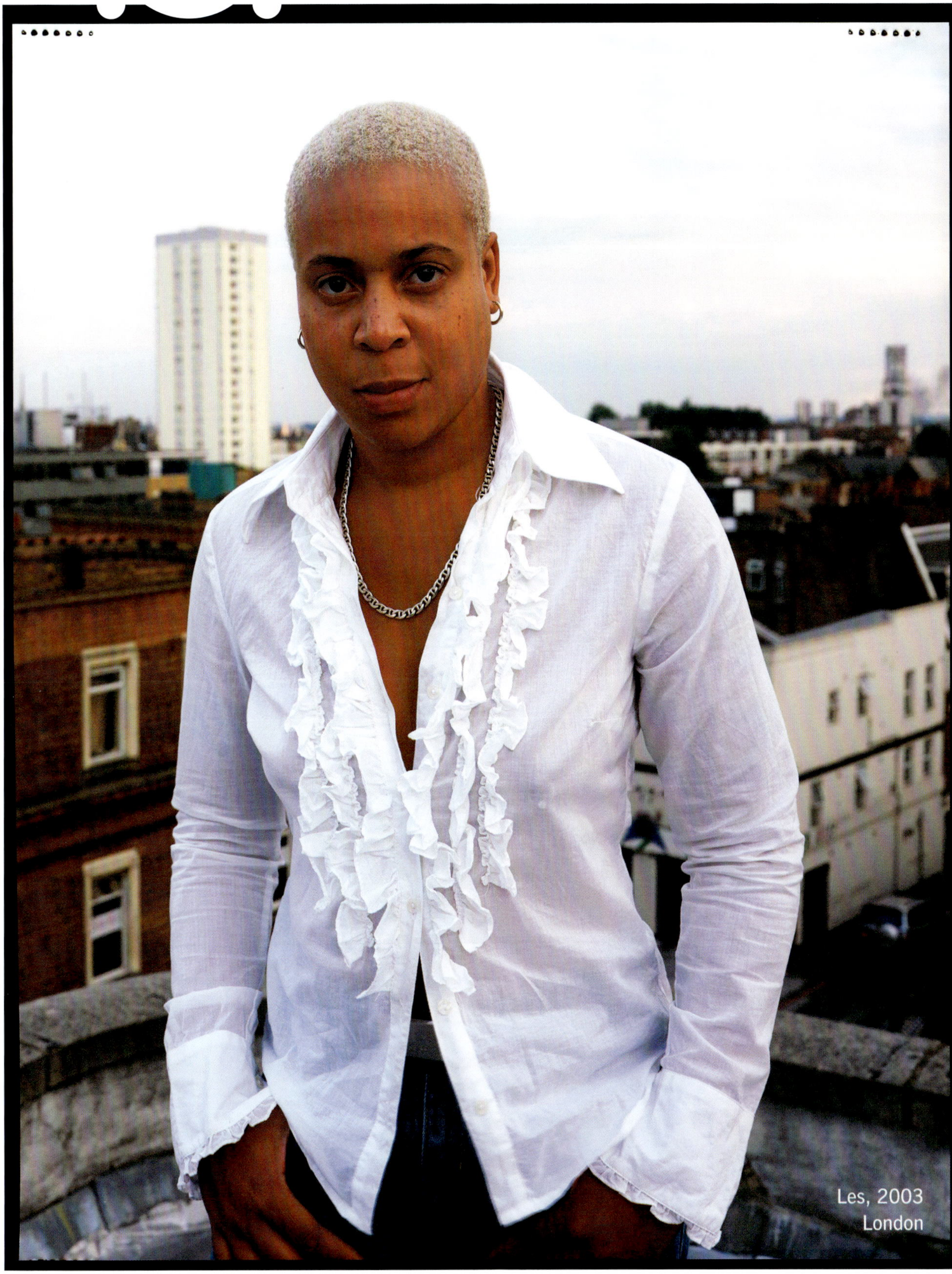

Les, 2003
London

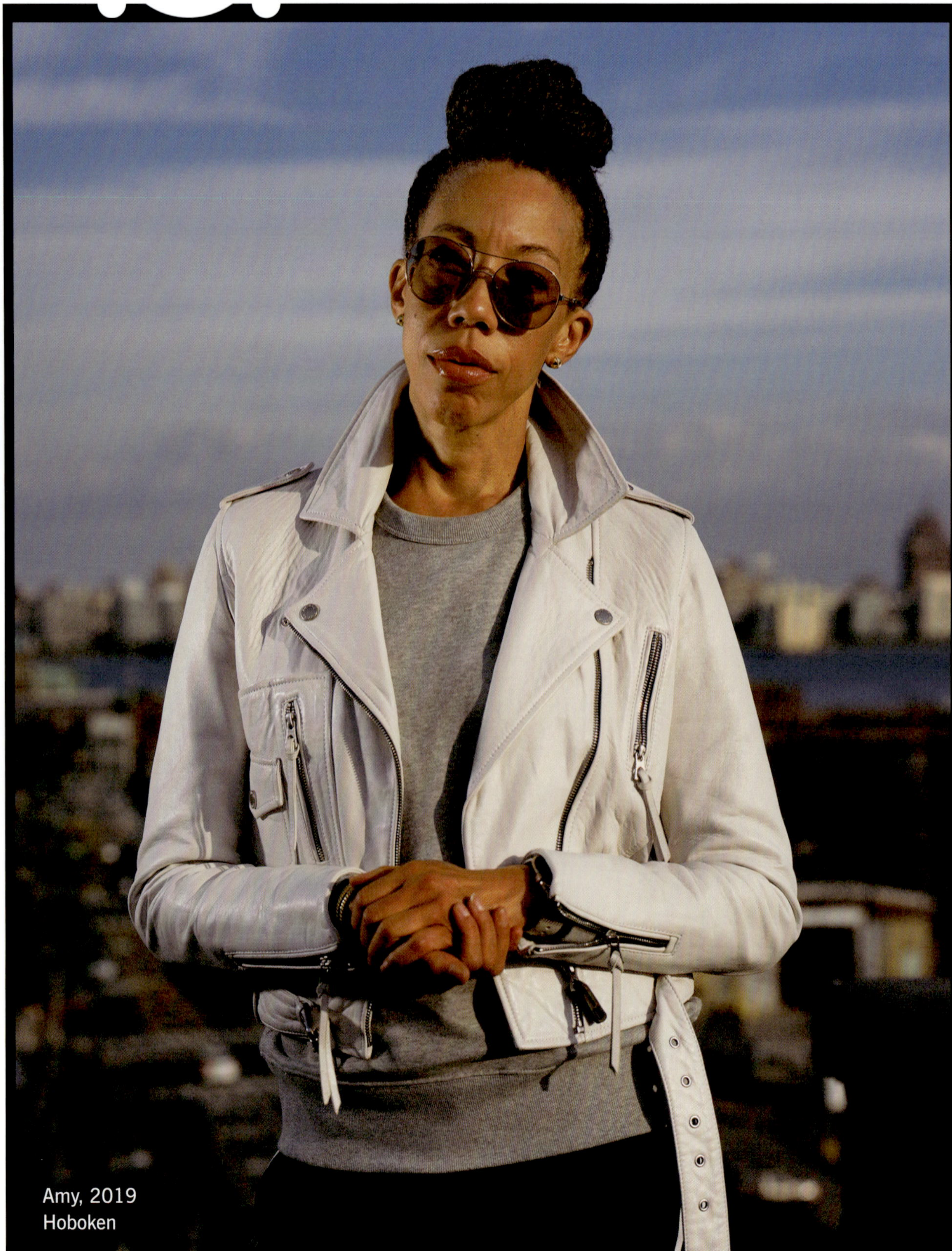

Amy, 2019
Hoboken

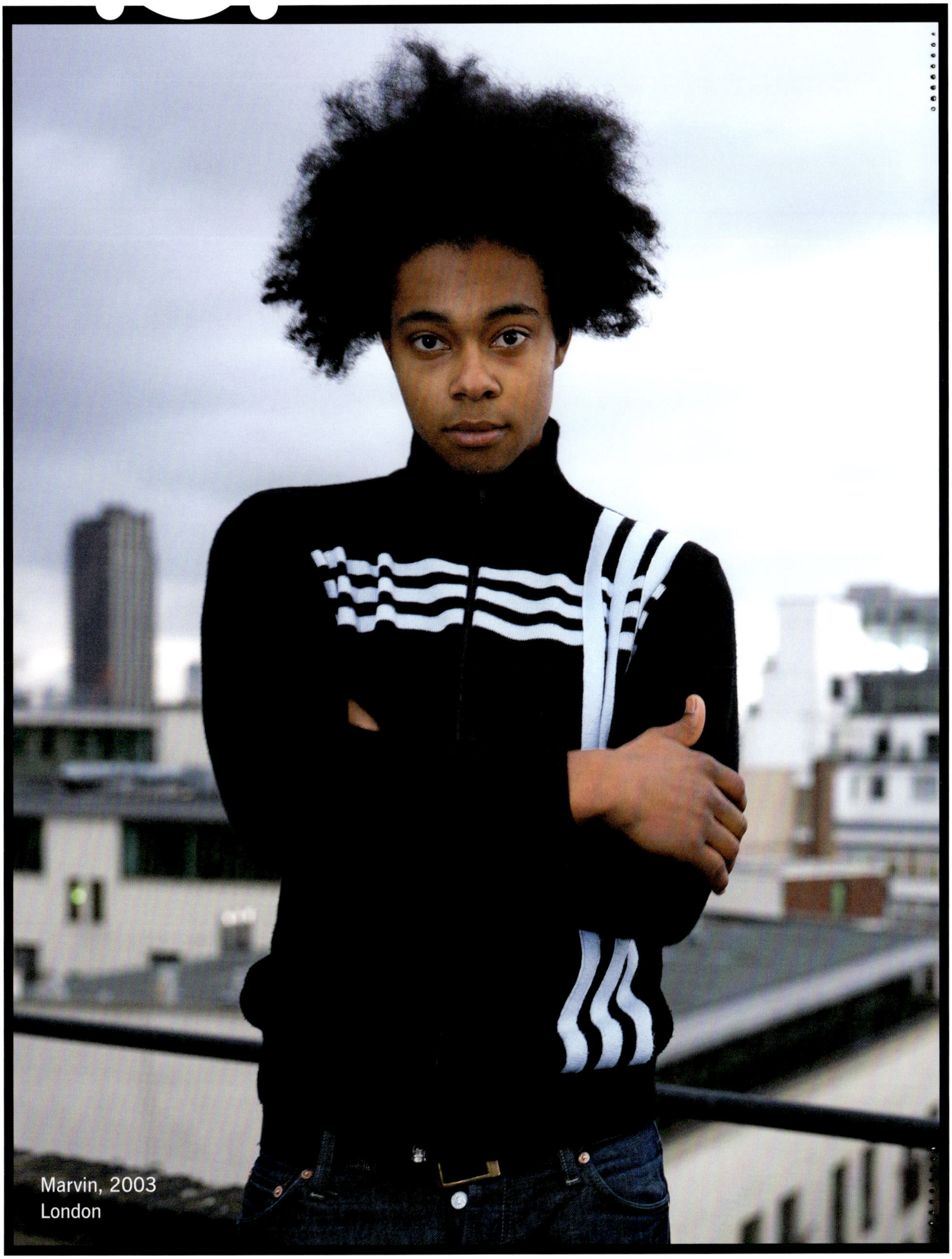
Marvin, 2003
London

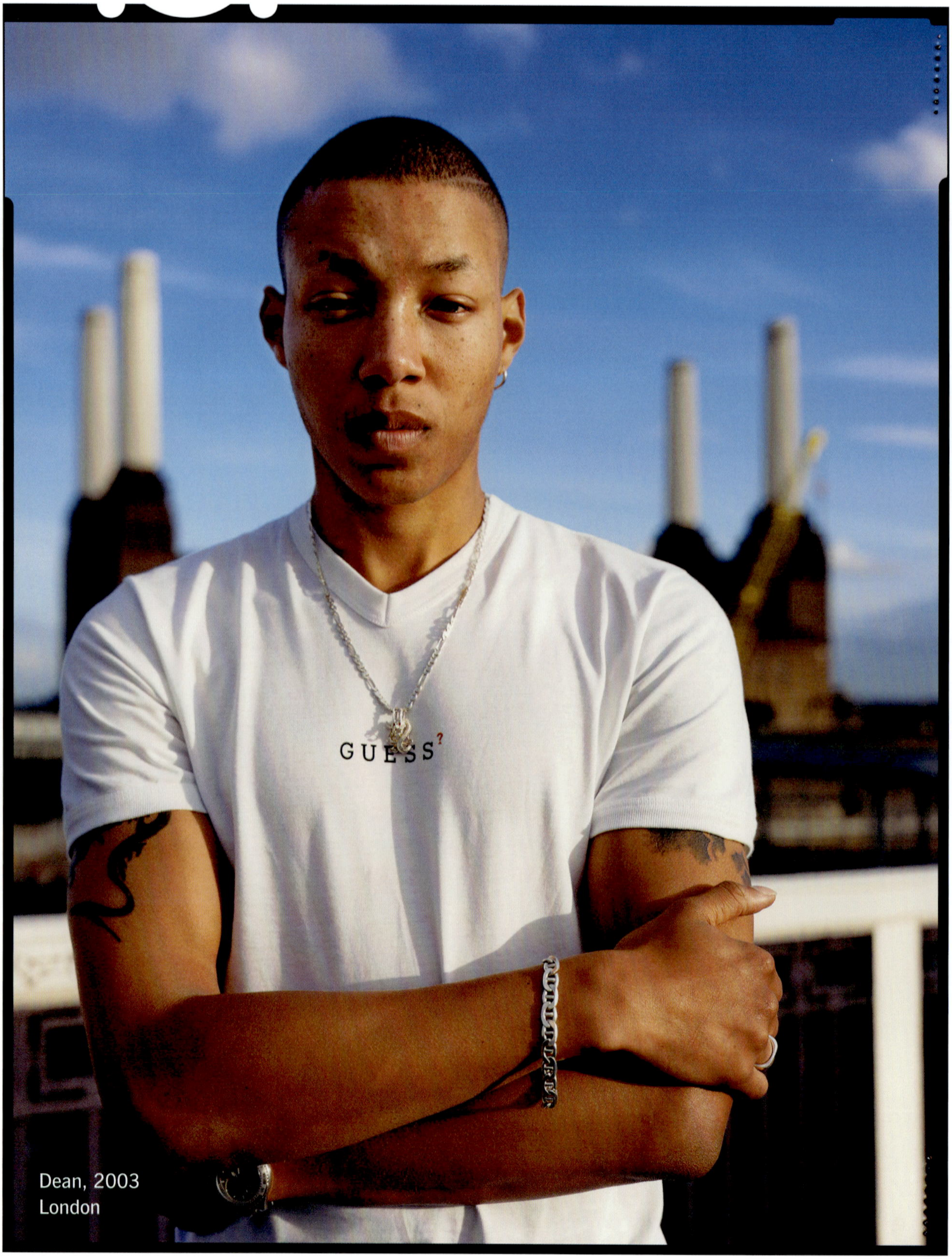

Dean, 2003
London

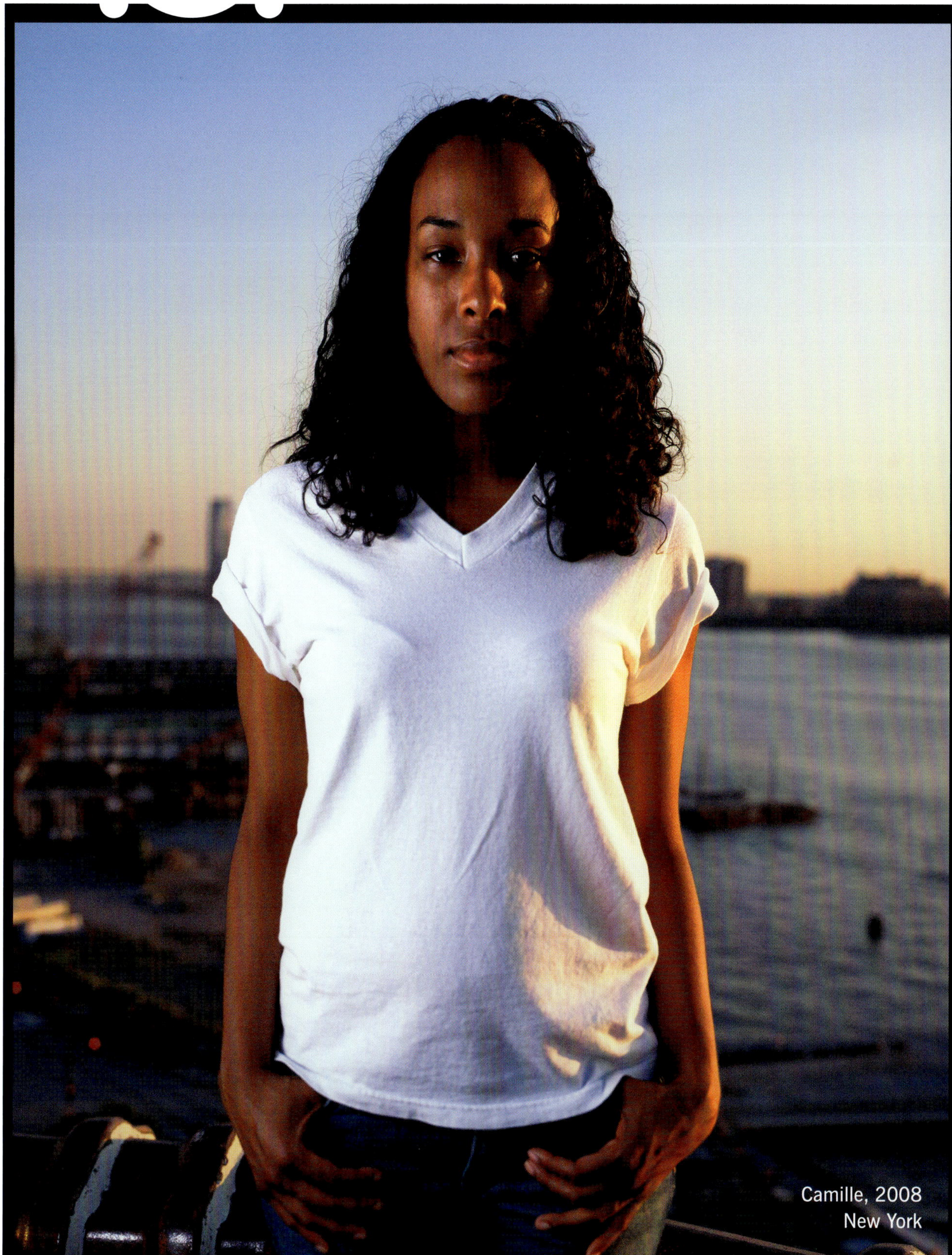

Camille, 2008
New York

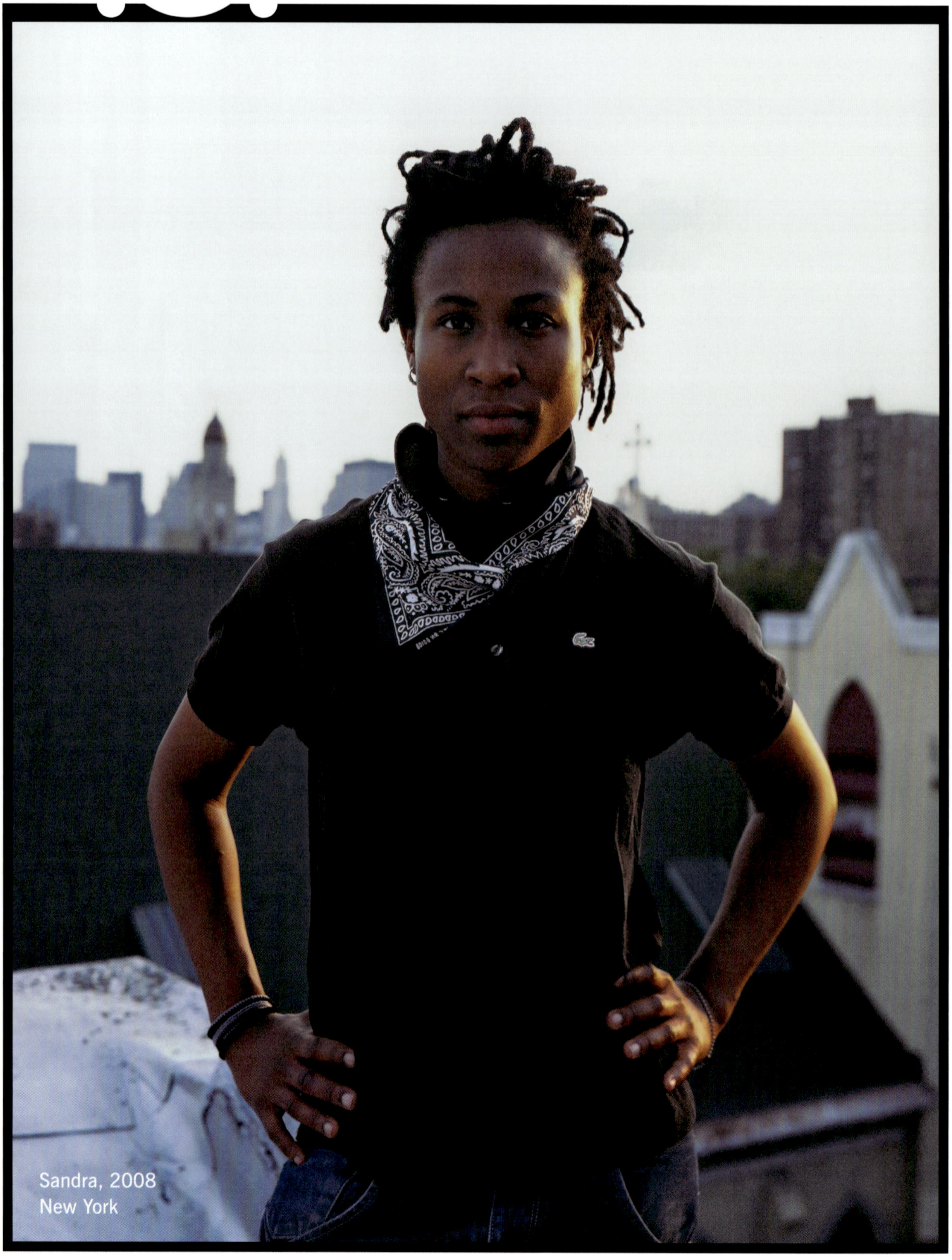

Sandra, 2008
New York

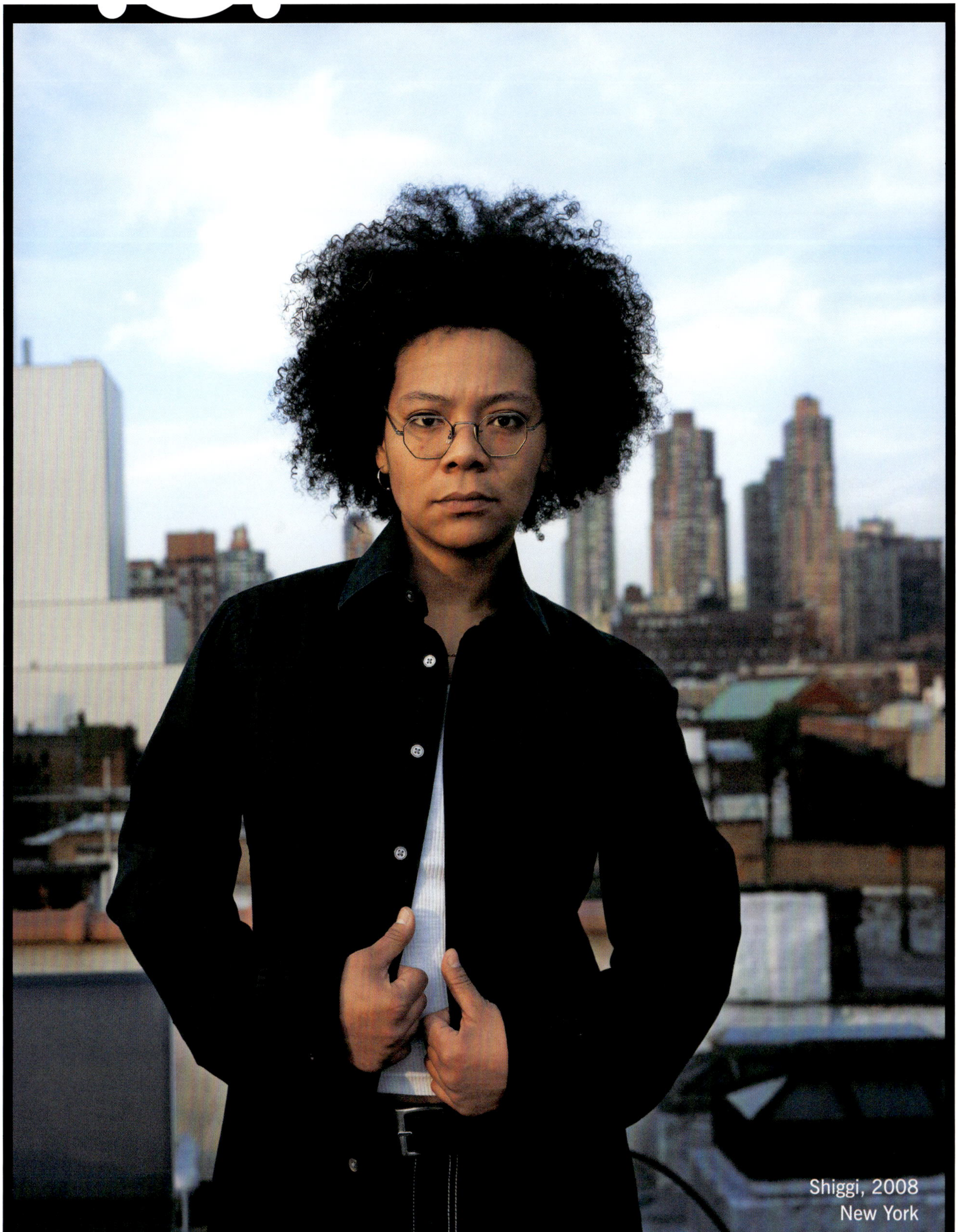

Shiggi, 2008
New York

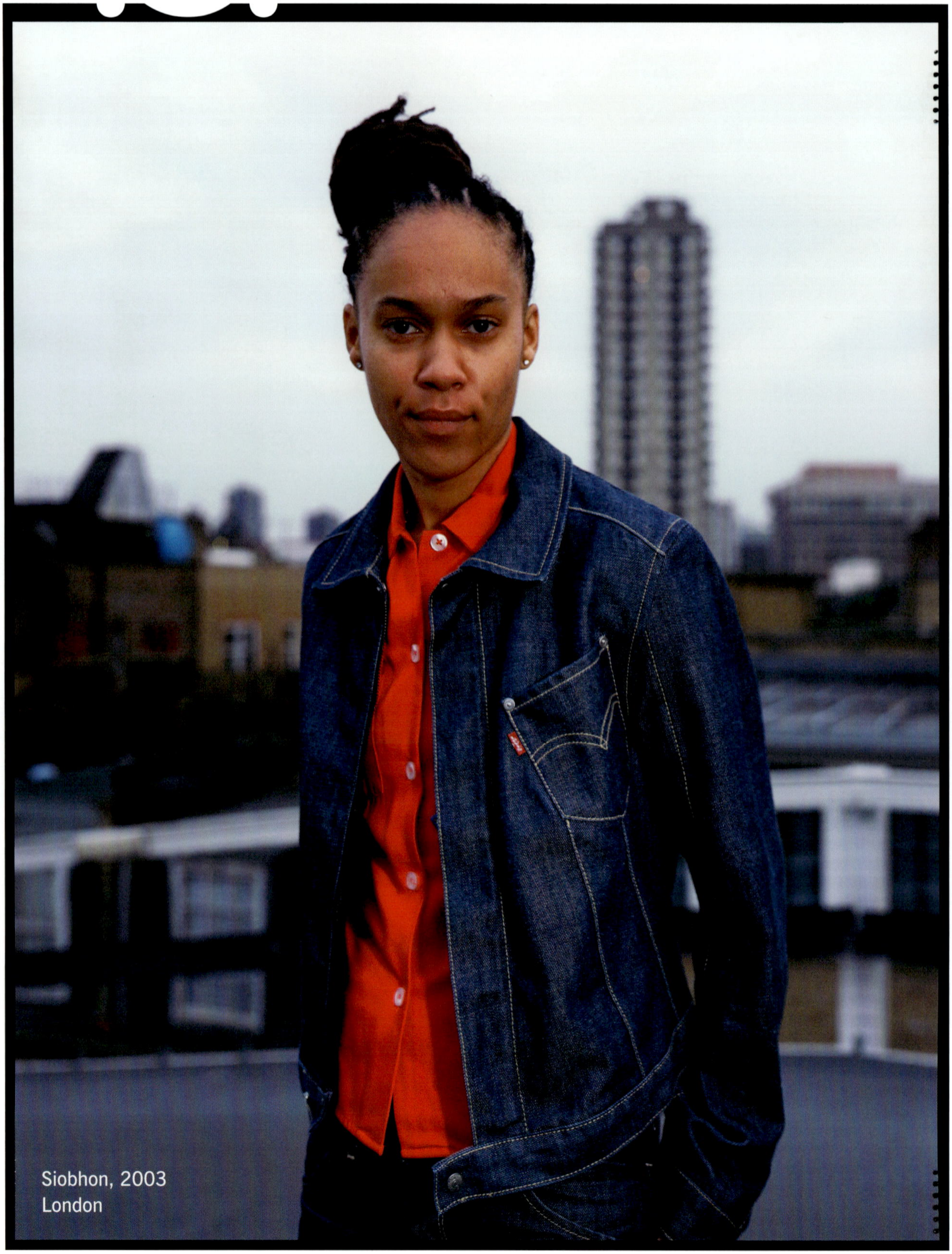

Siobhon, 2003
London

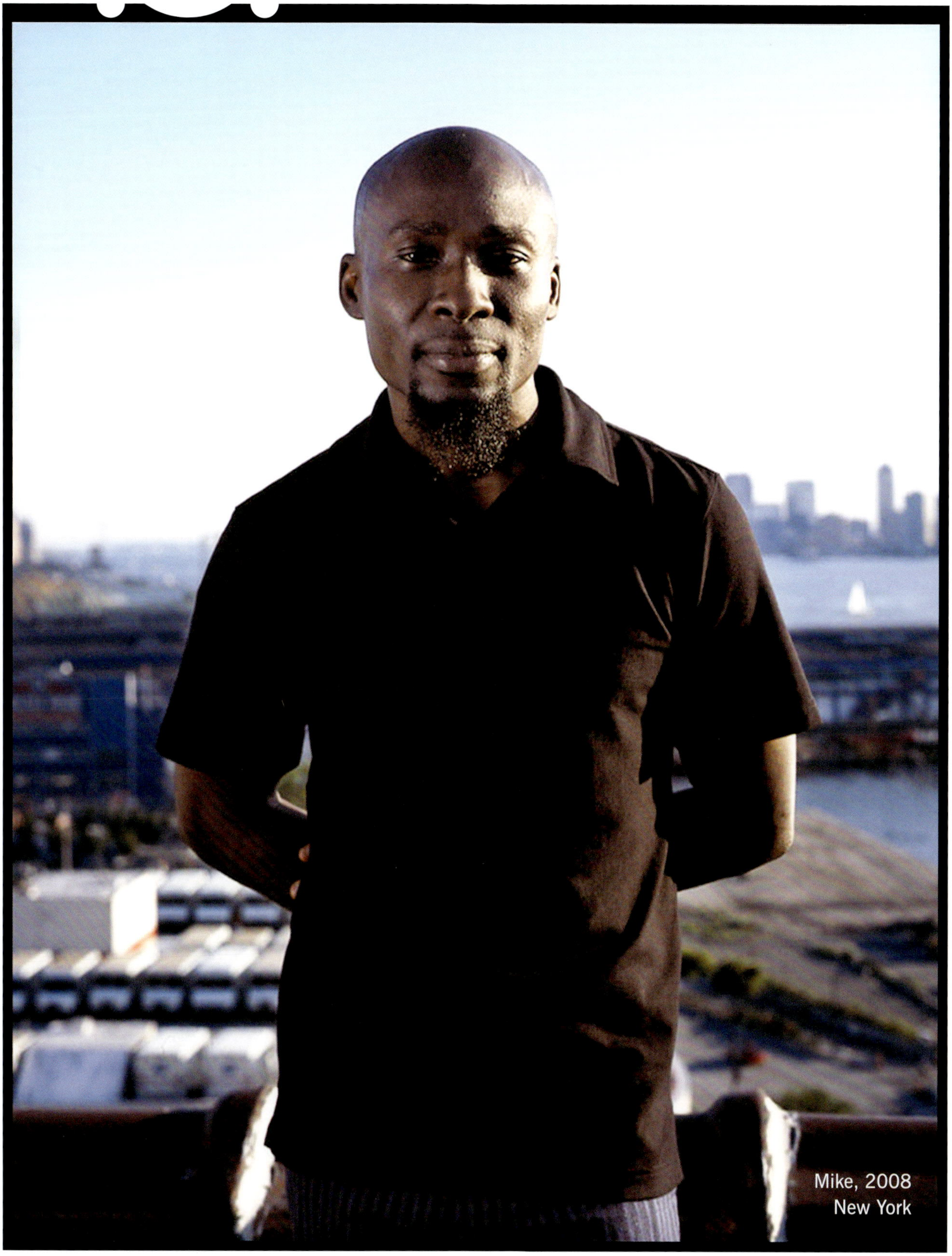

Mike, 2008
New York

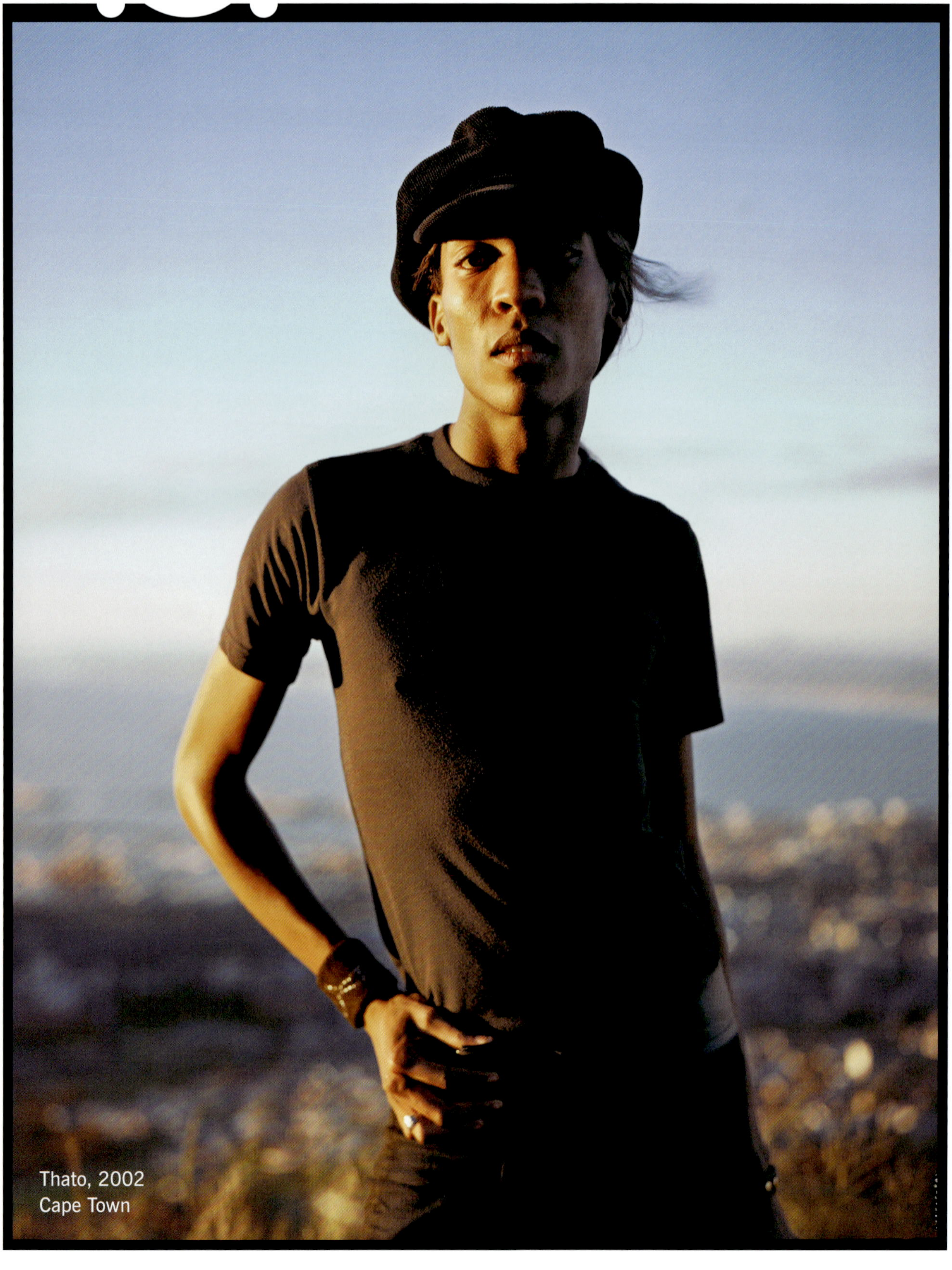

Thato, 2002
Cape Town

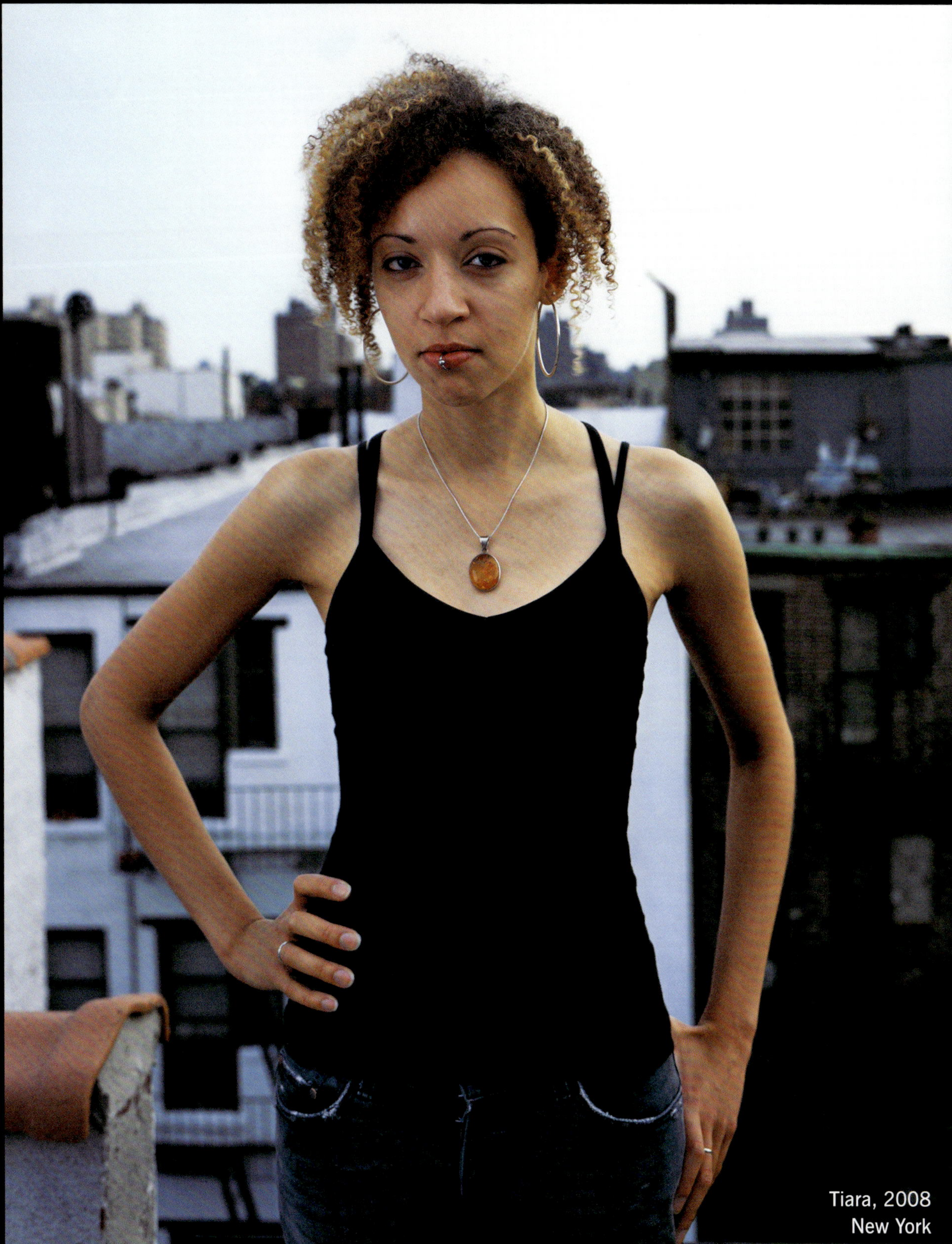

Tiara, 2008
New York

LEGENDS

These are the people who spear-headed a movement that wasn't a given. They are the trailblazers who presented an honest vision that clashed against societal norms, as we knew them. Where there was once no canon, each LEGEND in their own beautiful way, has harnessed a pride that transcends hate. They made it possible for the LGBTQ+ community to not only survive but to live a life of love.

Lina Bradford, 2016
New York

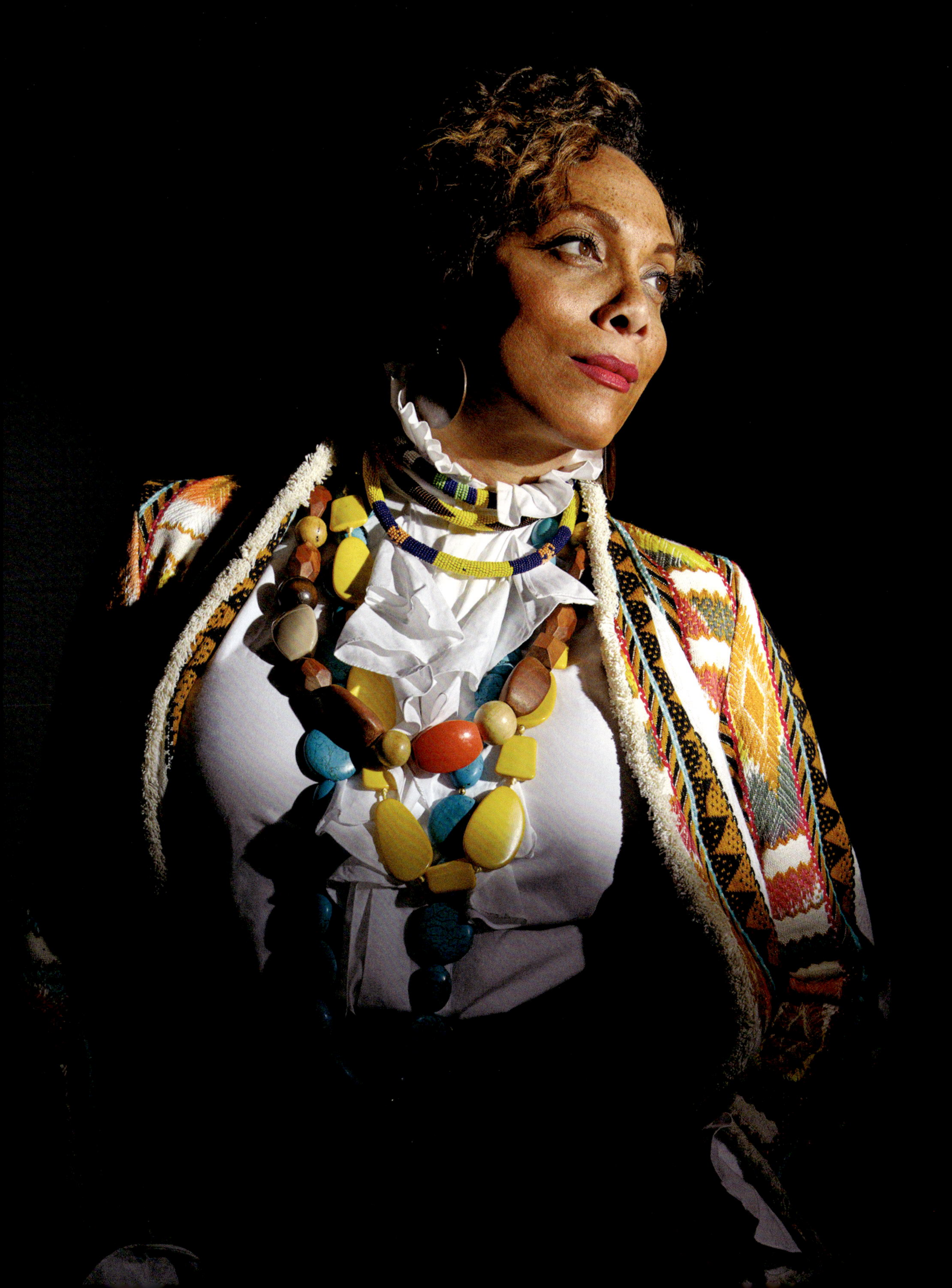

Juan Fernandez, 2017
Los Angeles

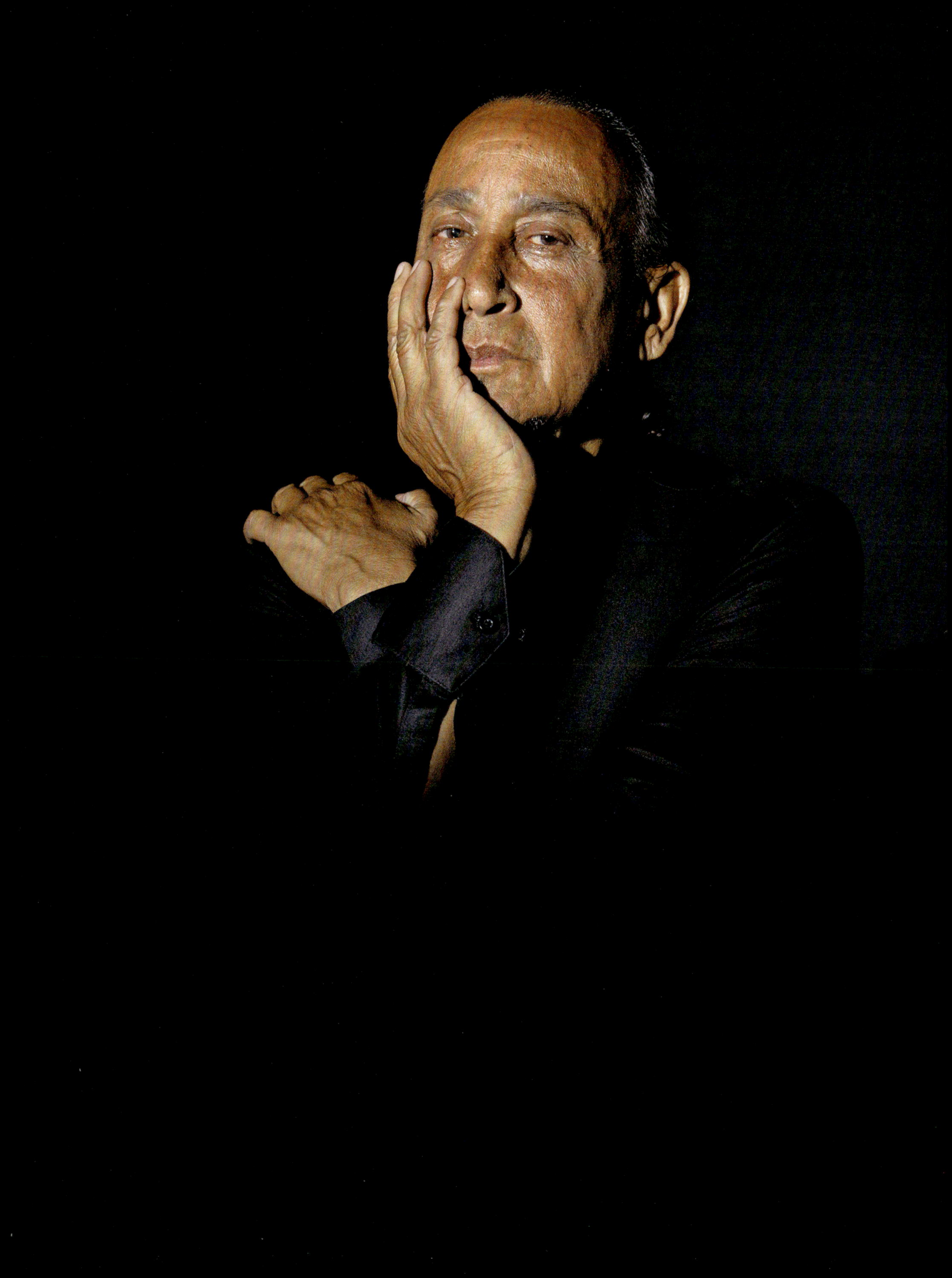

Sur Ron (Sur), 2017
New York

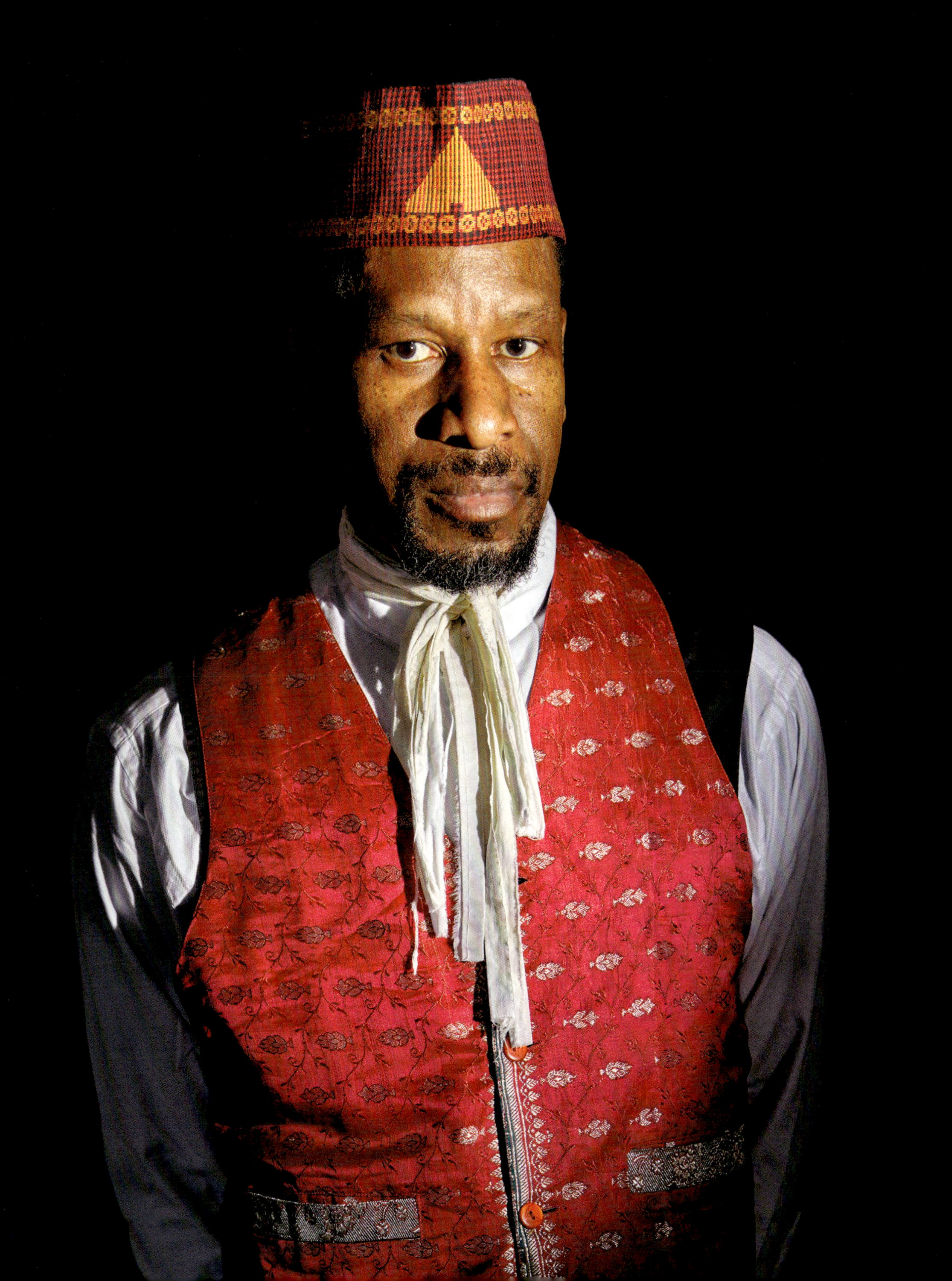

Guinevere Turner, 2017
New York

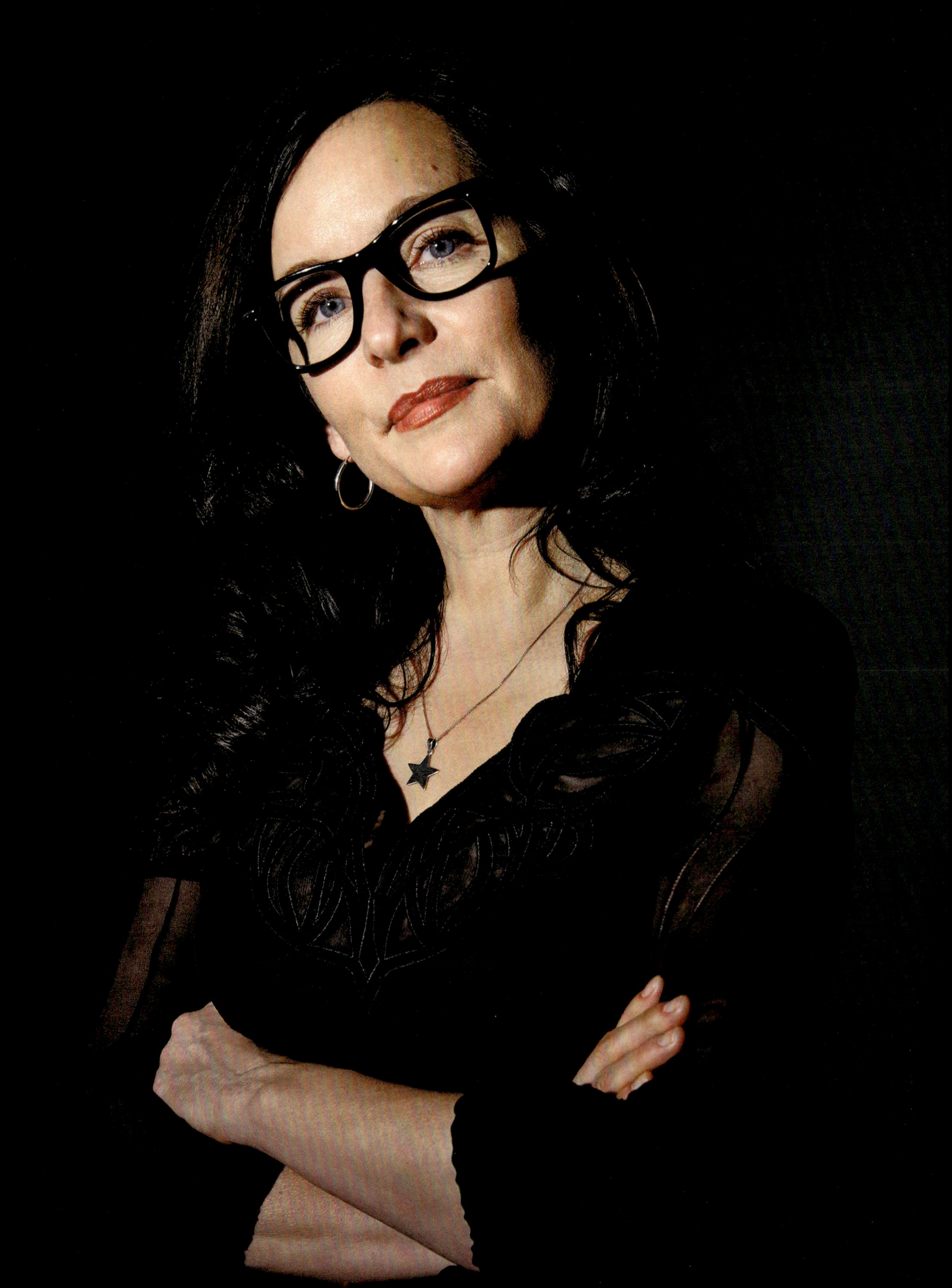

Cheryl Dunye, 2017
Los Angeles

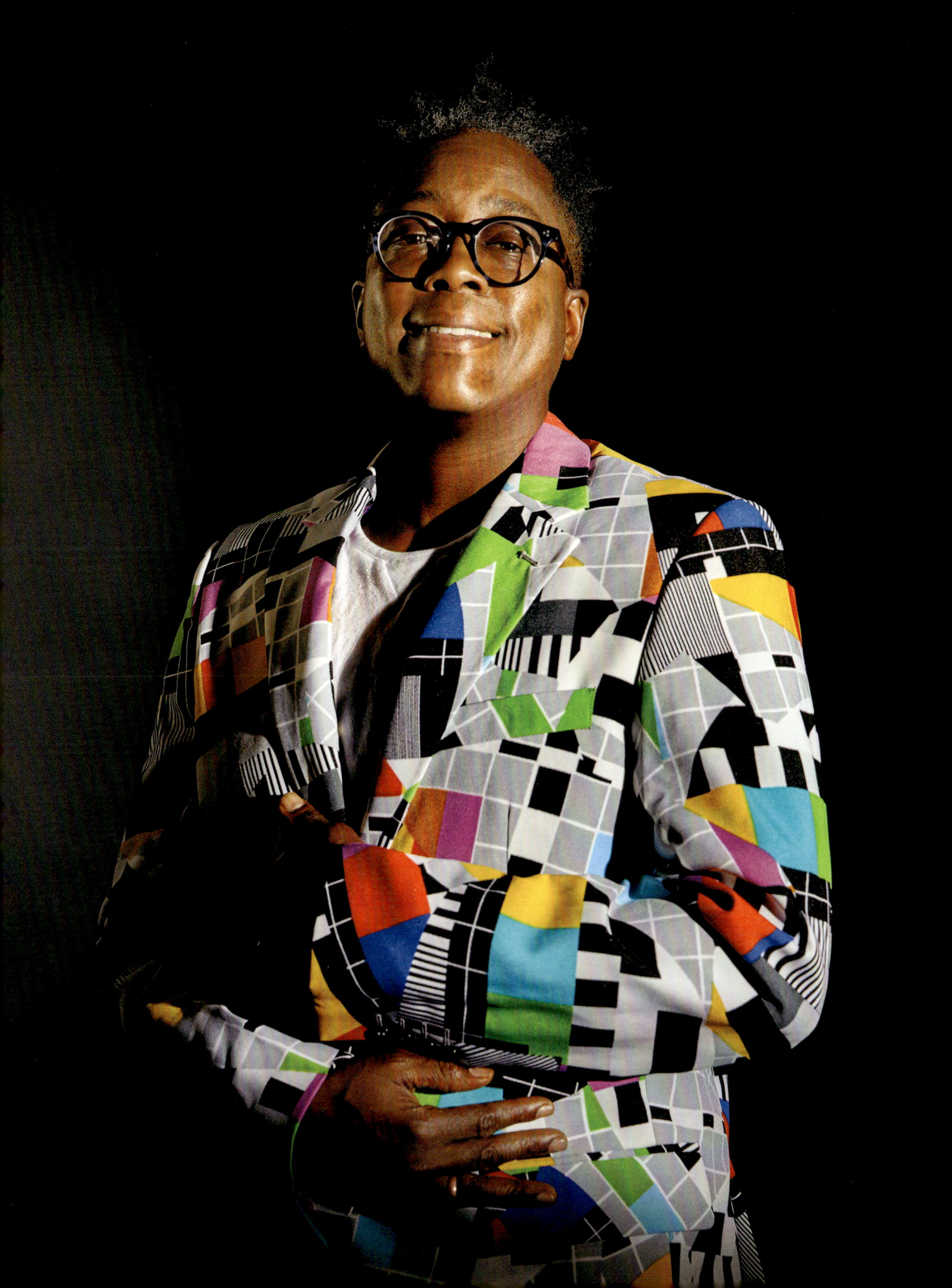

Murray Hill, 2016
New York

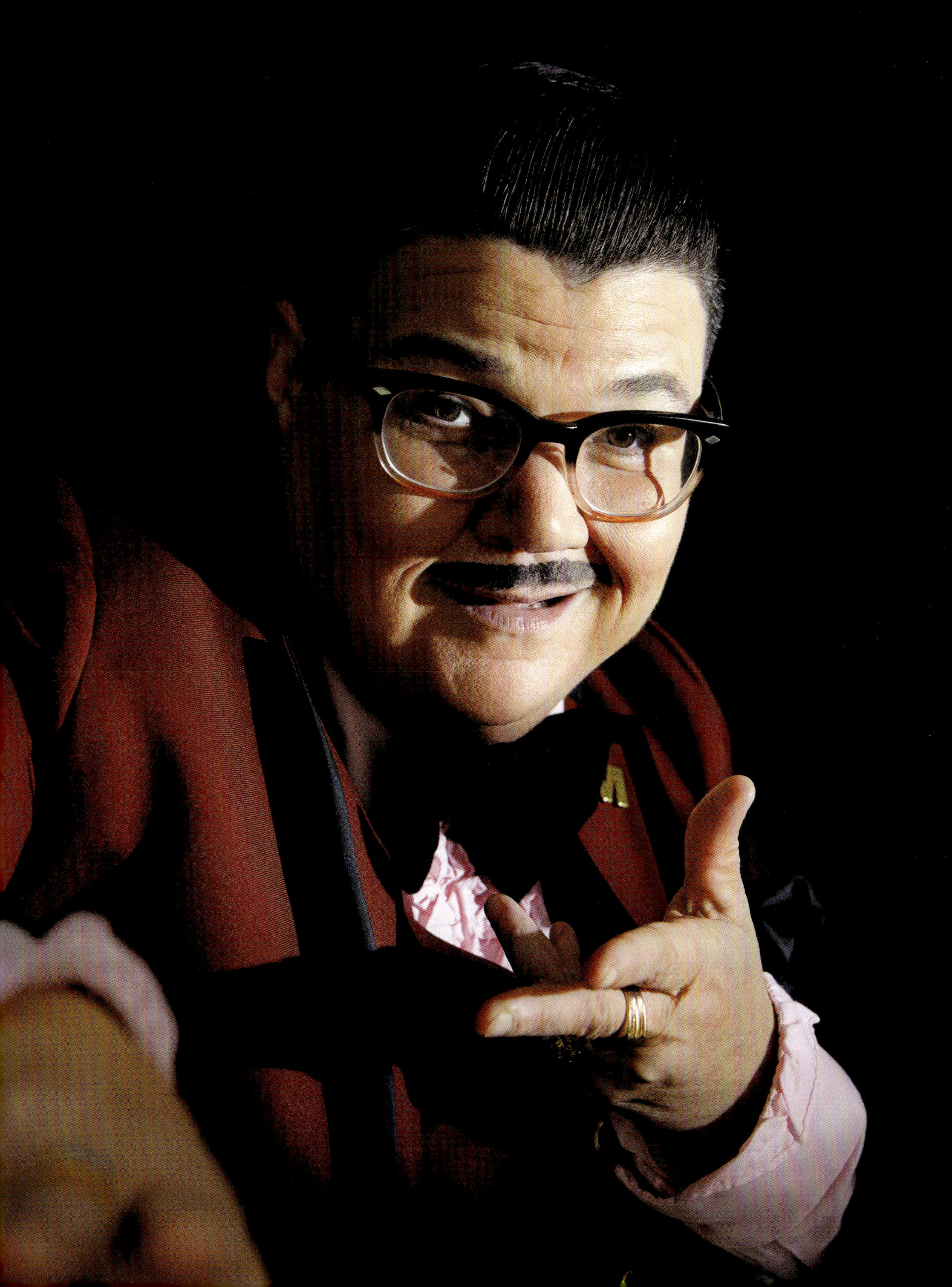

The Maine Attraction, 2016
New York

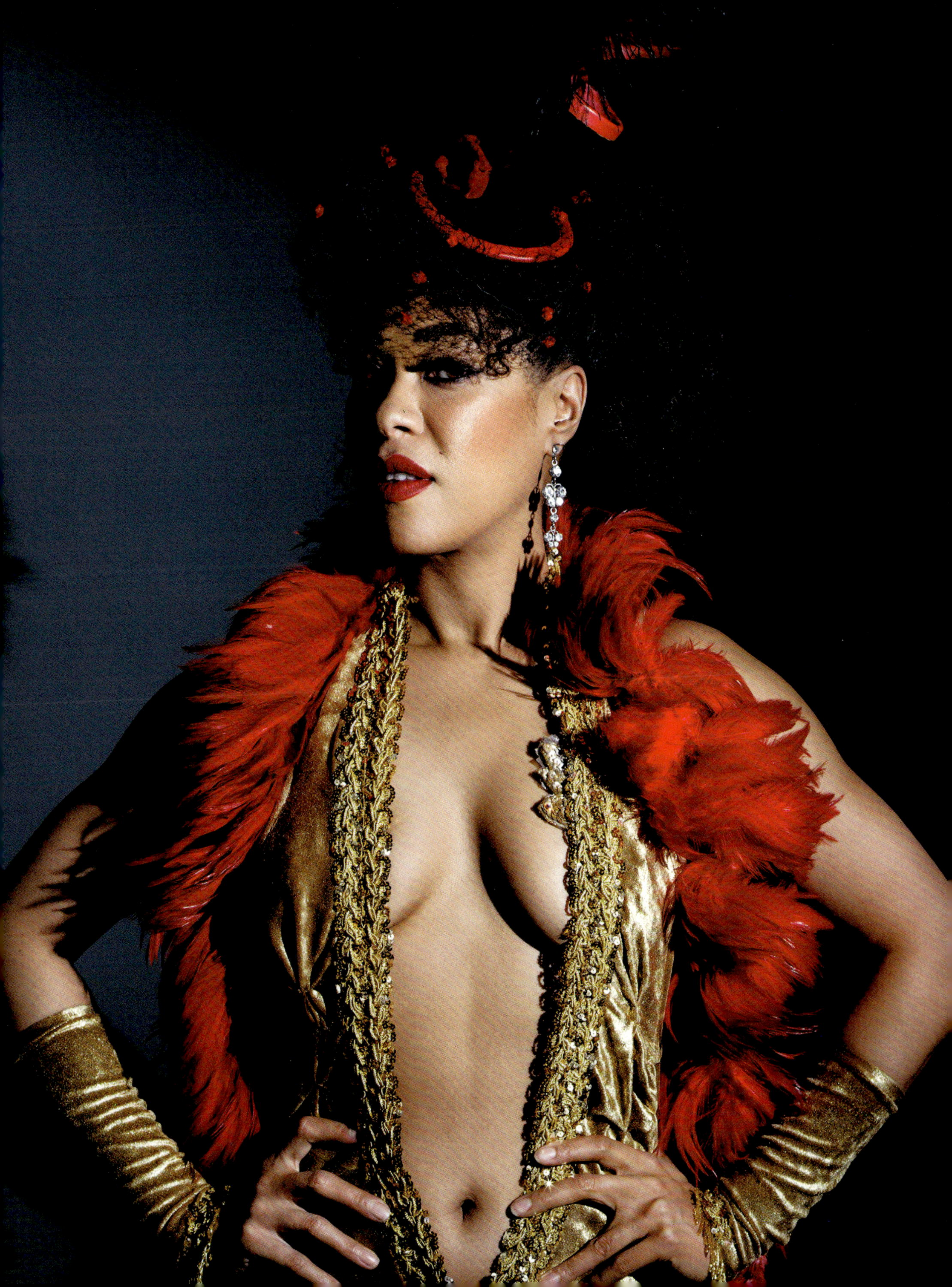

Kate Clinton, 2019
New York

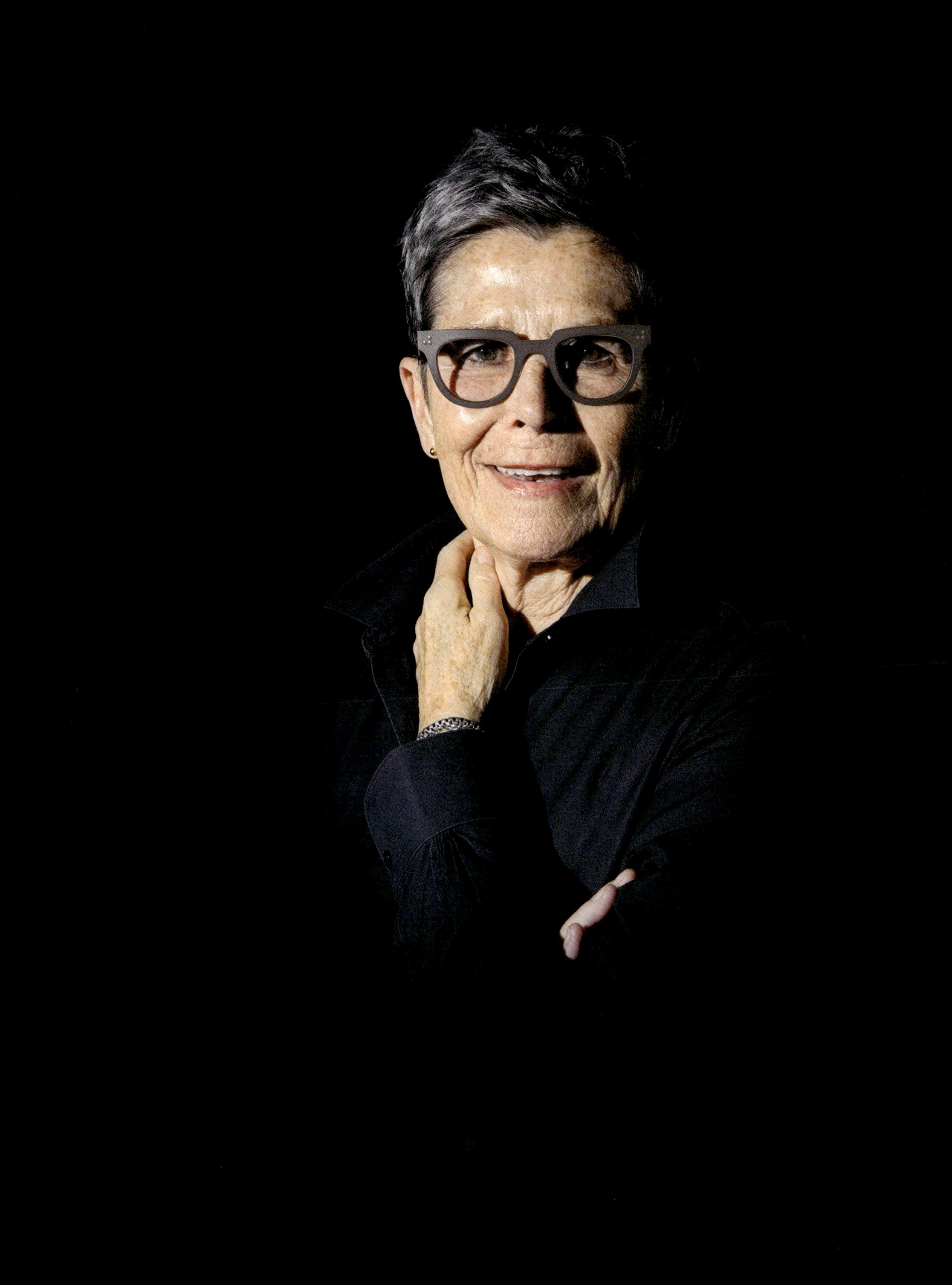

Sherry Vine, 2016
New York

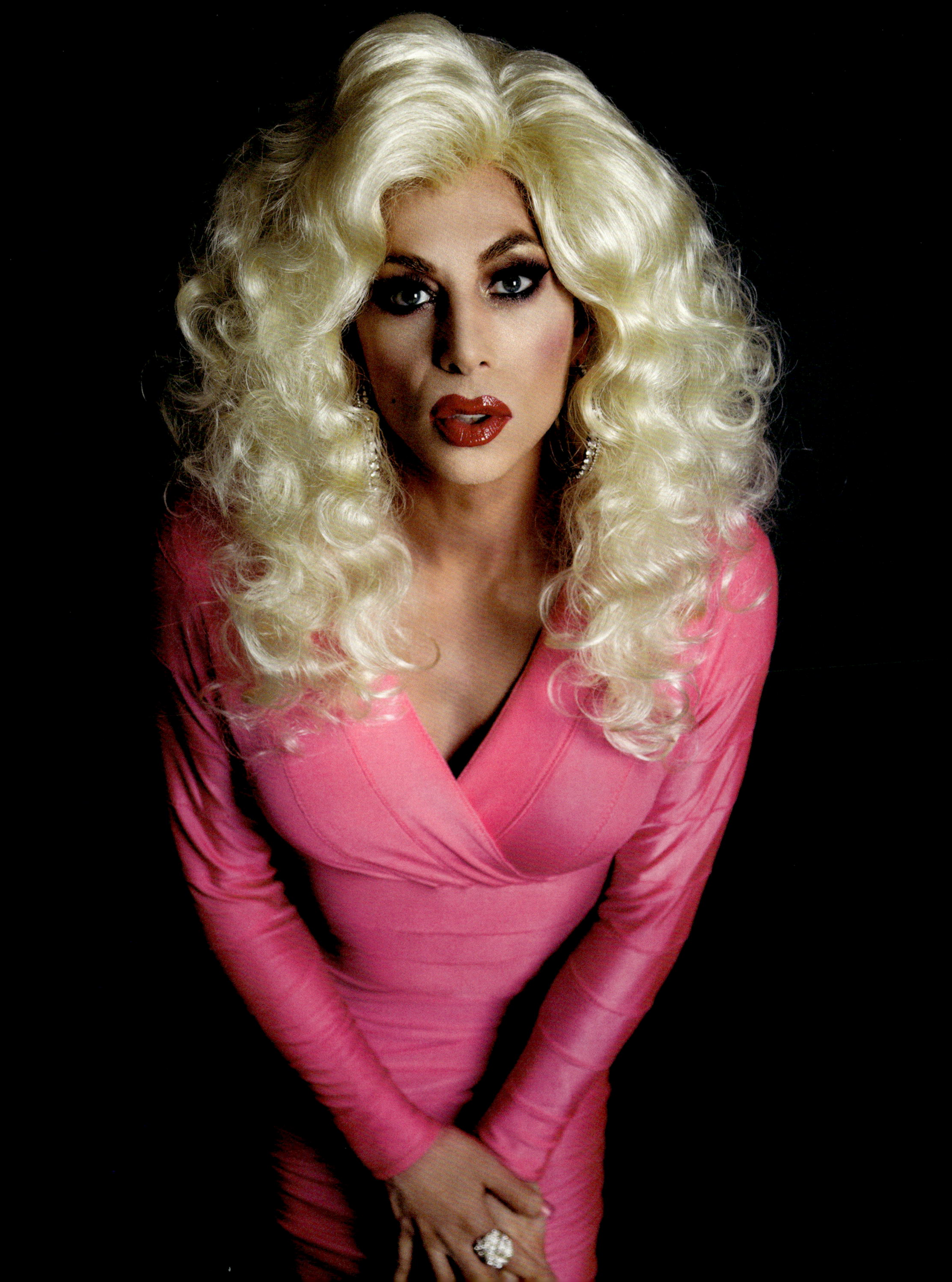

Bill Coleman, 2017
New York

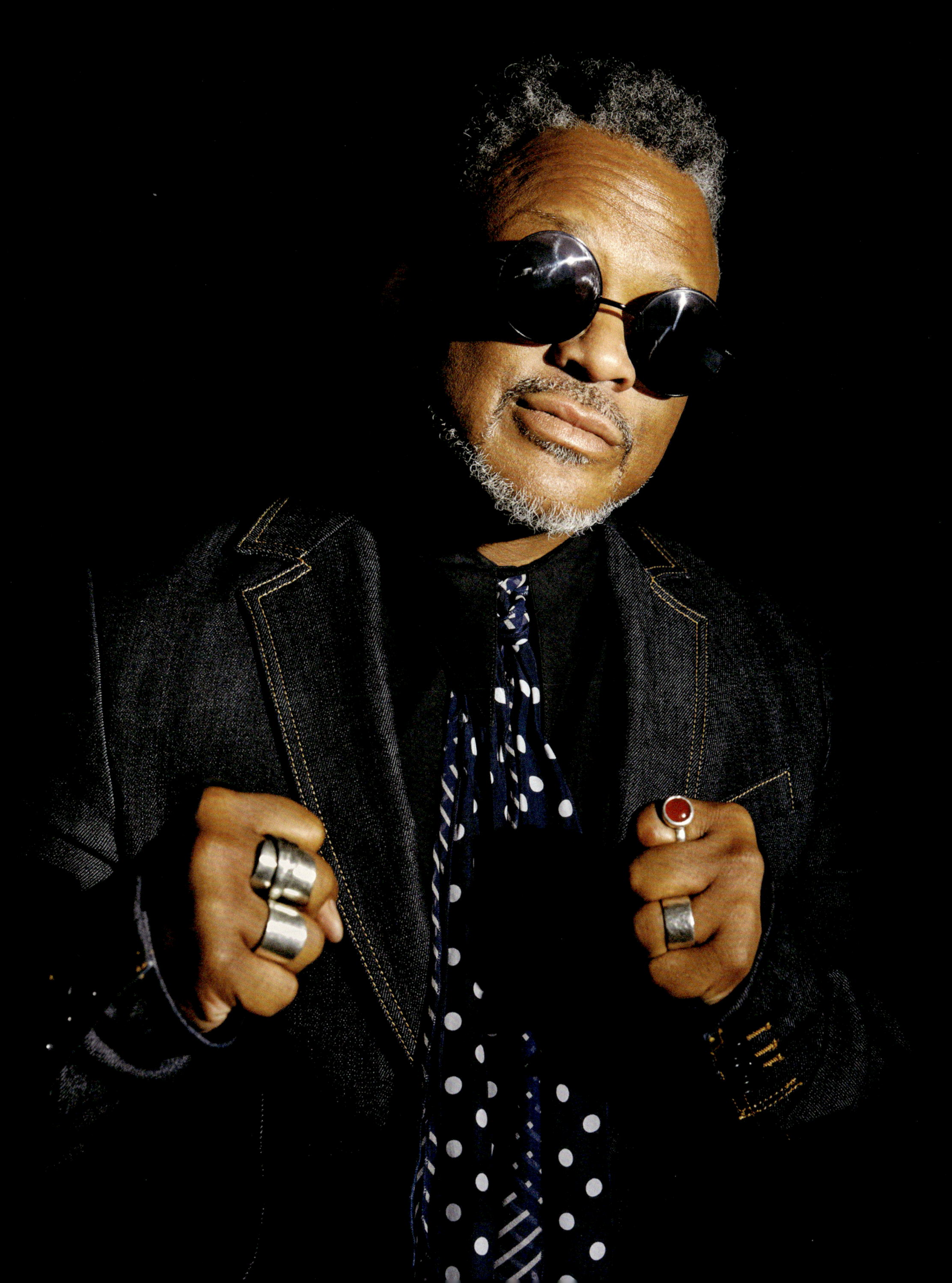

Pamela Sneed, 2017
New York

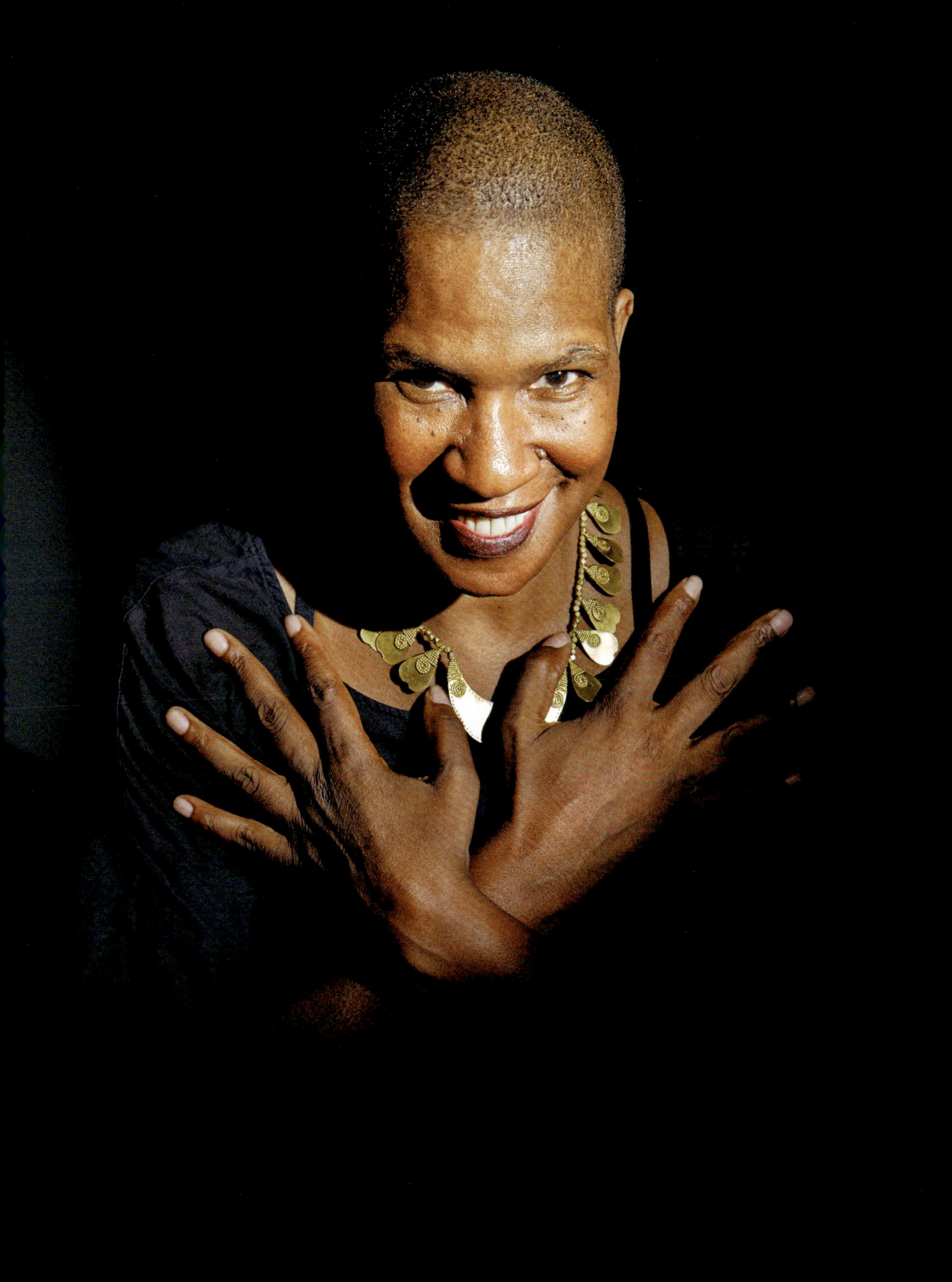

DJ Formika, 2016
New York

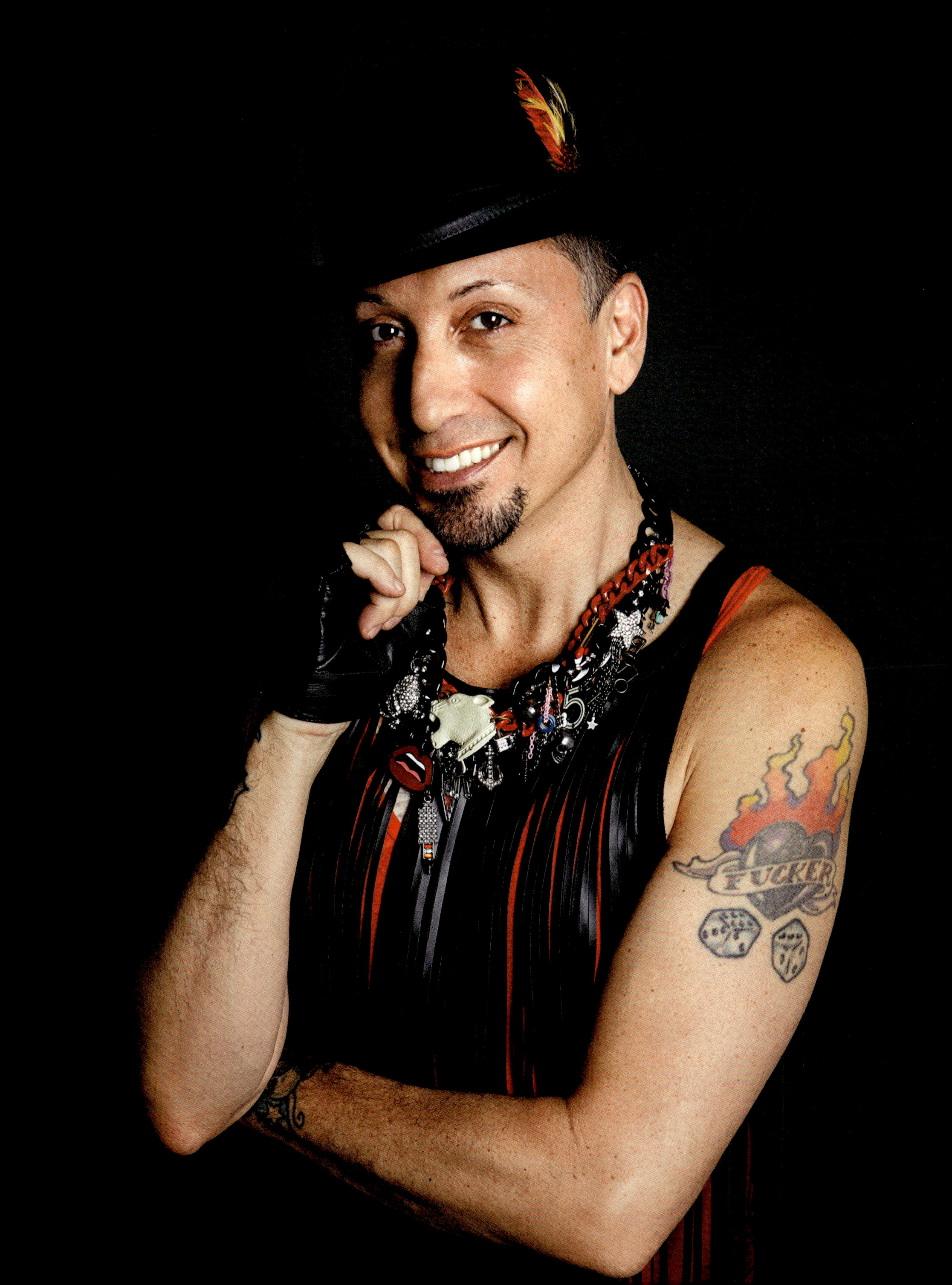
FUCKER

Heather Liteer, 2017
New York

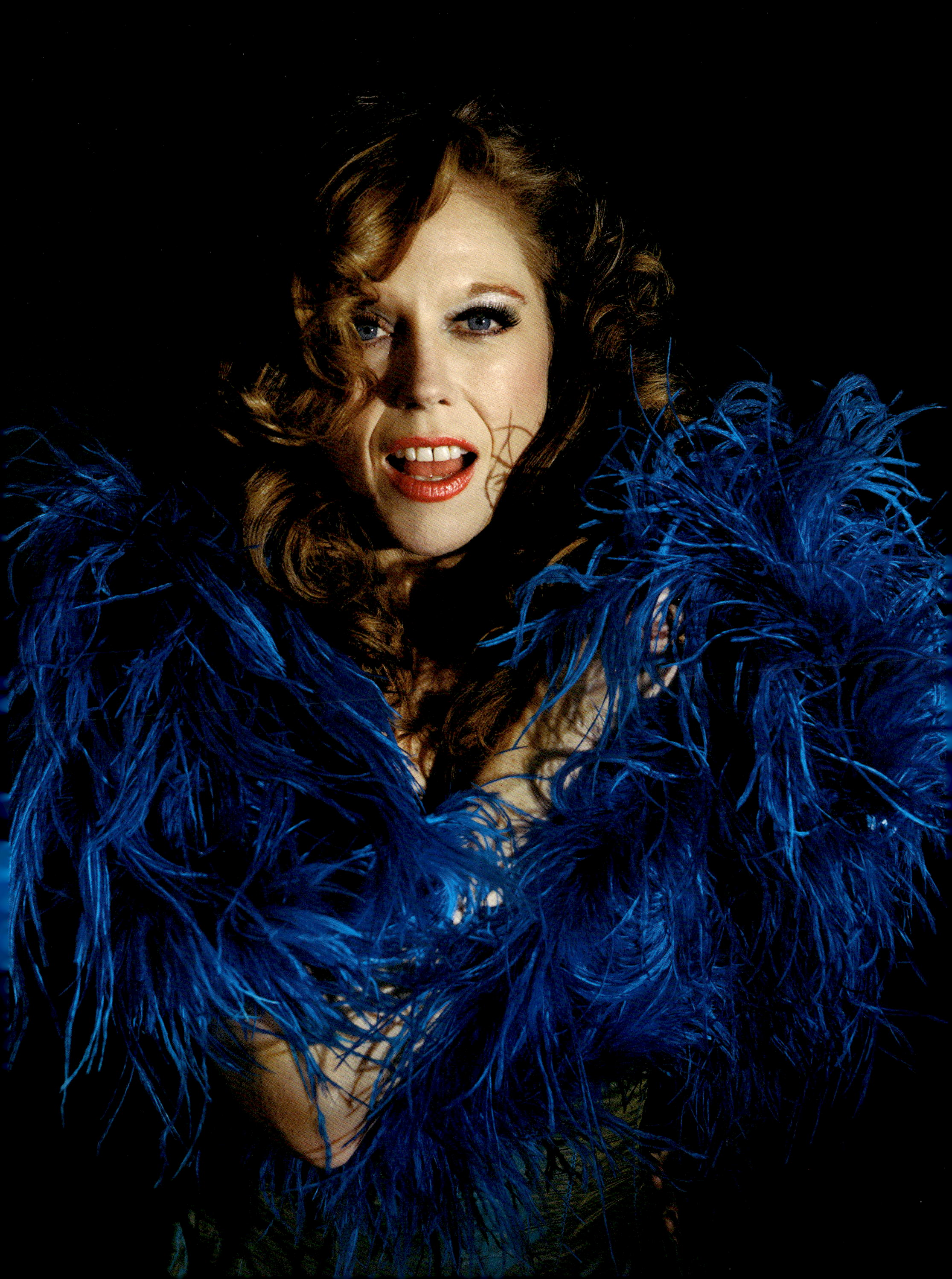

Buck Angel, 2017
Los Angeles

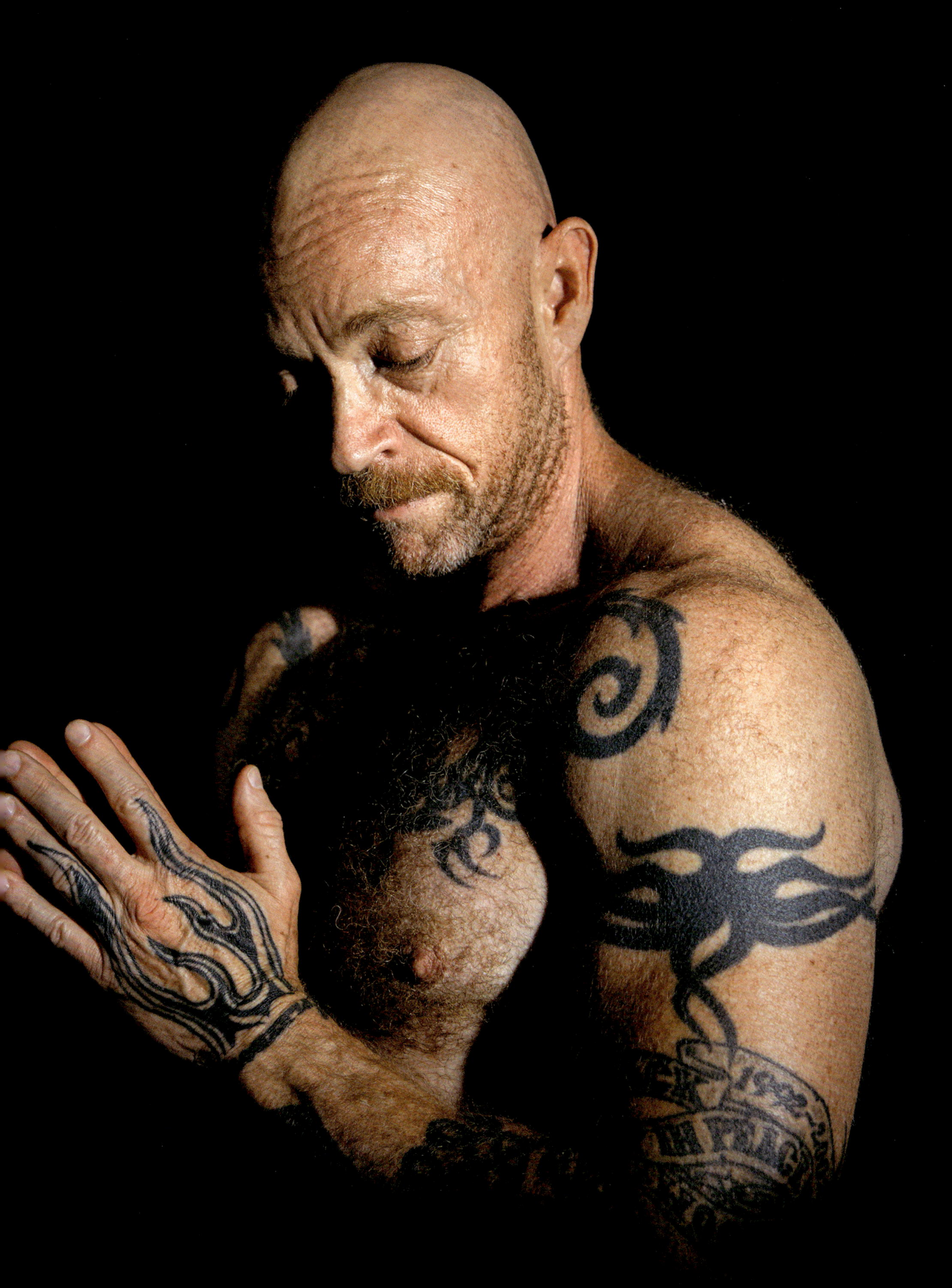

Tabboo, 2018
New York

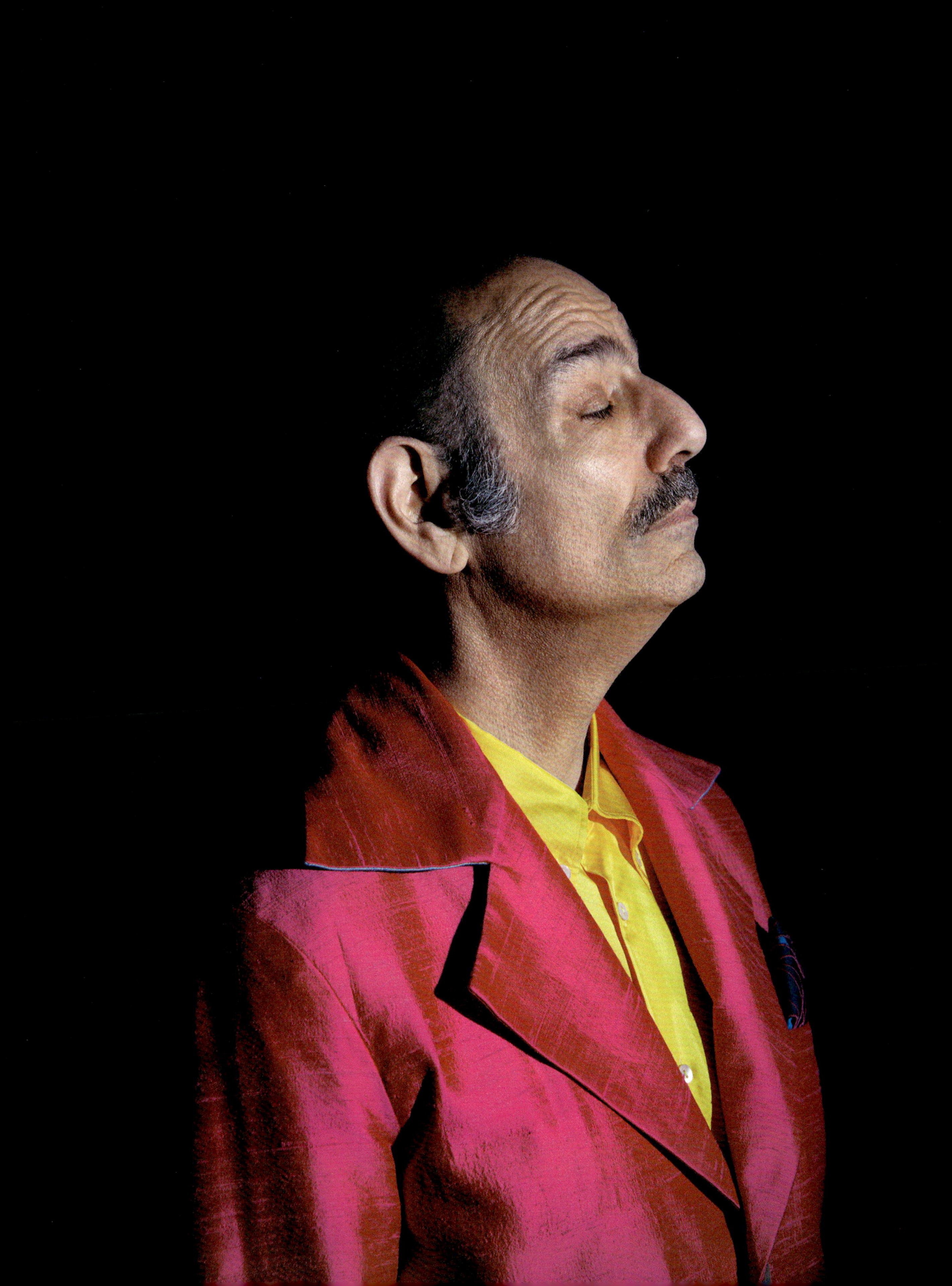

salt

Here, I have created portraits that feature iconic women who I strive to be like when I grow up. They are aged 70+ years and still fiercely engaged in their life's work. In a culture where beauty is equated with youth, these women are not only beautiful but accomplished and still making significant contributions to society.

Maria, 2011
Puerto Rico

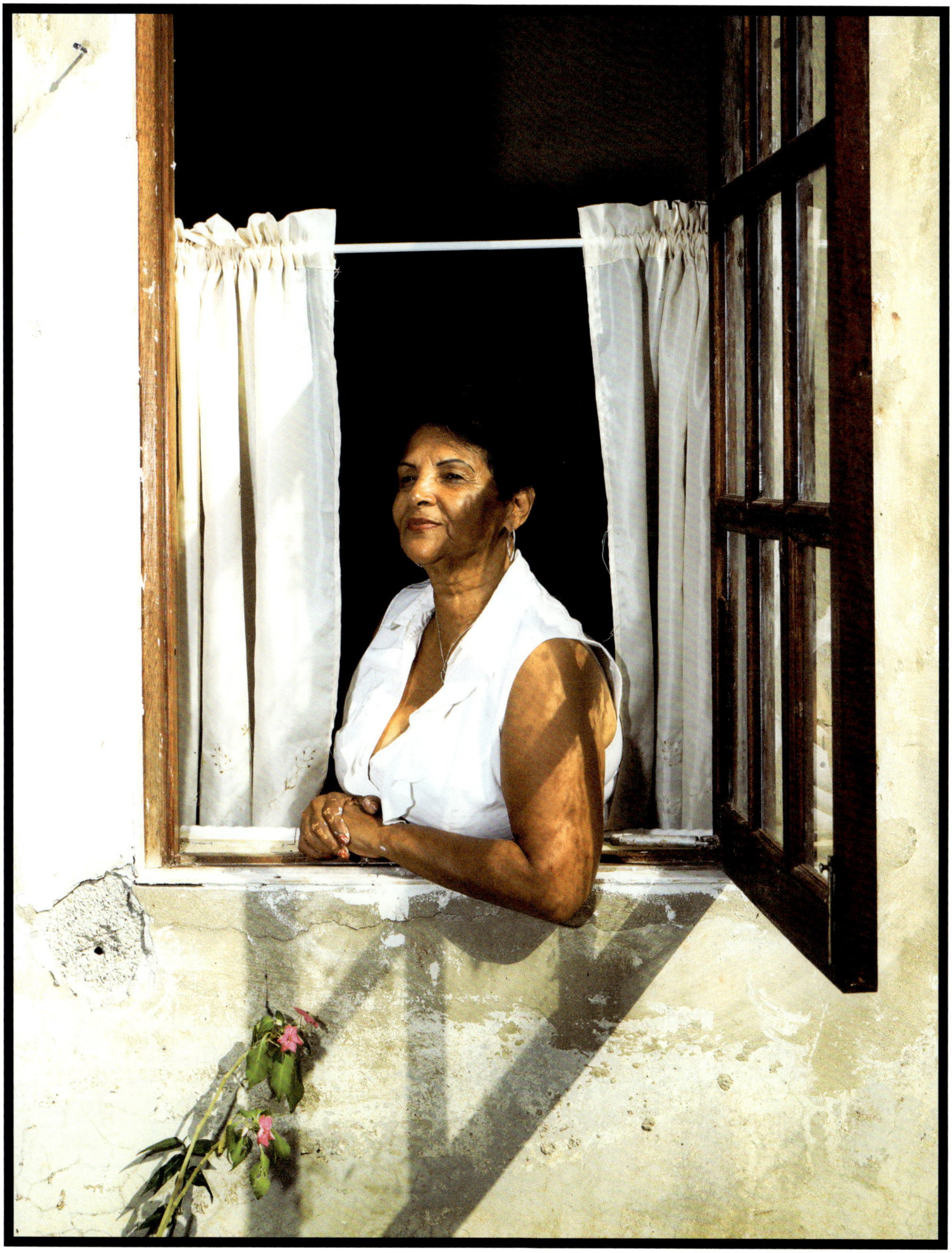

Toni, 2011
Torquay

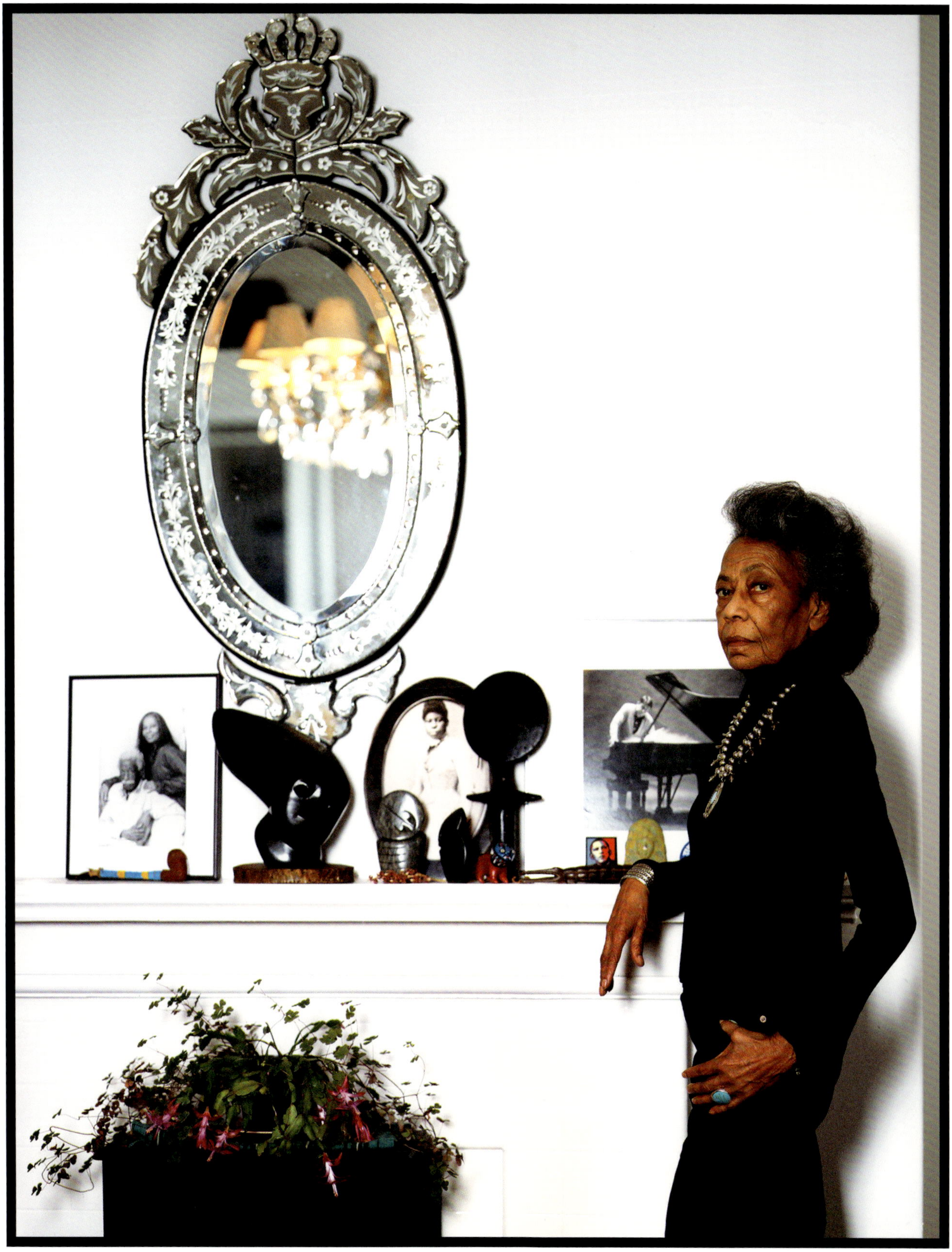

Esther, 2013
Brooklyn

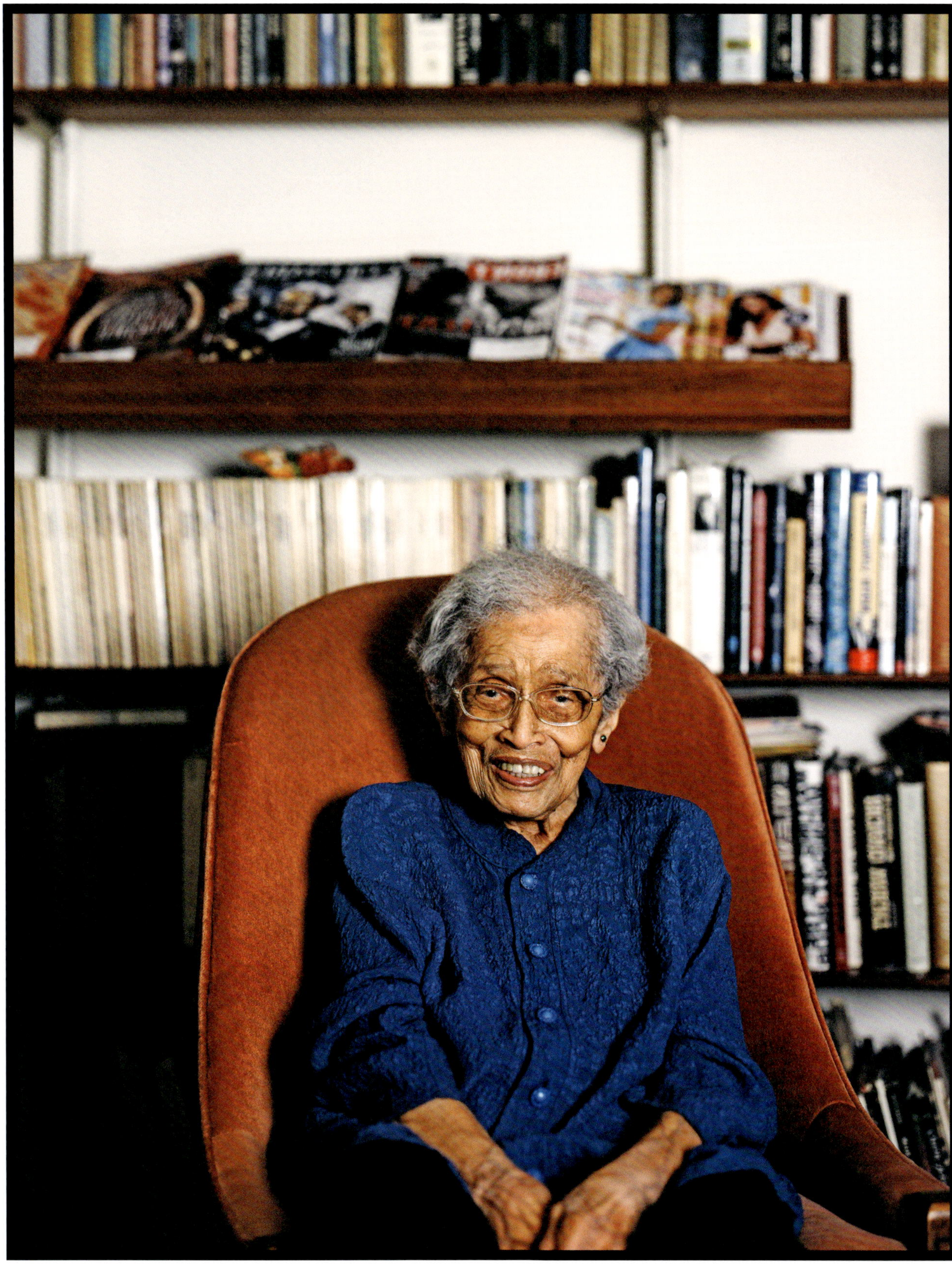

Nettie, 2015
Maplewood

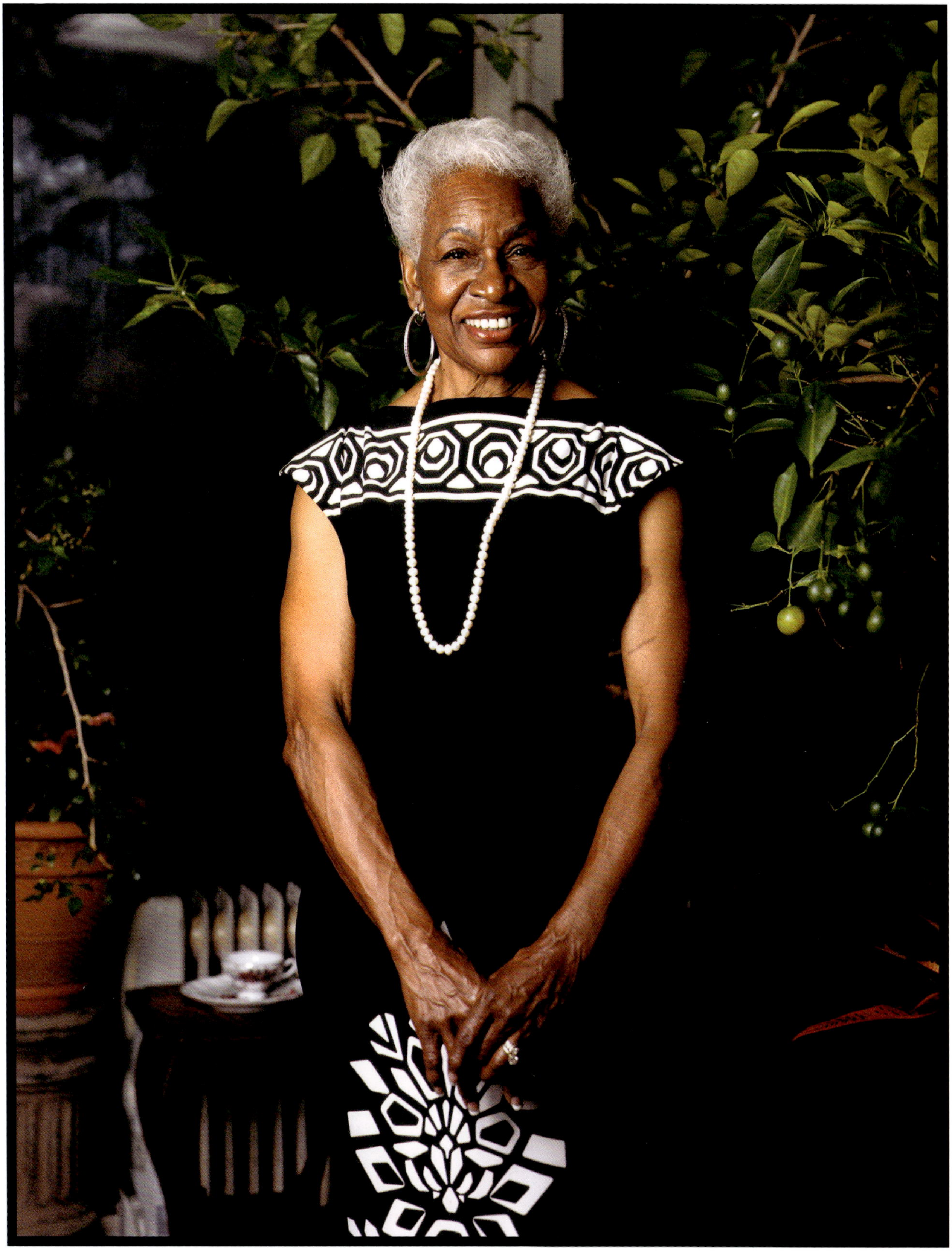

Agnes, 2015
New York

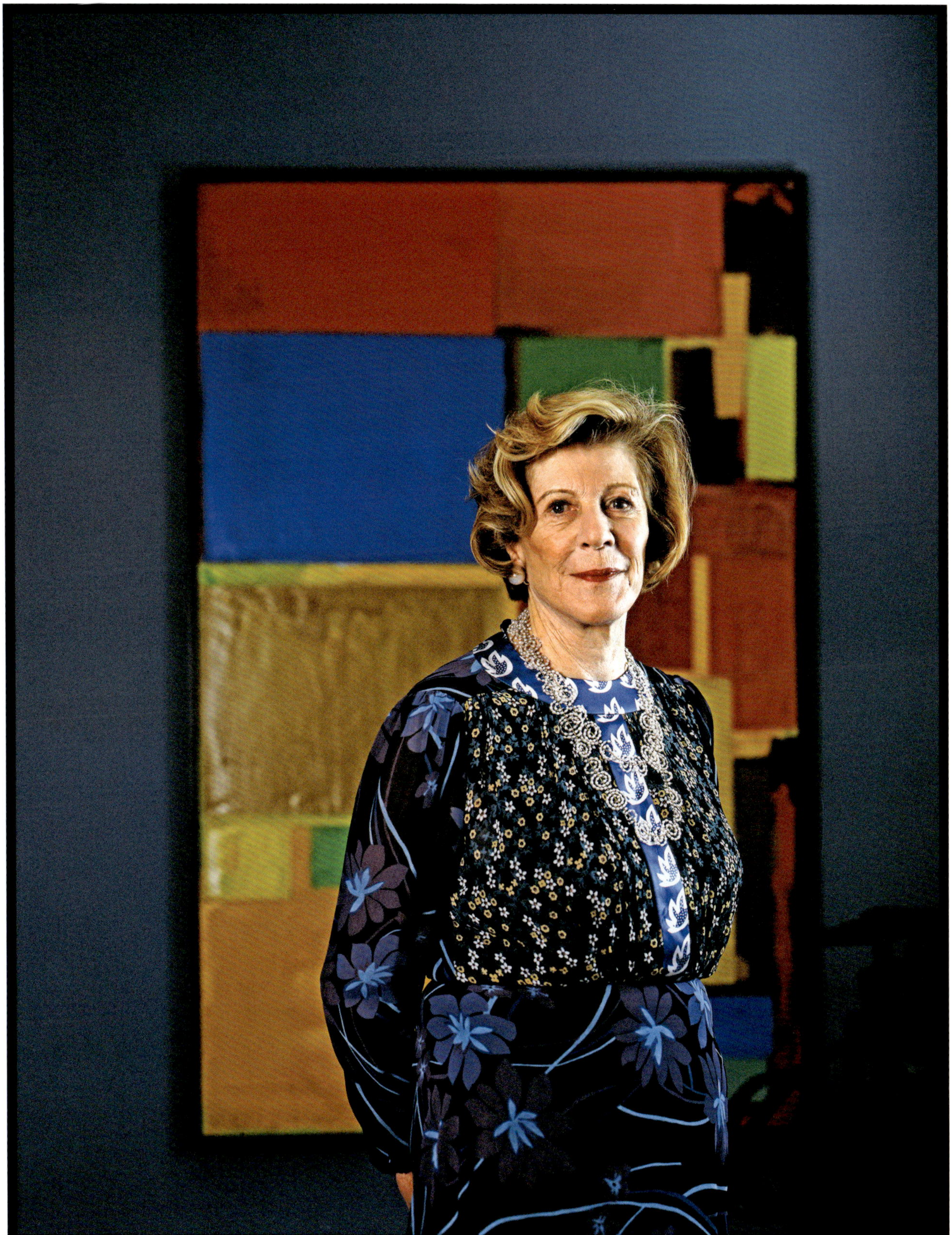

Ilona, 2012
New York

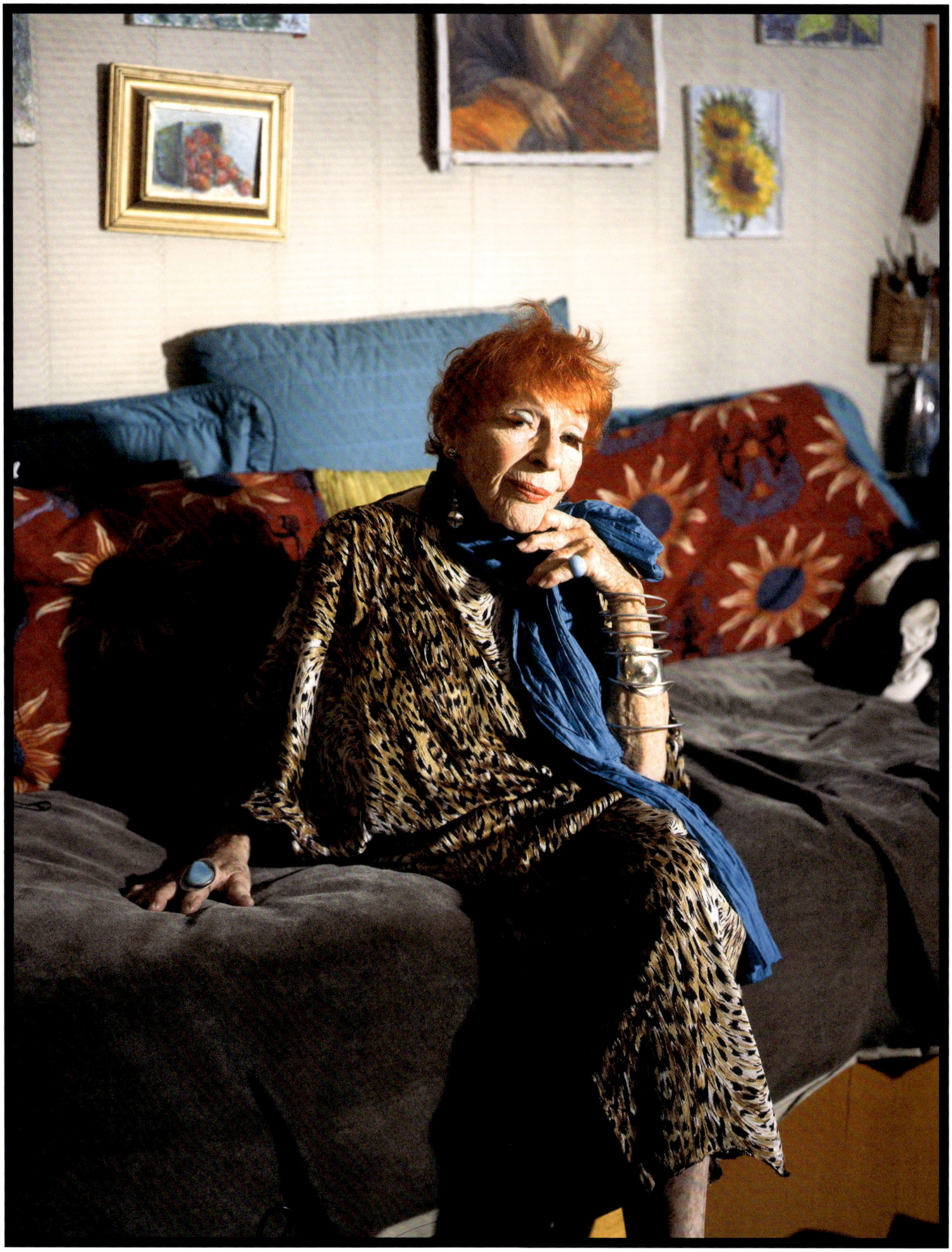

Gai, 2017
Los Angeles

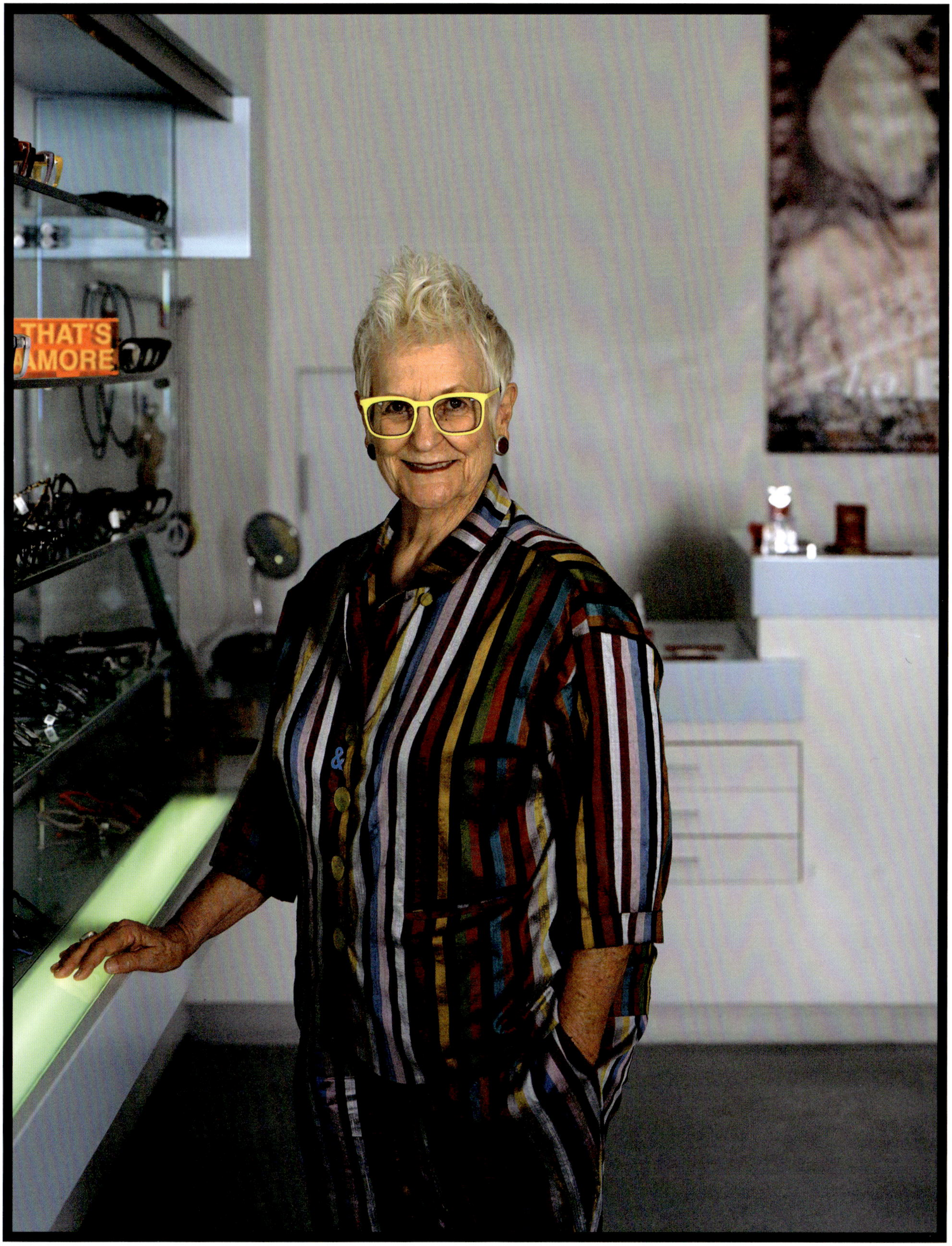
THAT'S
AMORE

Koho, 2013
New York

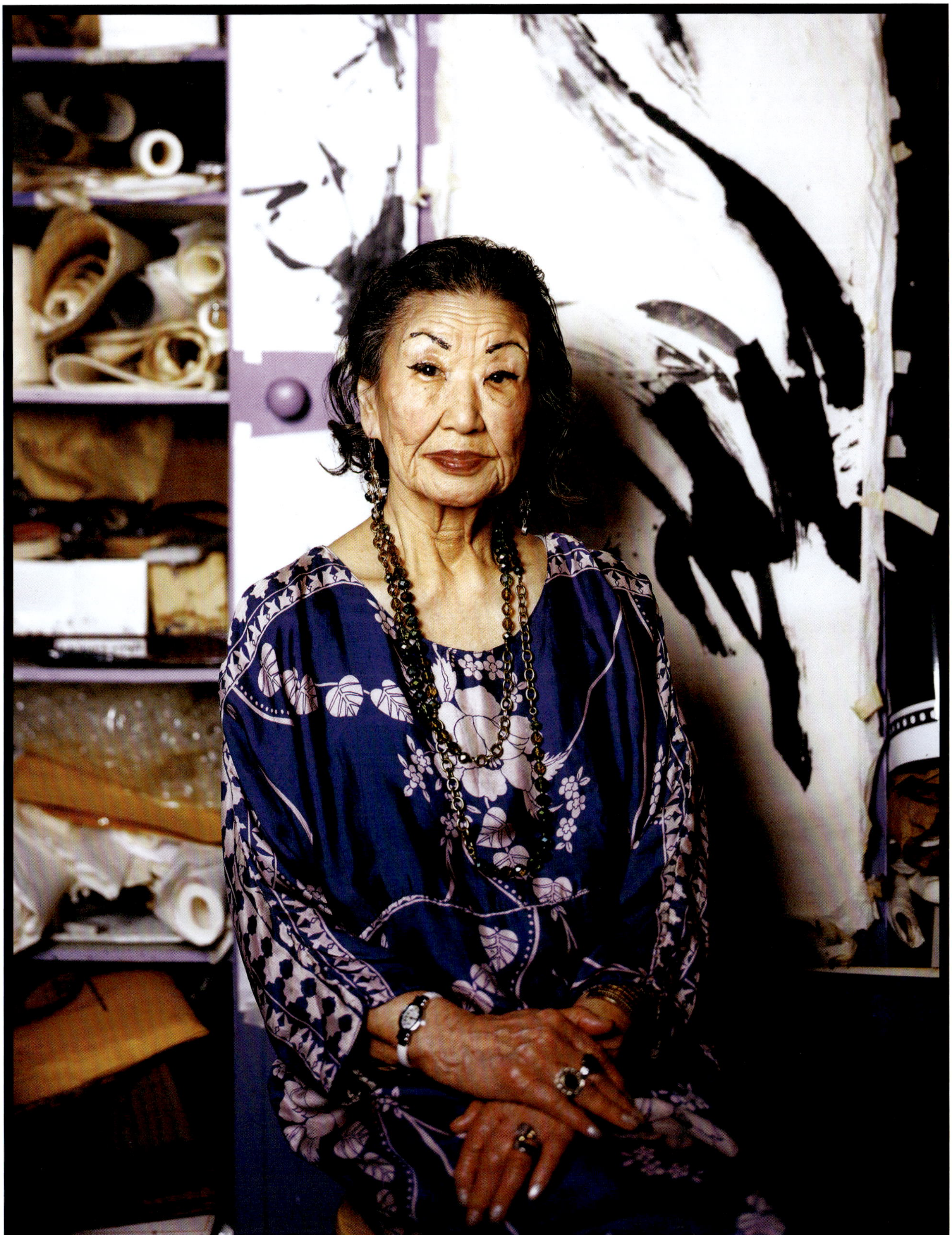

surmise

Surmise is an insiders' account of the many ways the LGBTQIA+ community is perceived and how certain images have adversely affected our psyche. These brave subjects reveal an alternative appearance, which creates a bold departure from the status quo.

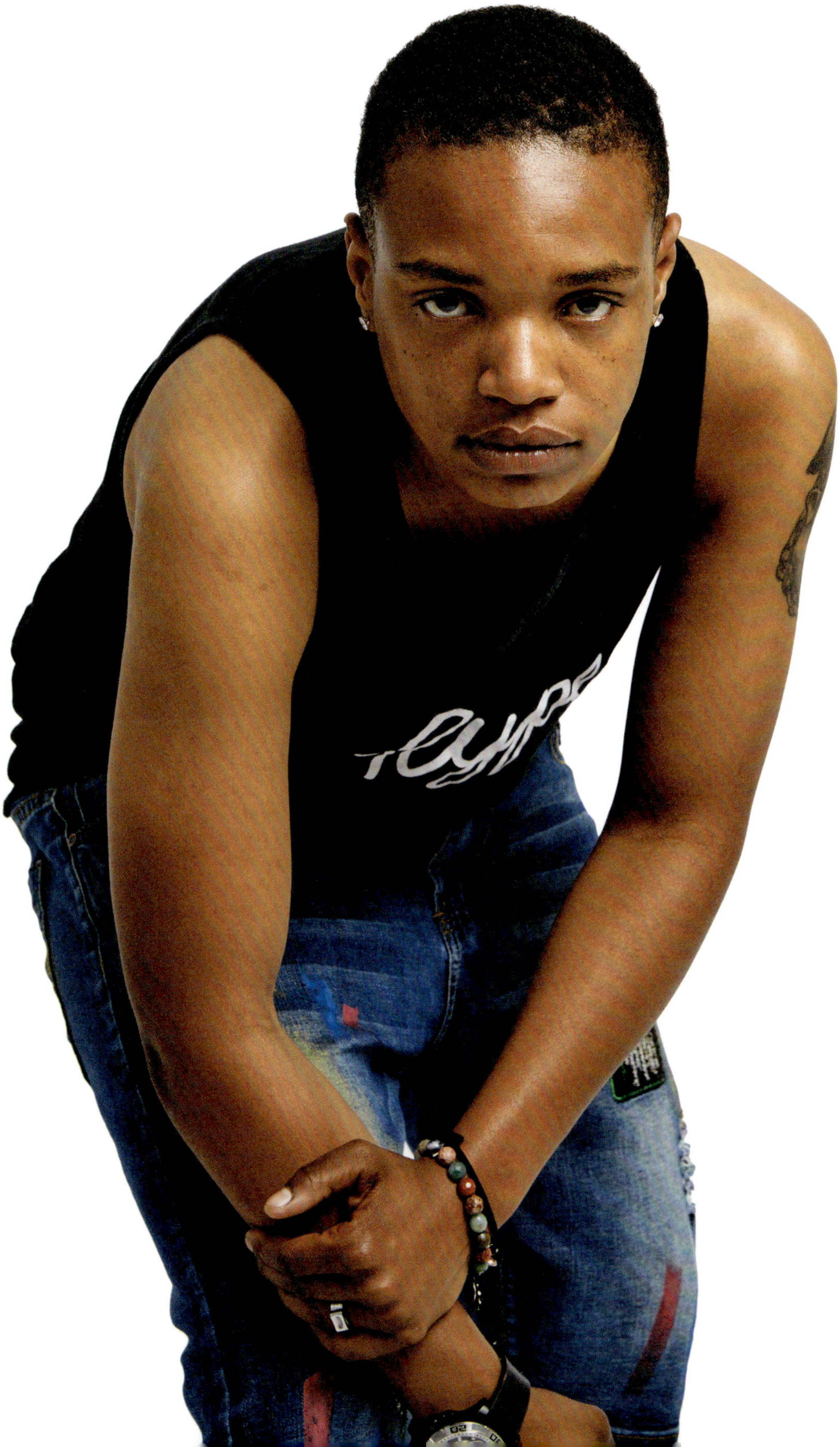

Joe, 2021
New York

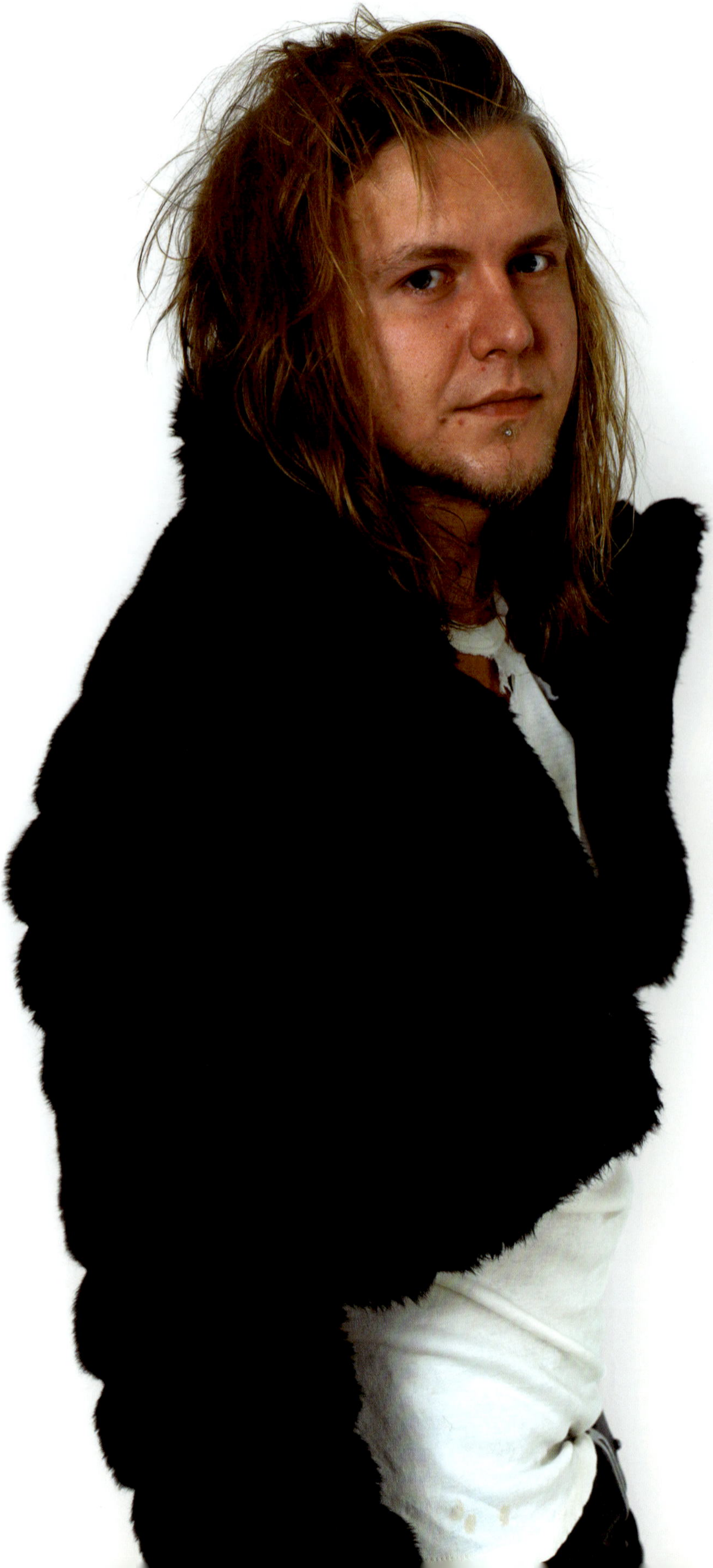

Lucas, 2008
New York

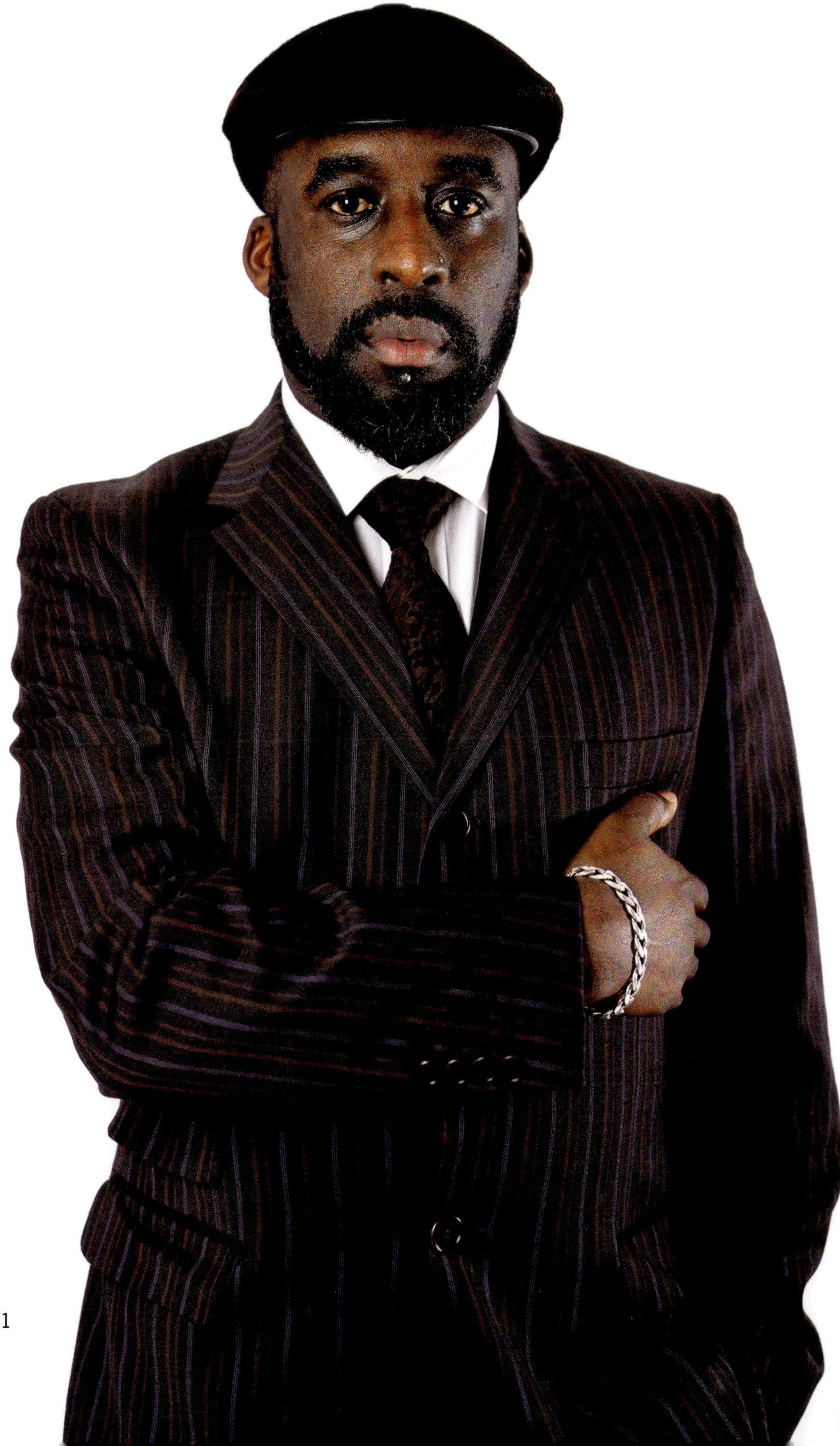

Ajamu, 2011
London

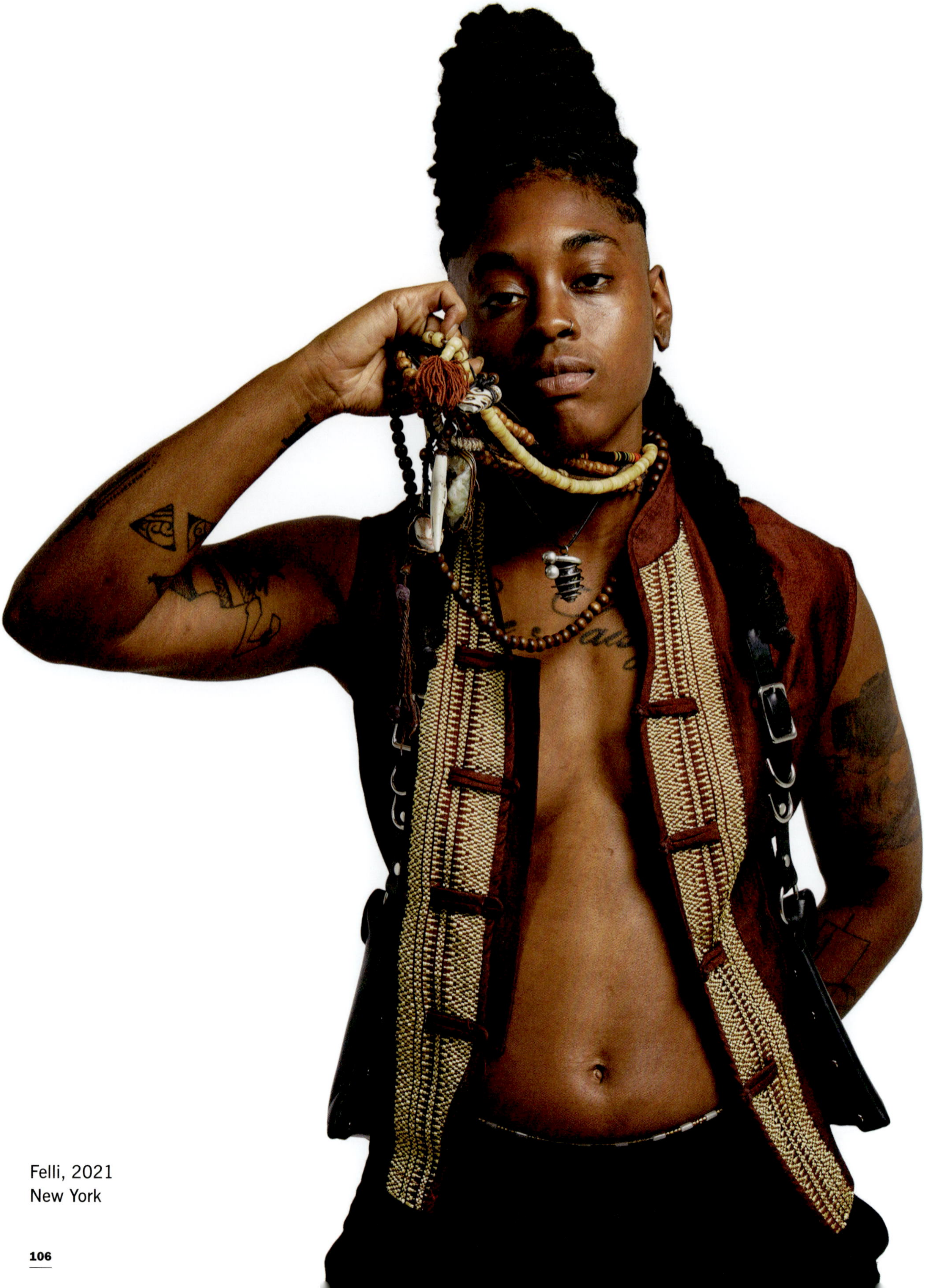

Felli, 2021
New York

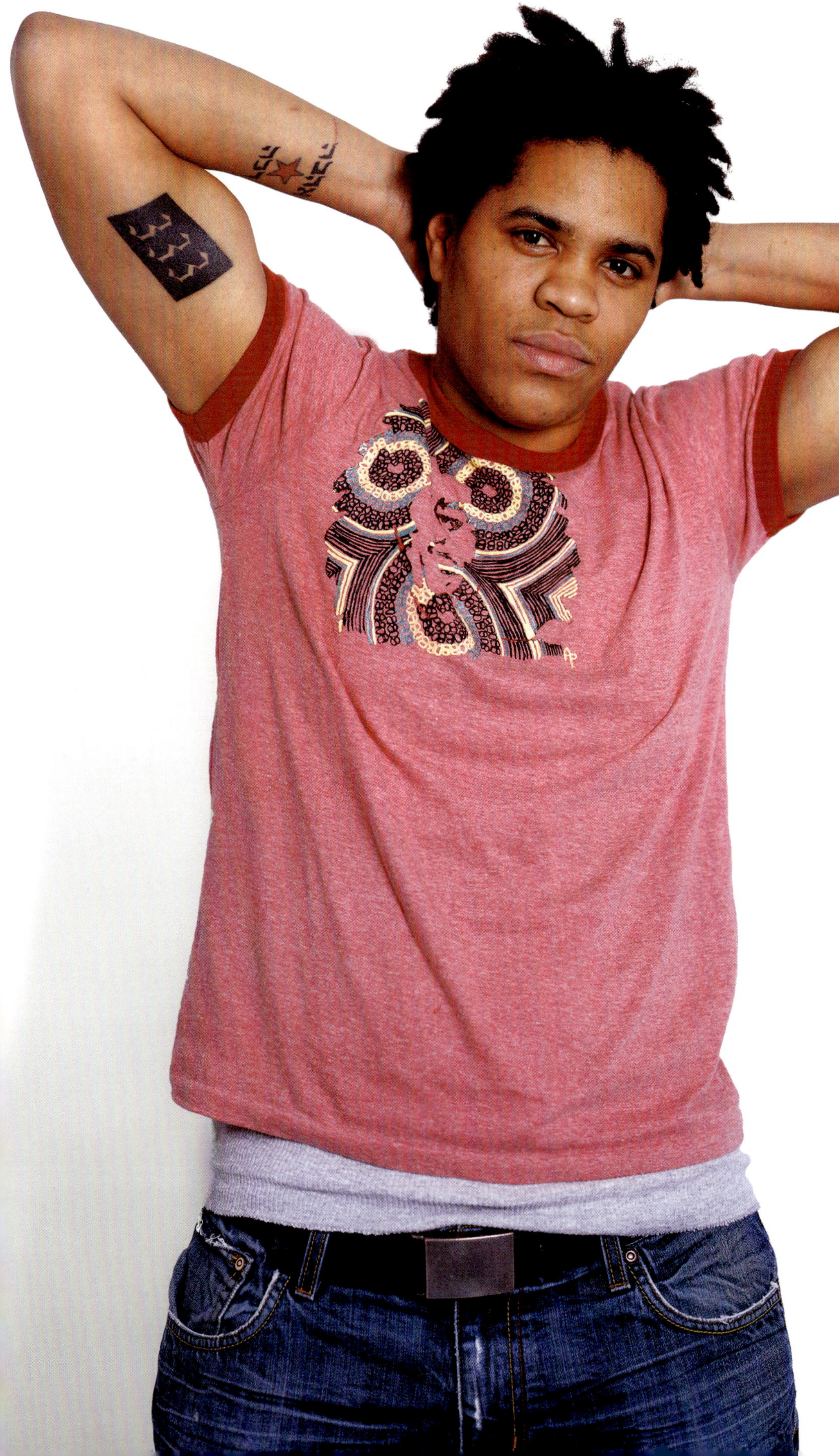

Kerri, 2008
New York

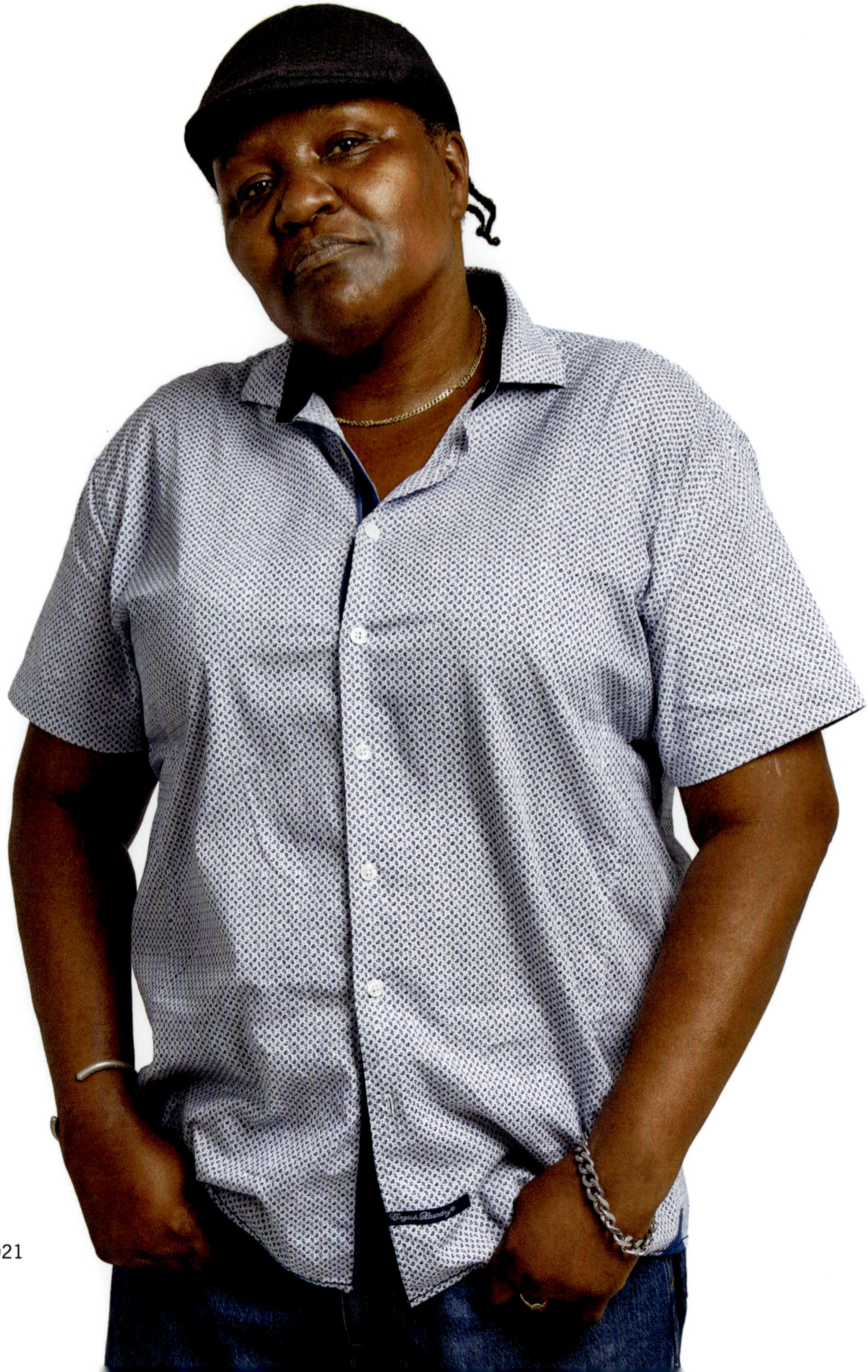

Michele, 2021
New York

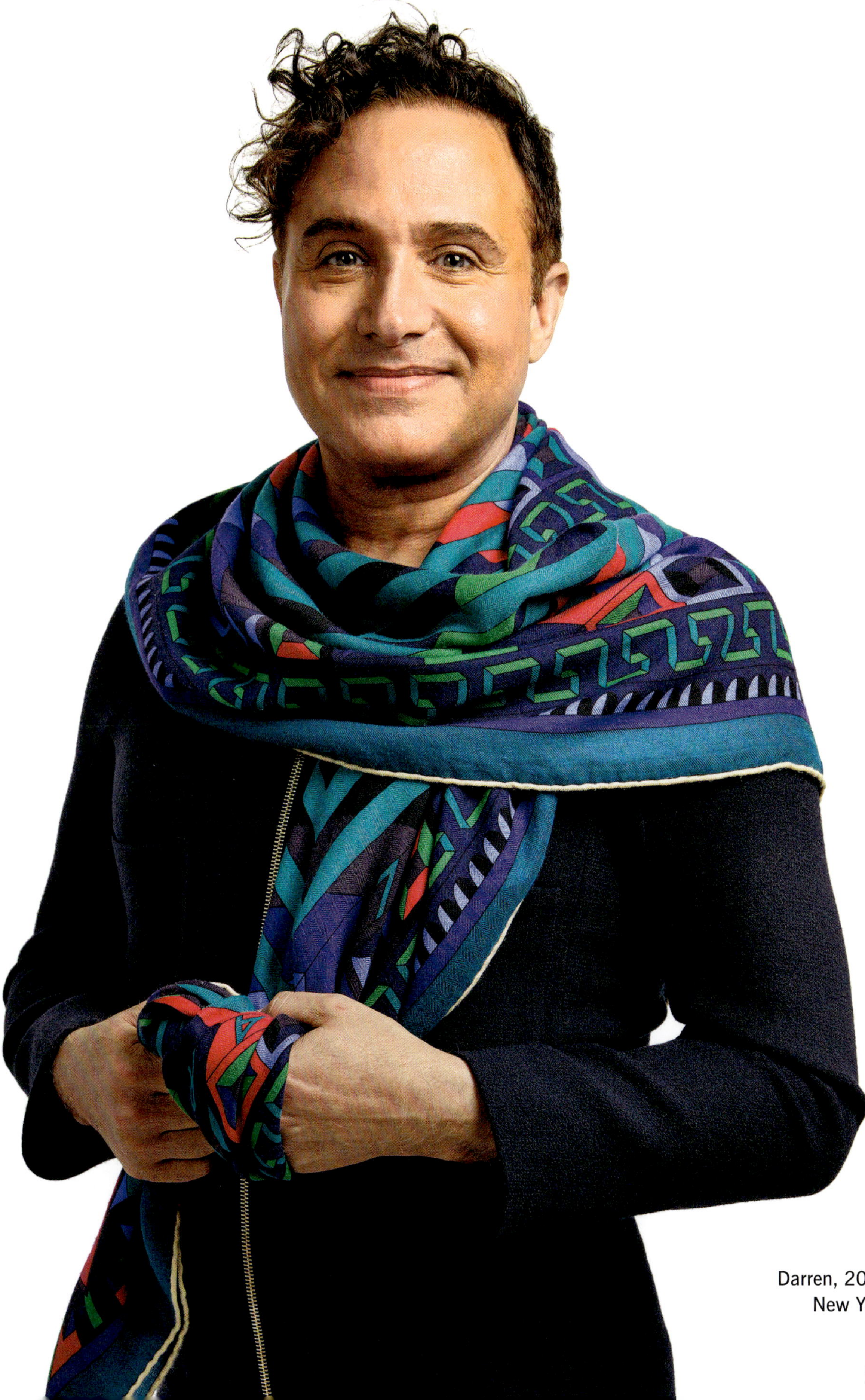

Darren, 2021
New York

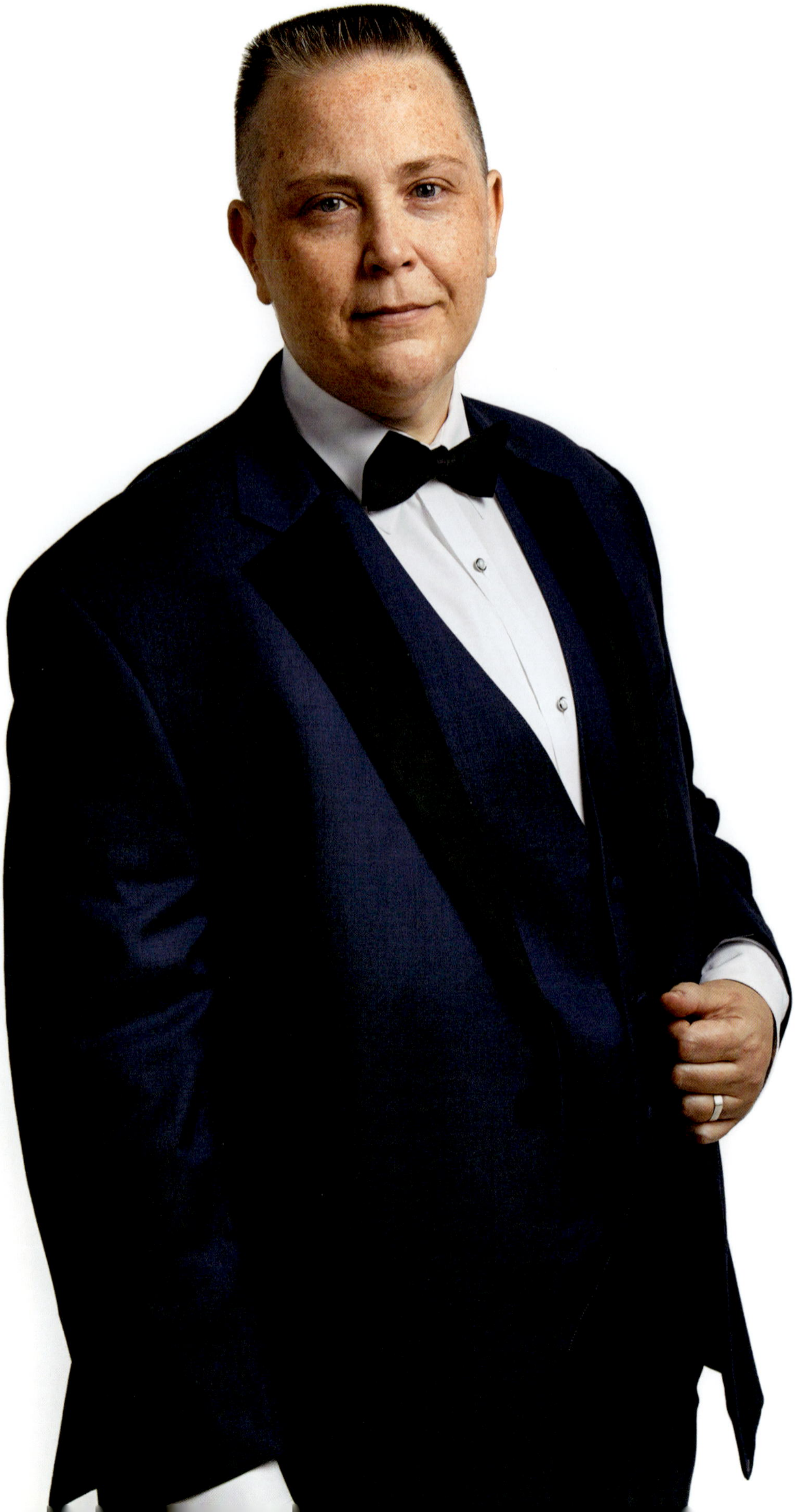

Marty, 2021
New York

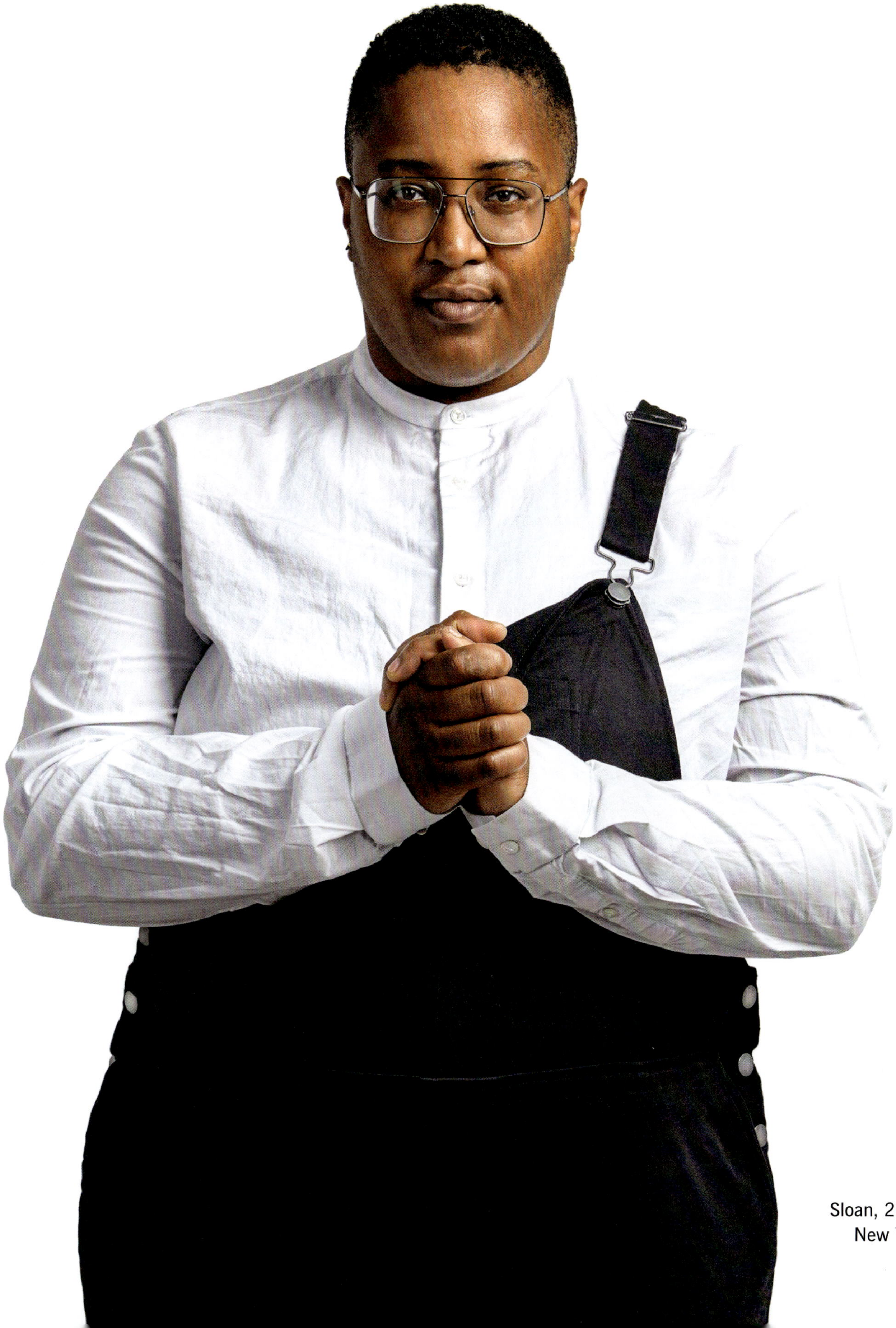

Sloan, 2021
New York

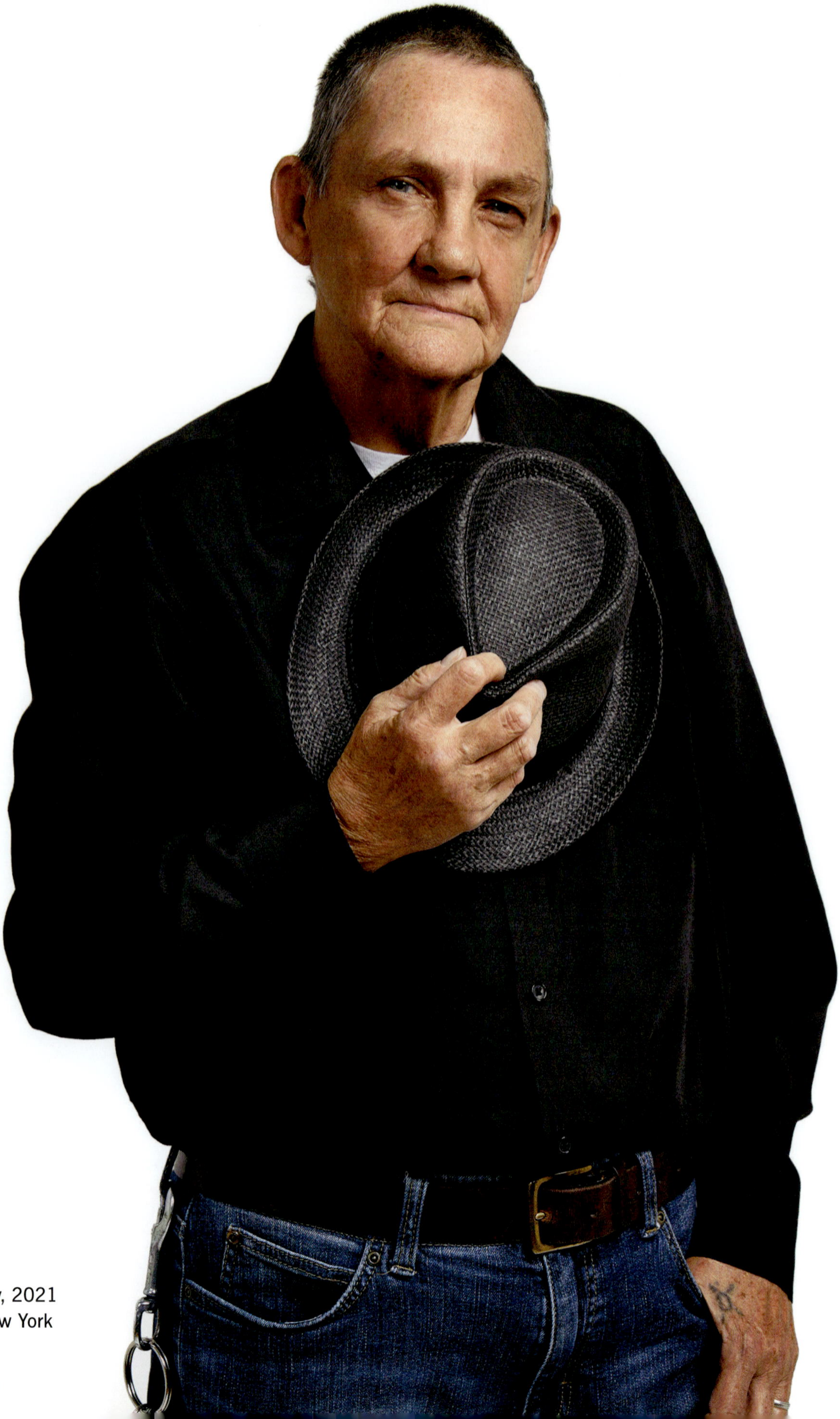

Jay, 2021
New York

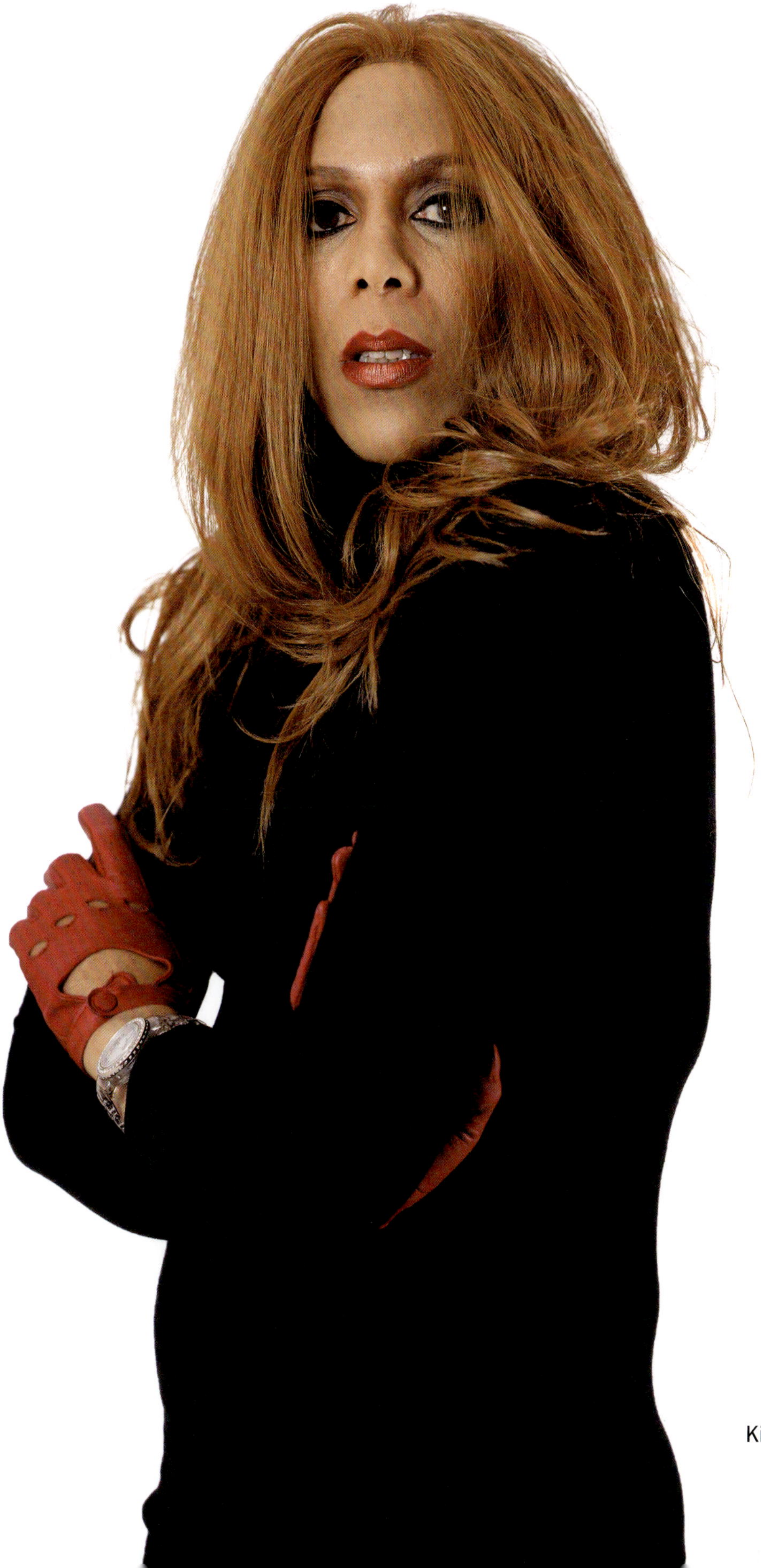

Kimberly, 2011
London

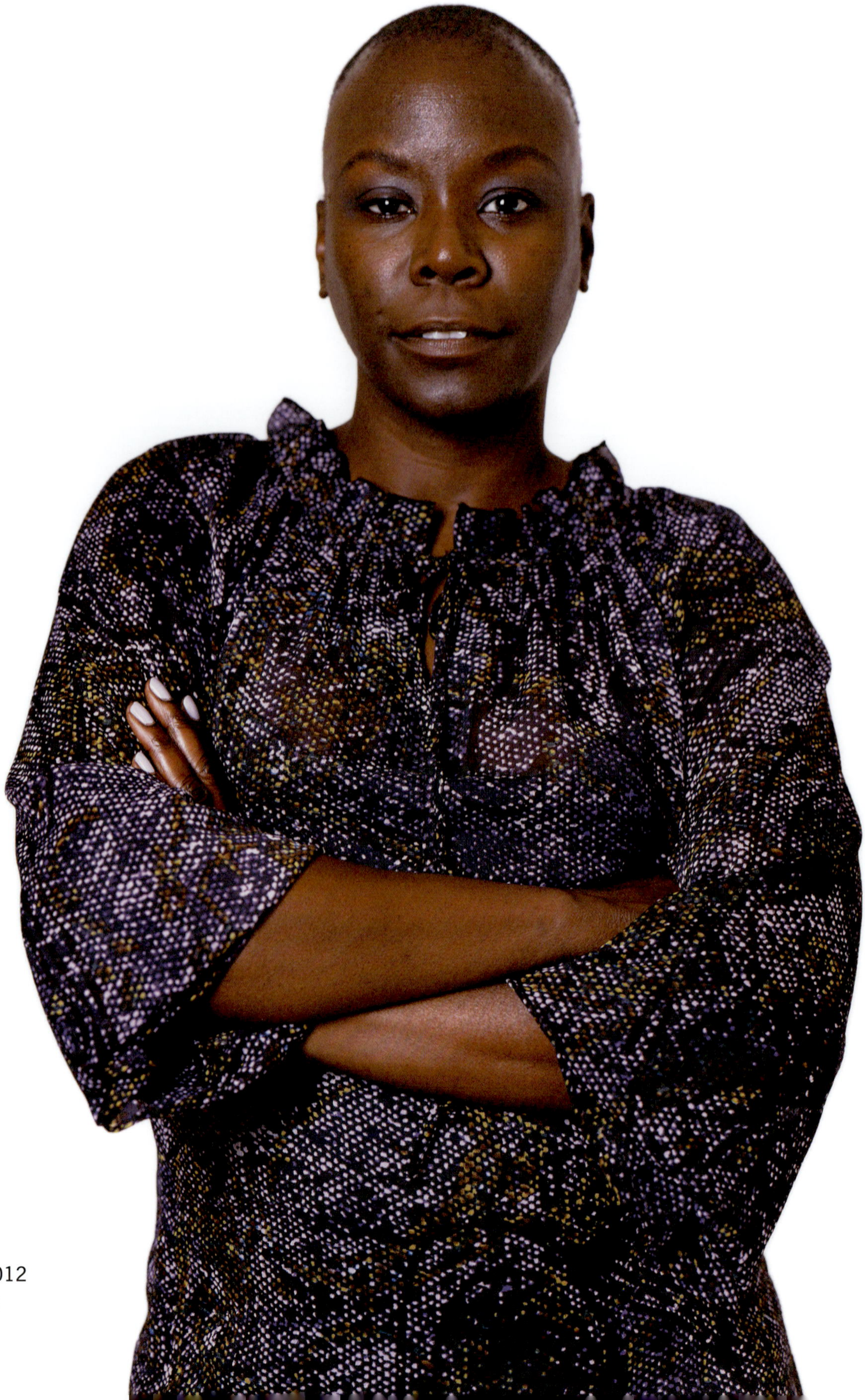

Shelly, 2012
New York

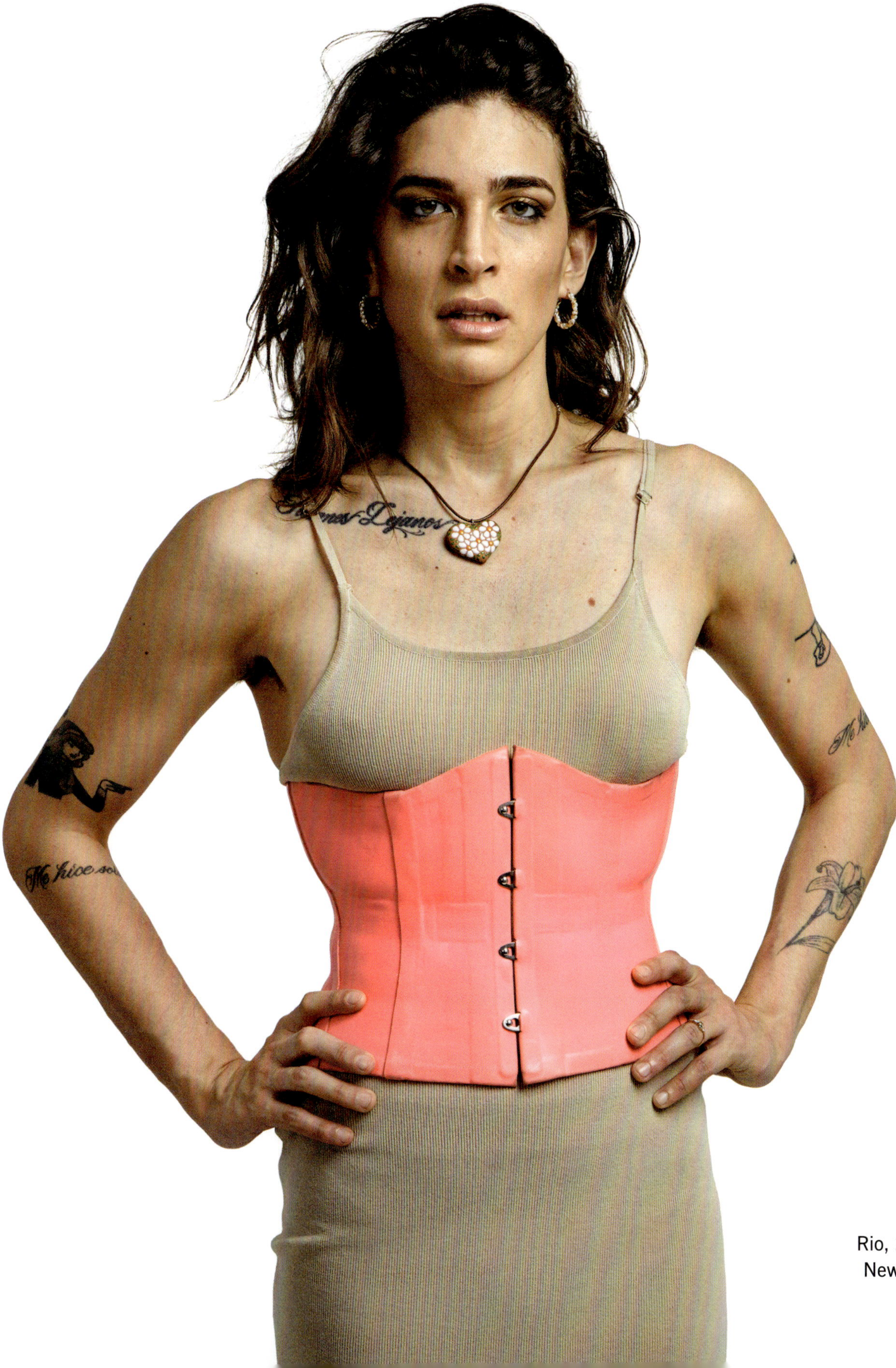

Rio, 2021
New York

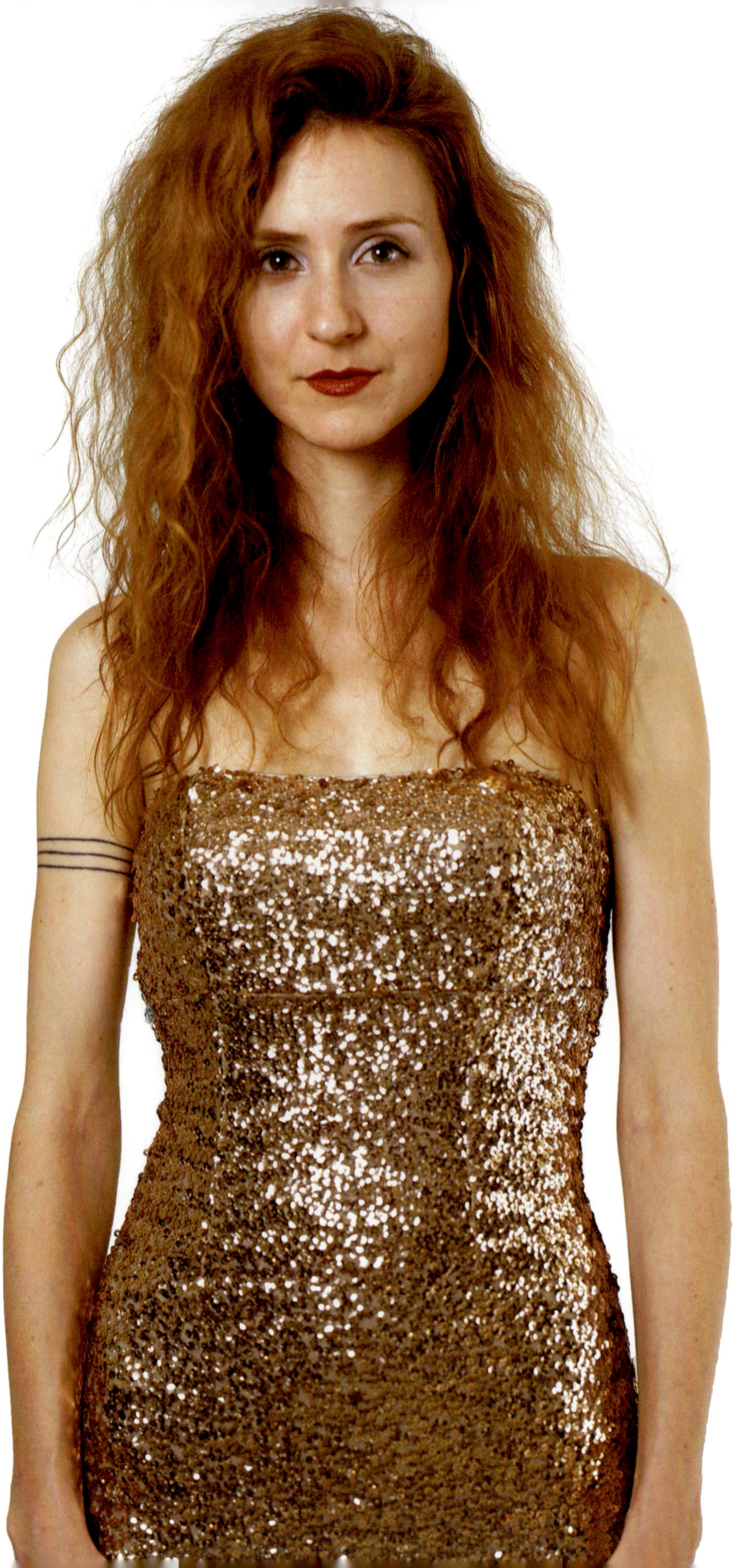

Sophie, 2011
New York

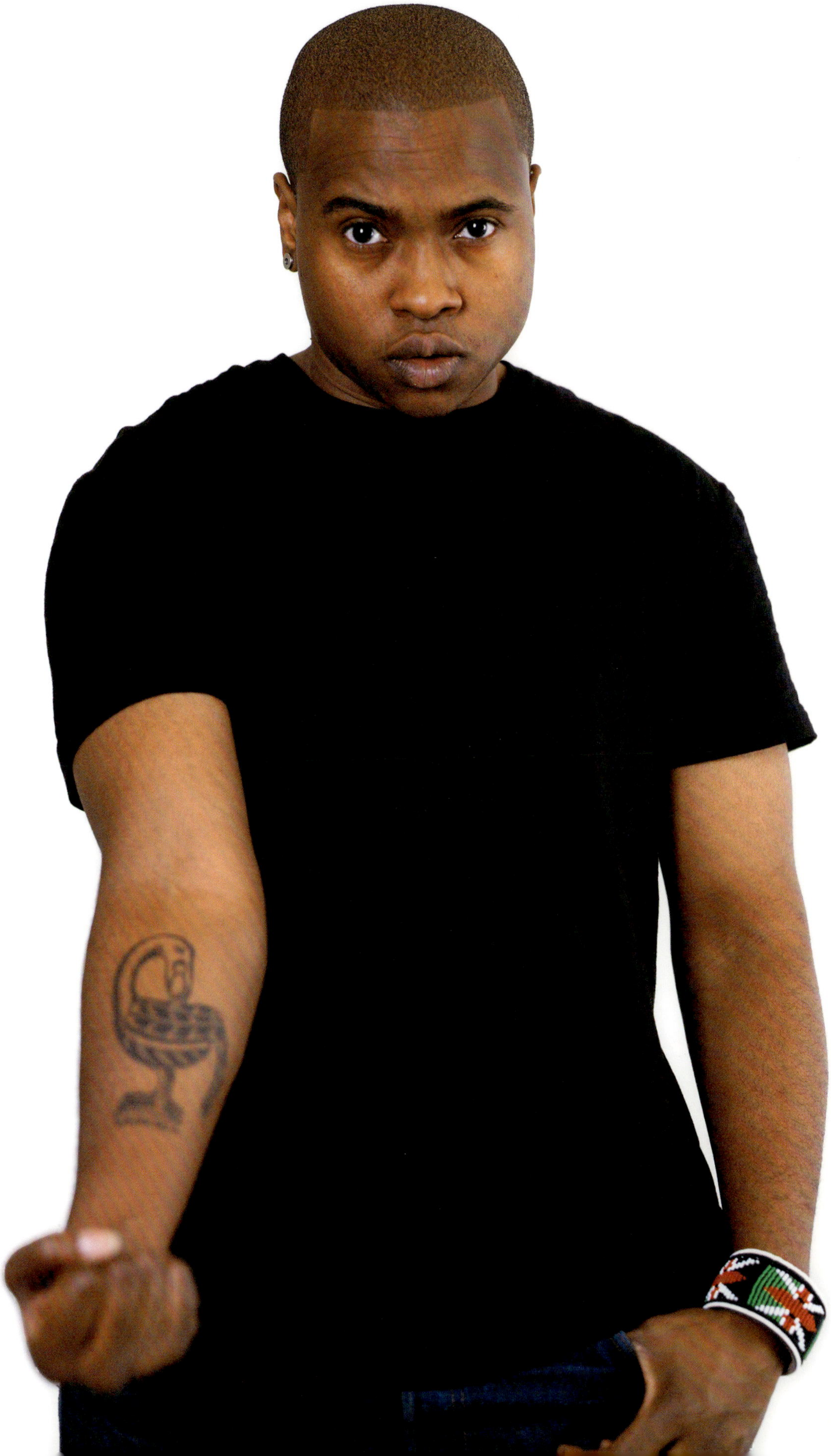

Tiq, 2012
New York

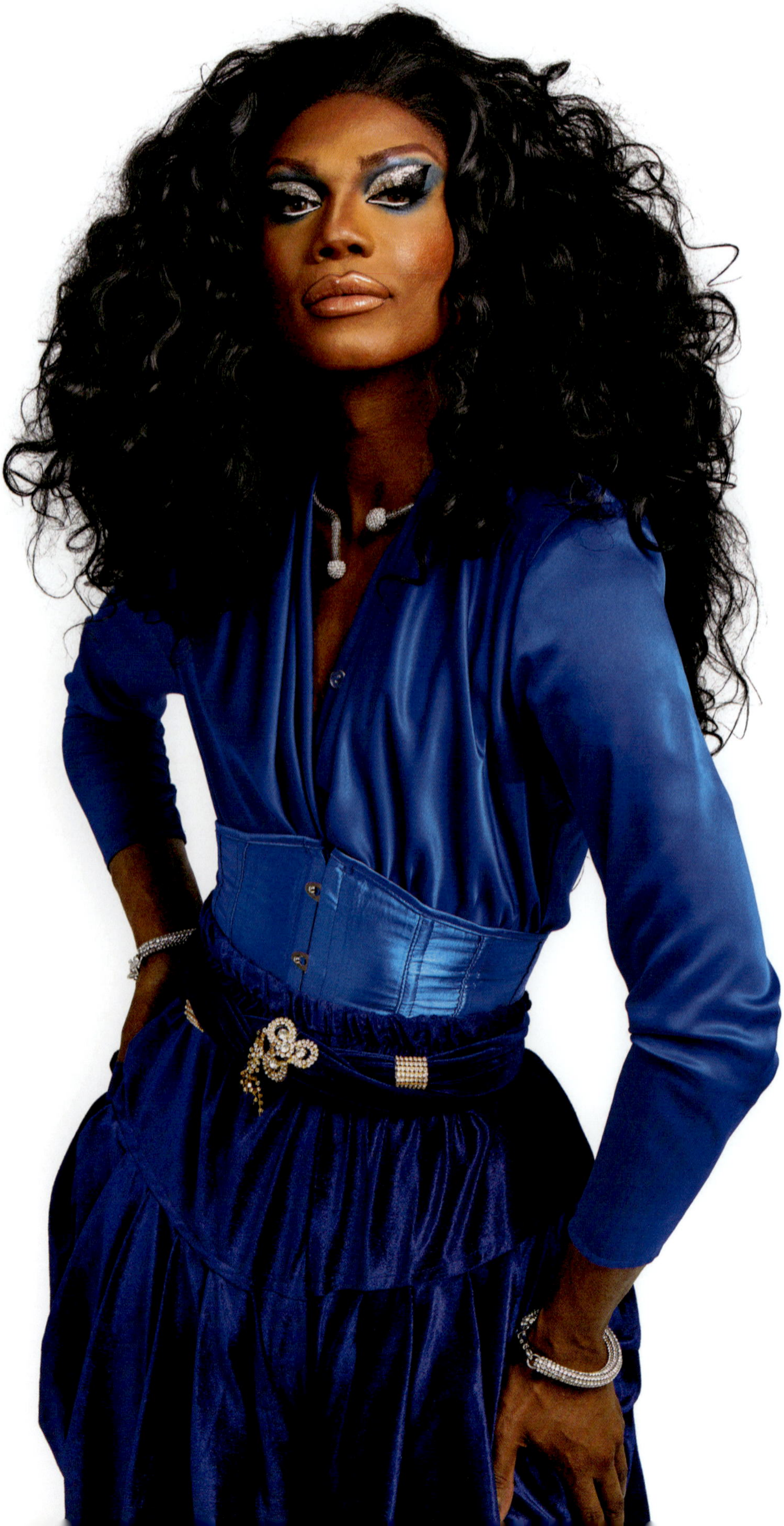

Xunami, 2021
New York

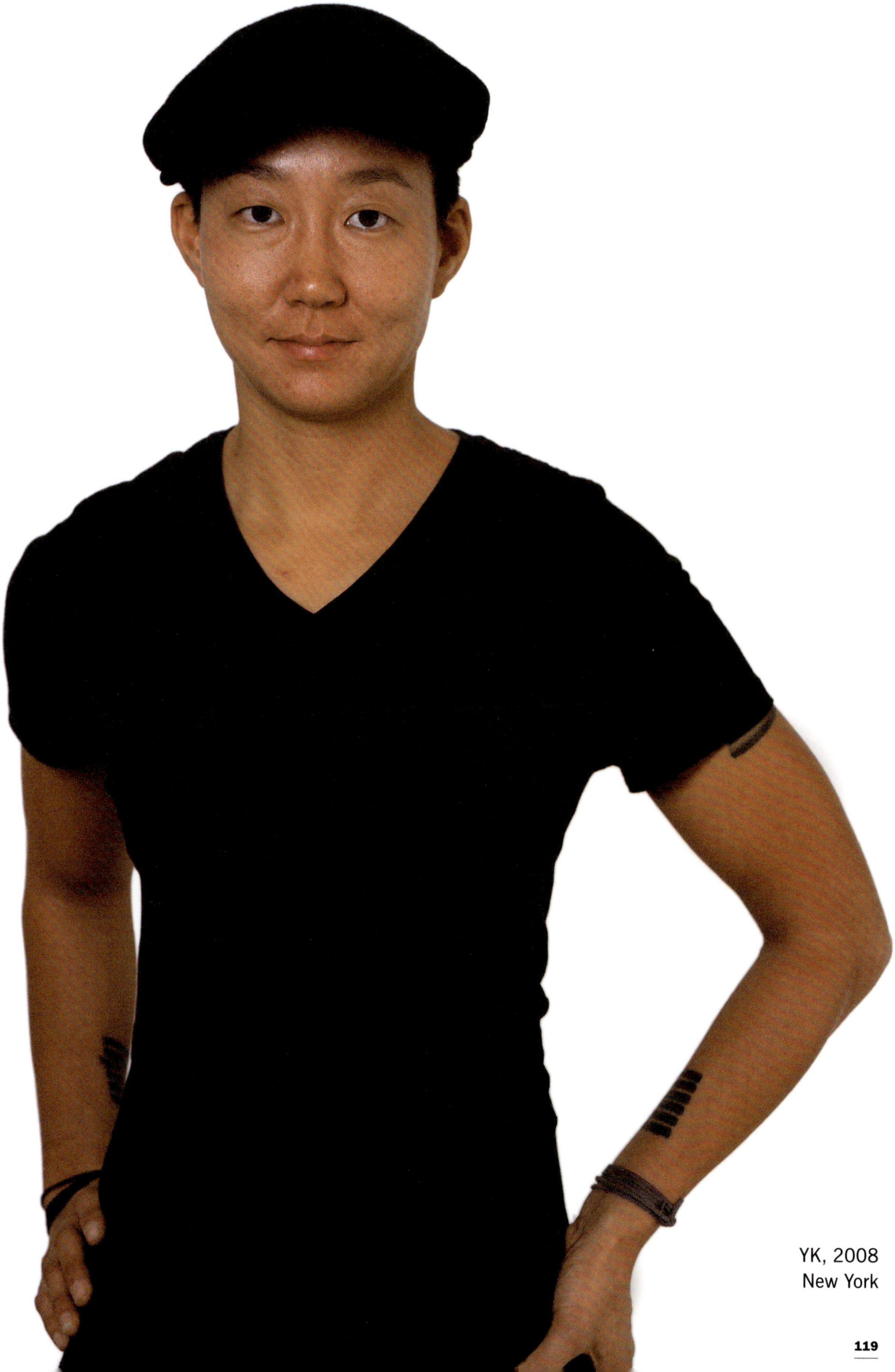

YK, 2008
New York

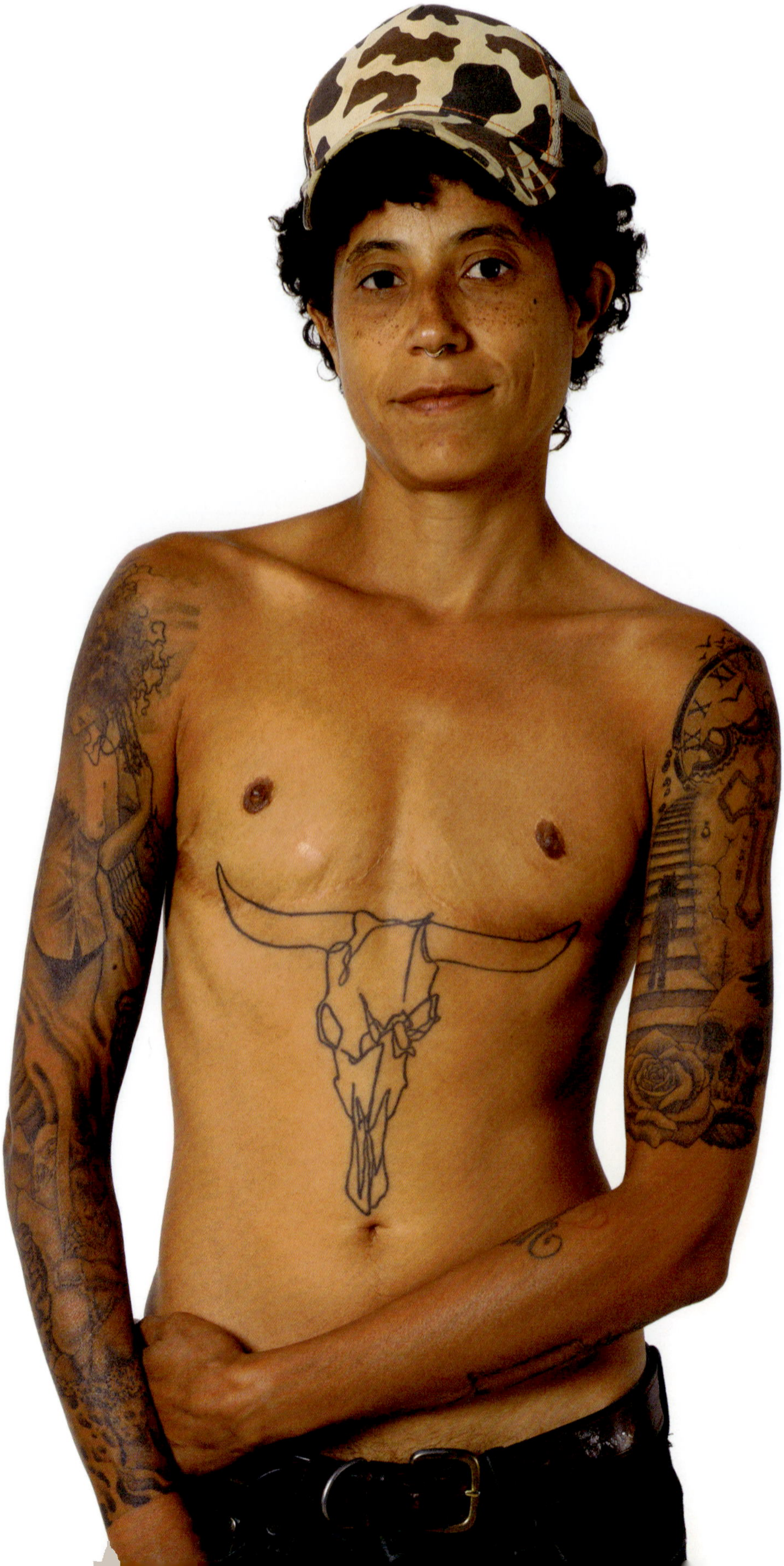

Utah, 2017
New York

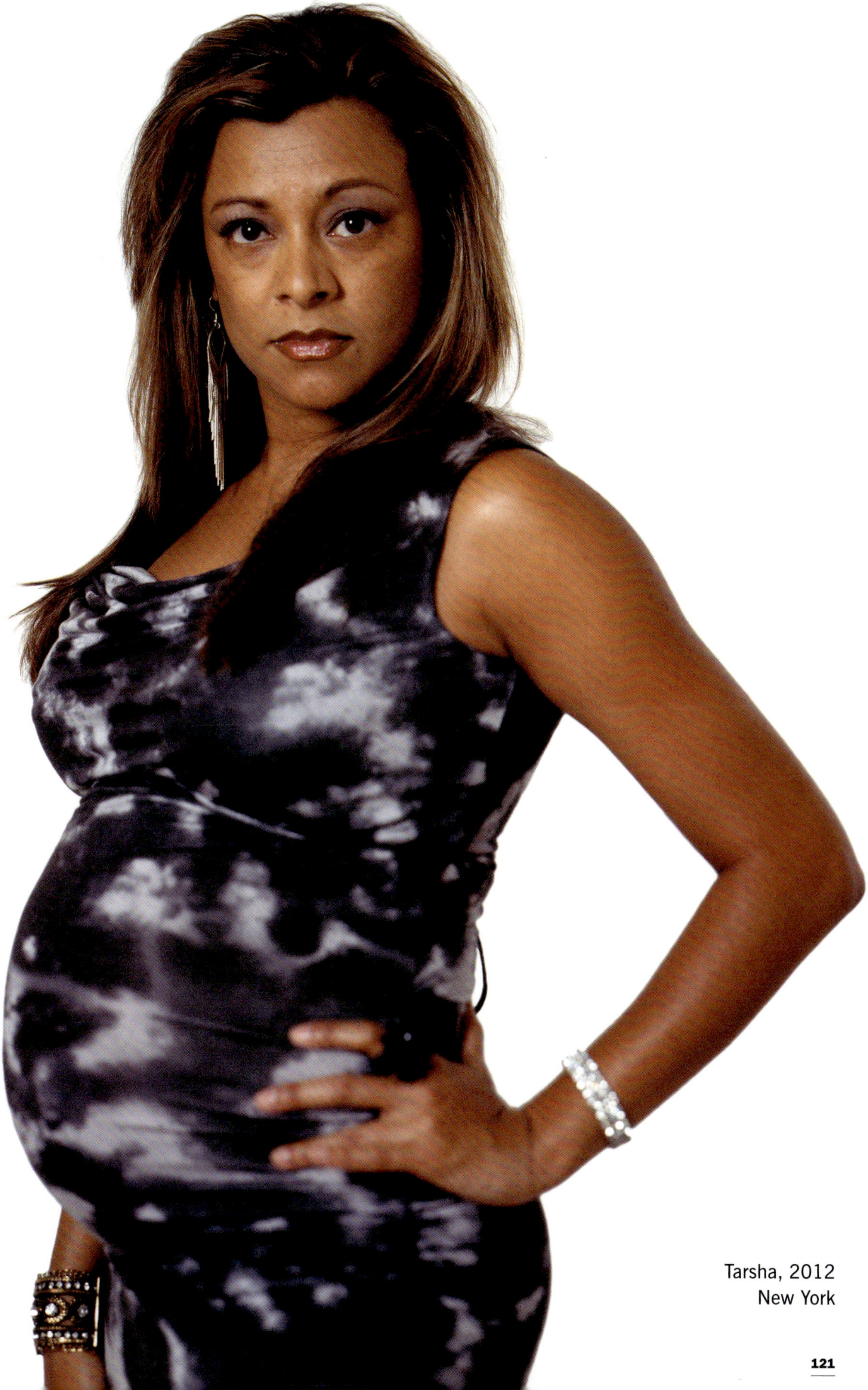

Tarsha, 2012
New York

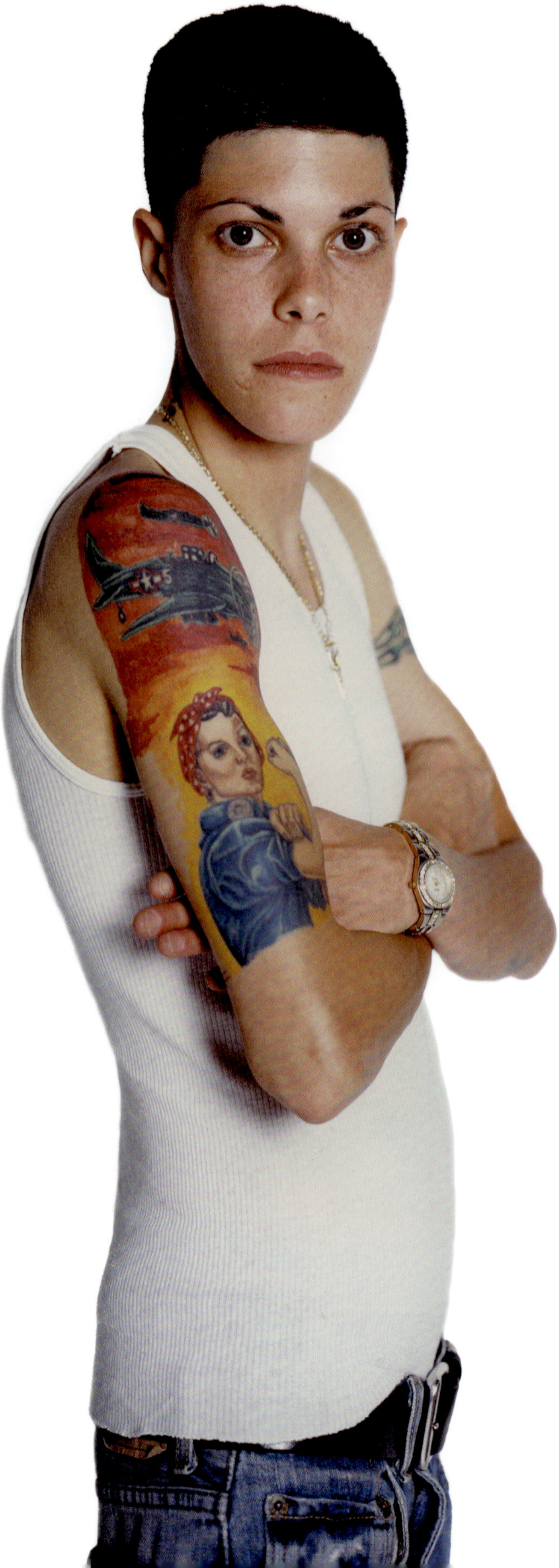

Tanya, 2008
Syracuse

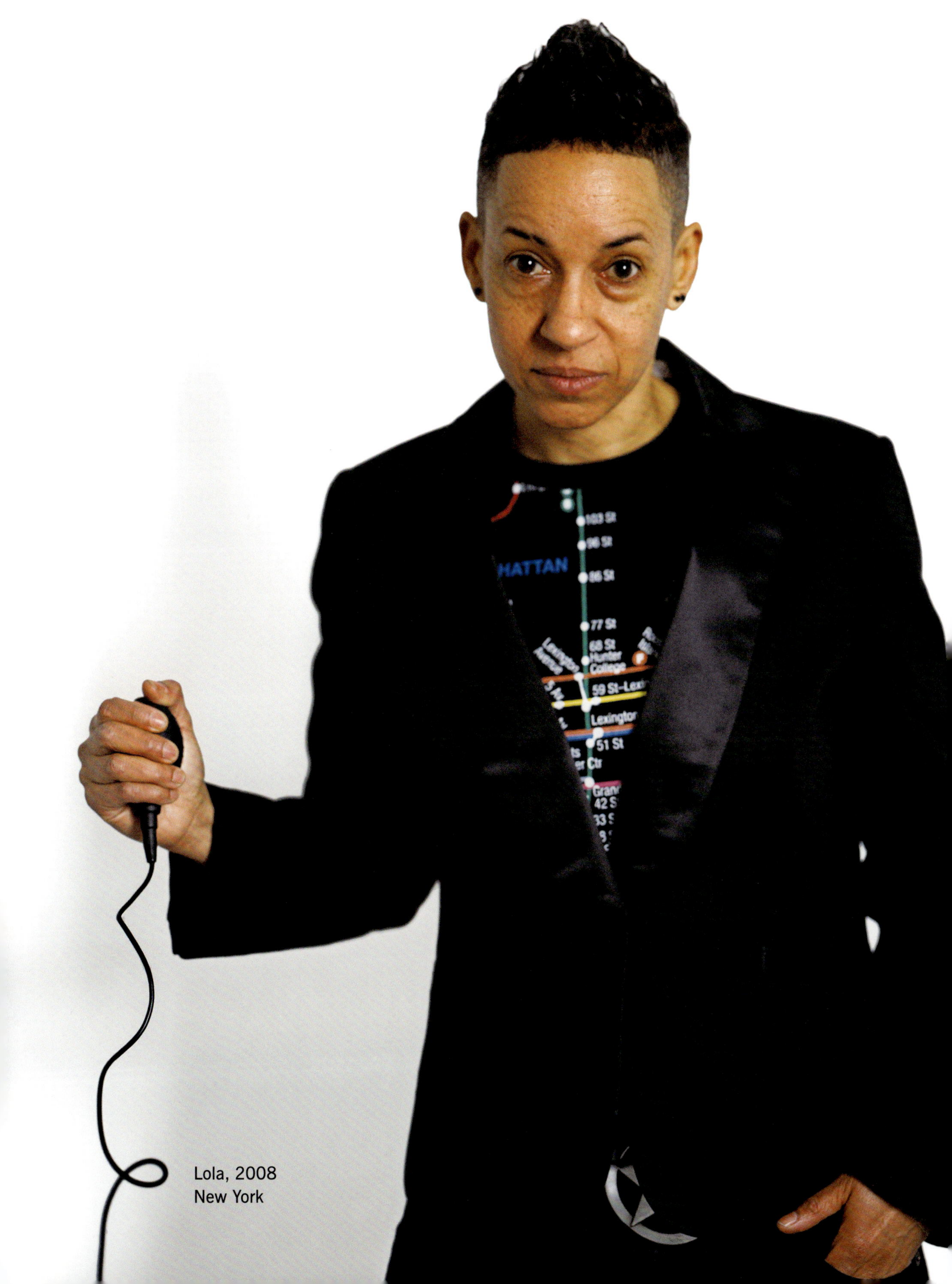

Lola, 2008
New York

syzygy, the vision

This is a self-portrait series that examines far-reaching facets of intersectional disadvantage, which manifest through an enduring history of unsettling cultural conflicts and legacies. This series defines and memorializes a universal cosmos of a conscious past, present, and future as an adaptable contemplation of Afrofuturism for the twenty-first century.

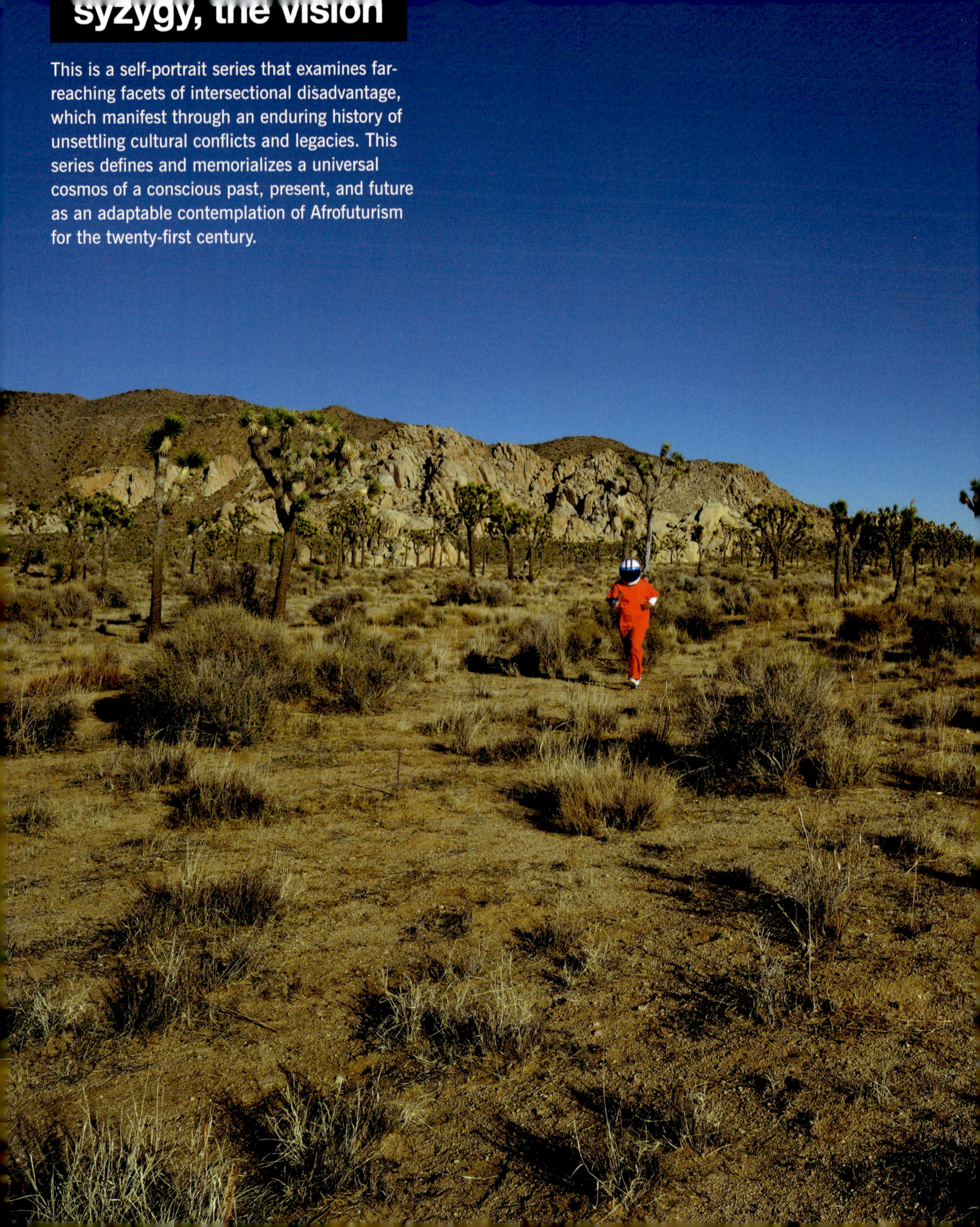

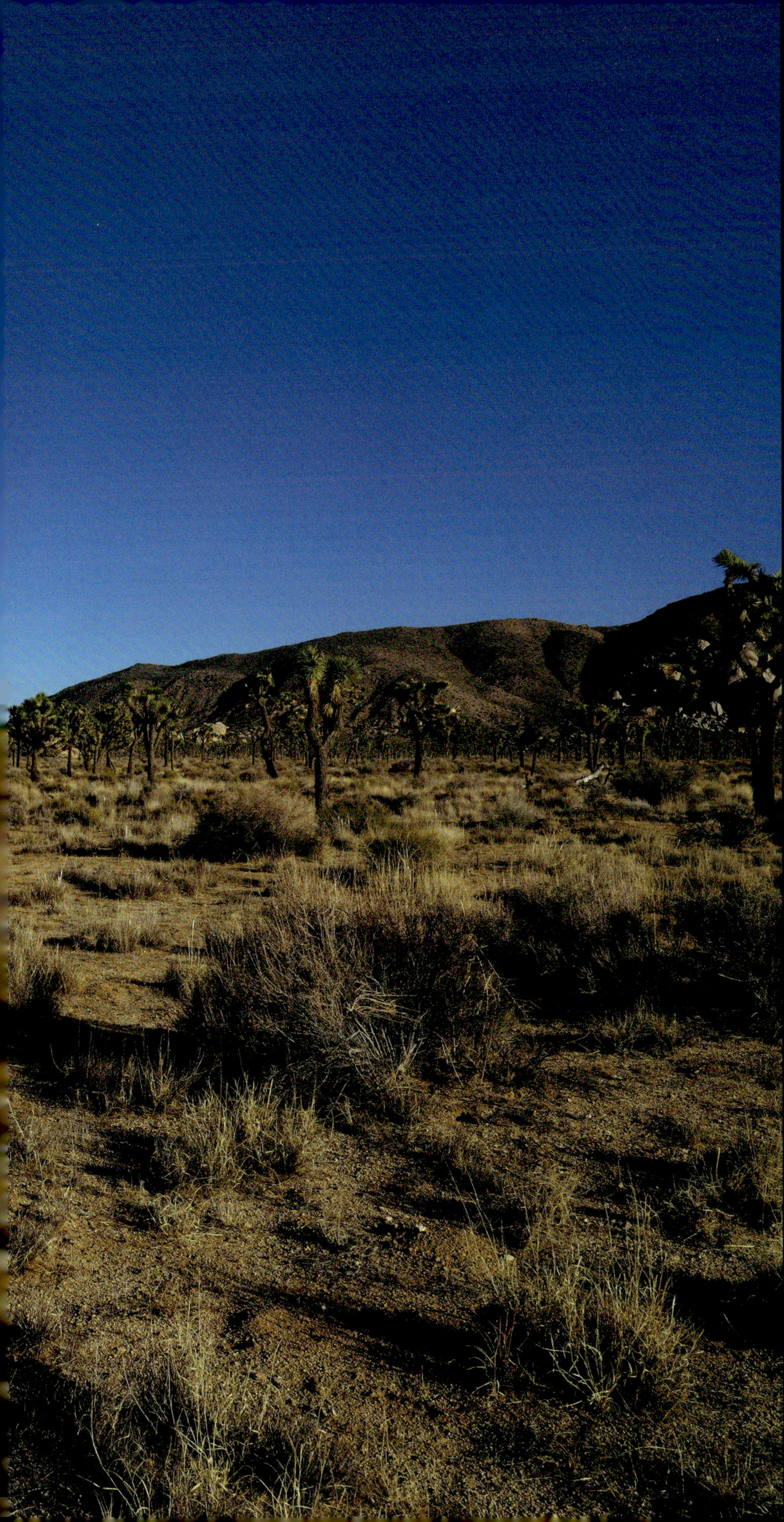

2022
Joshua Tree

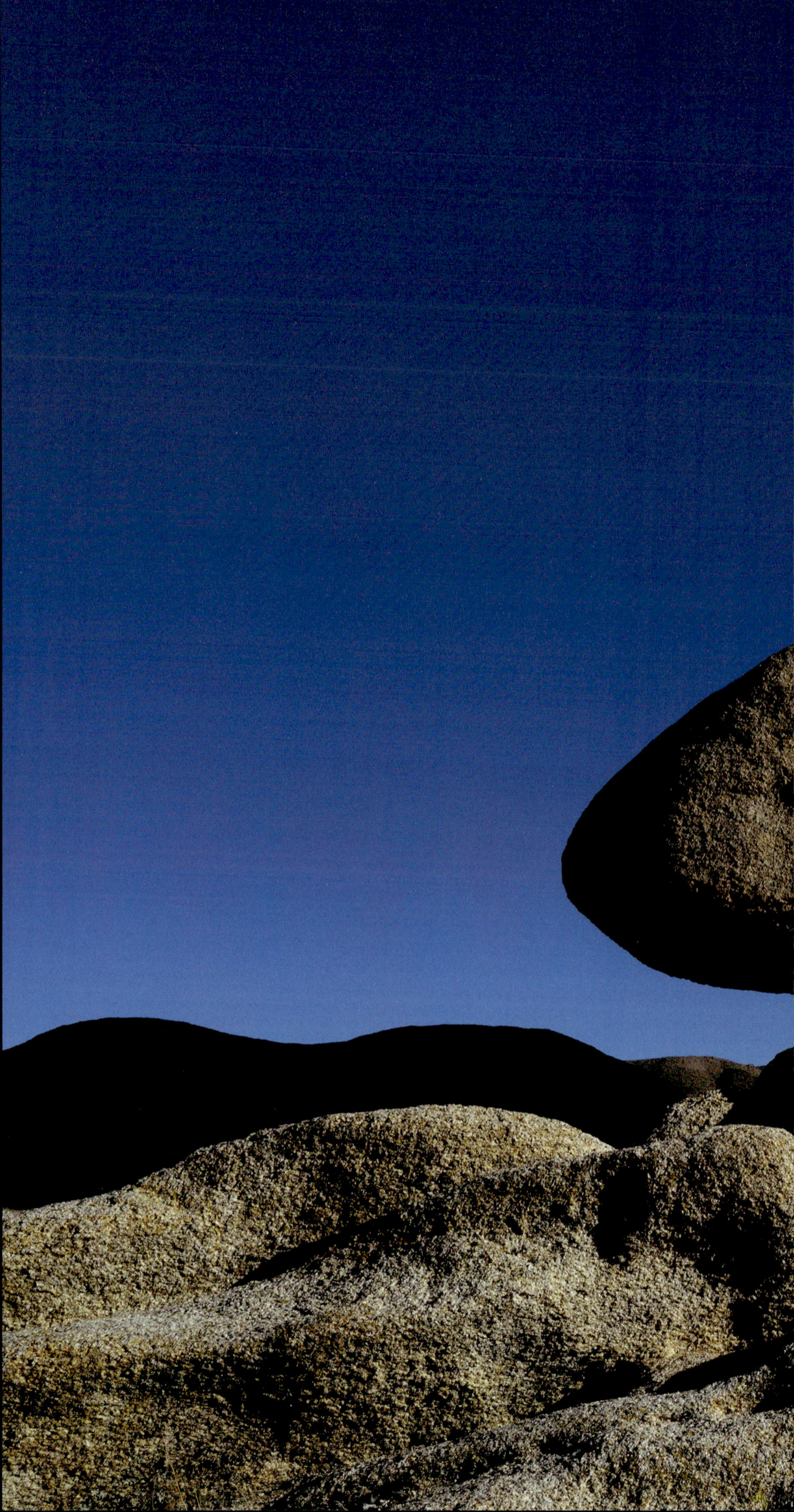

2022
Joshua Tree

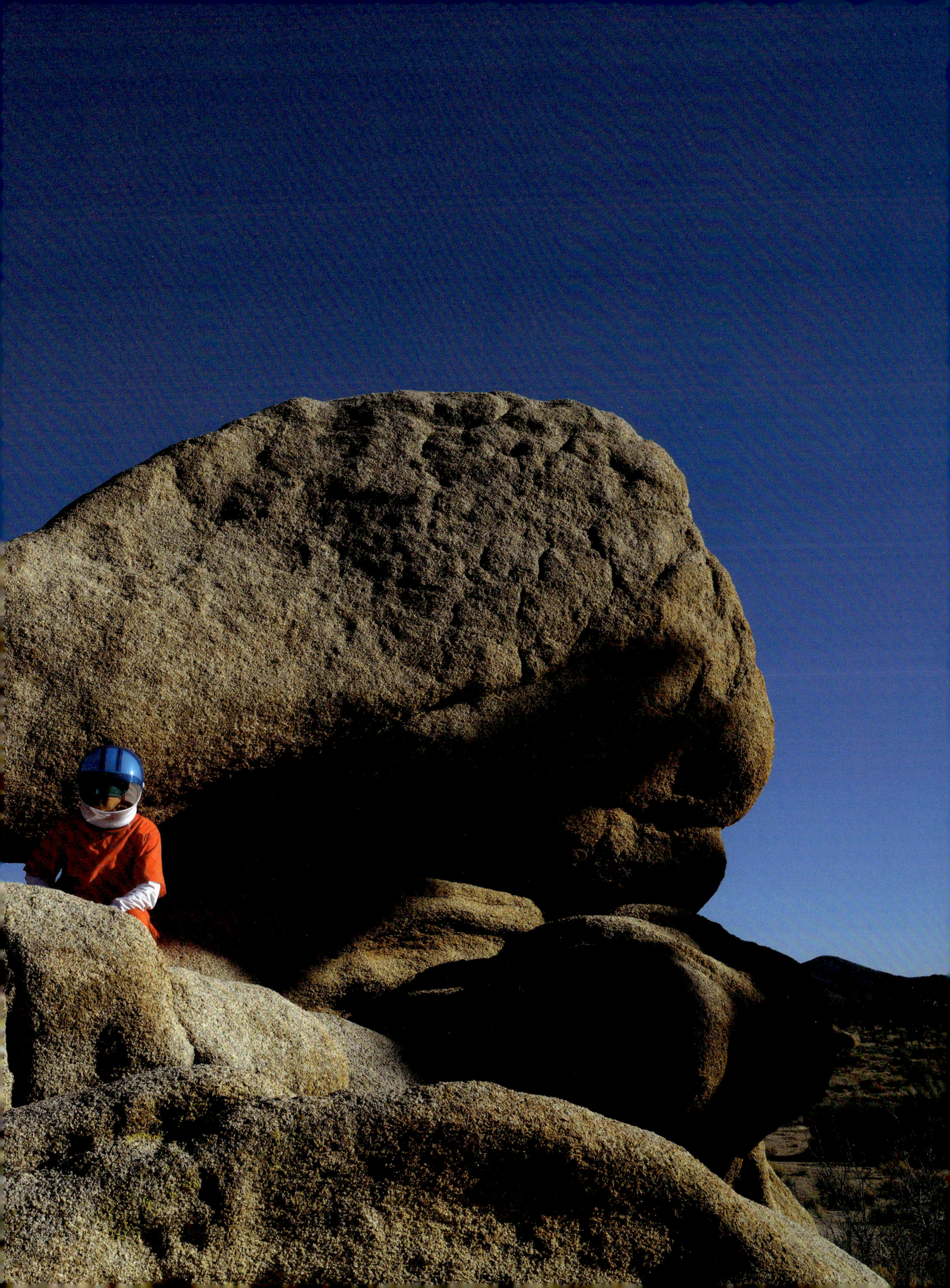

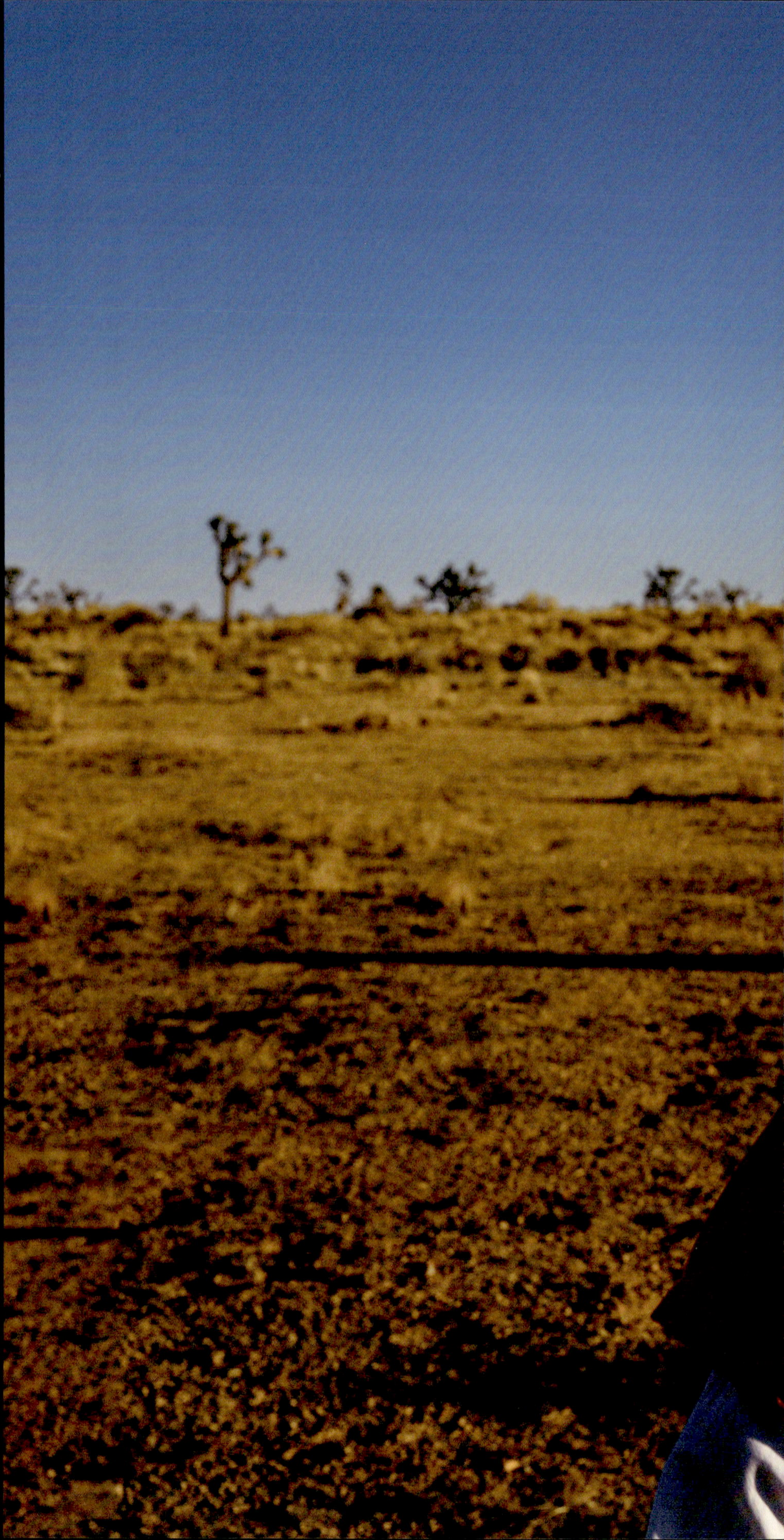

2022
Joshua Tree

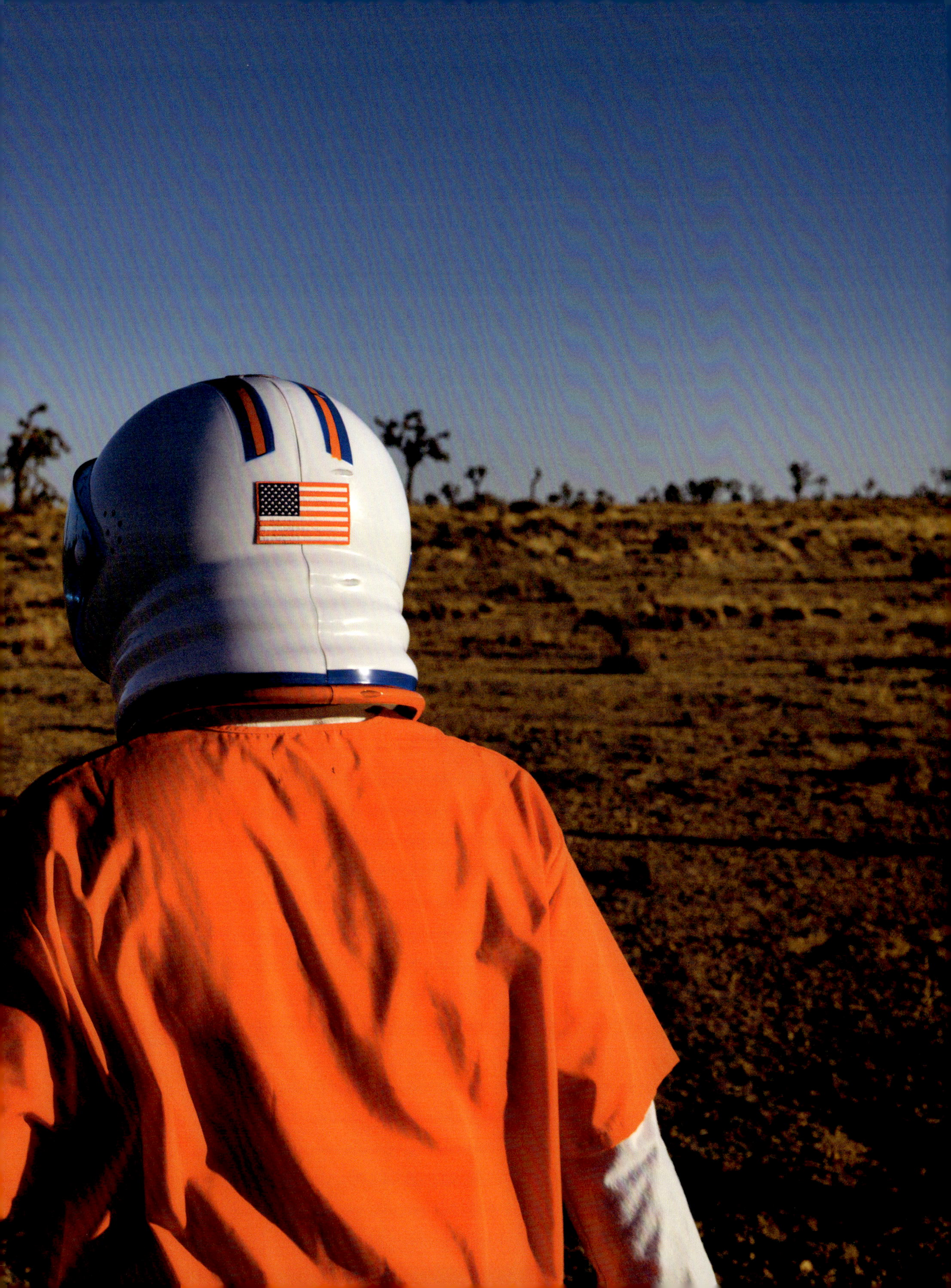

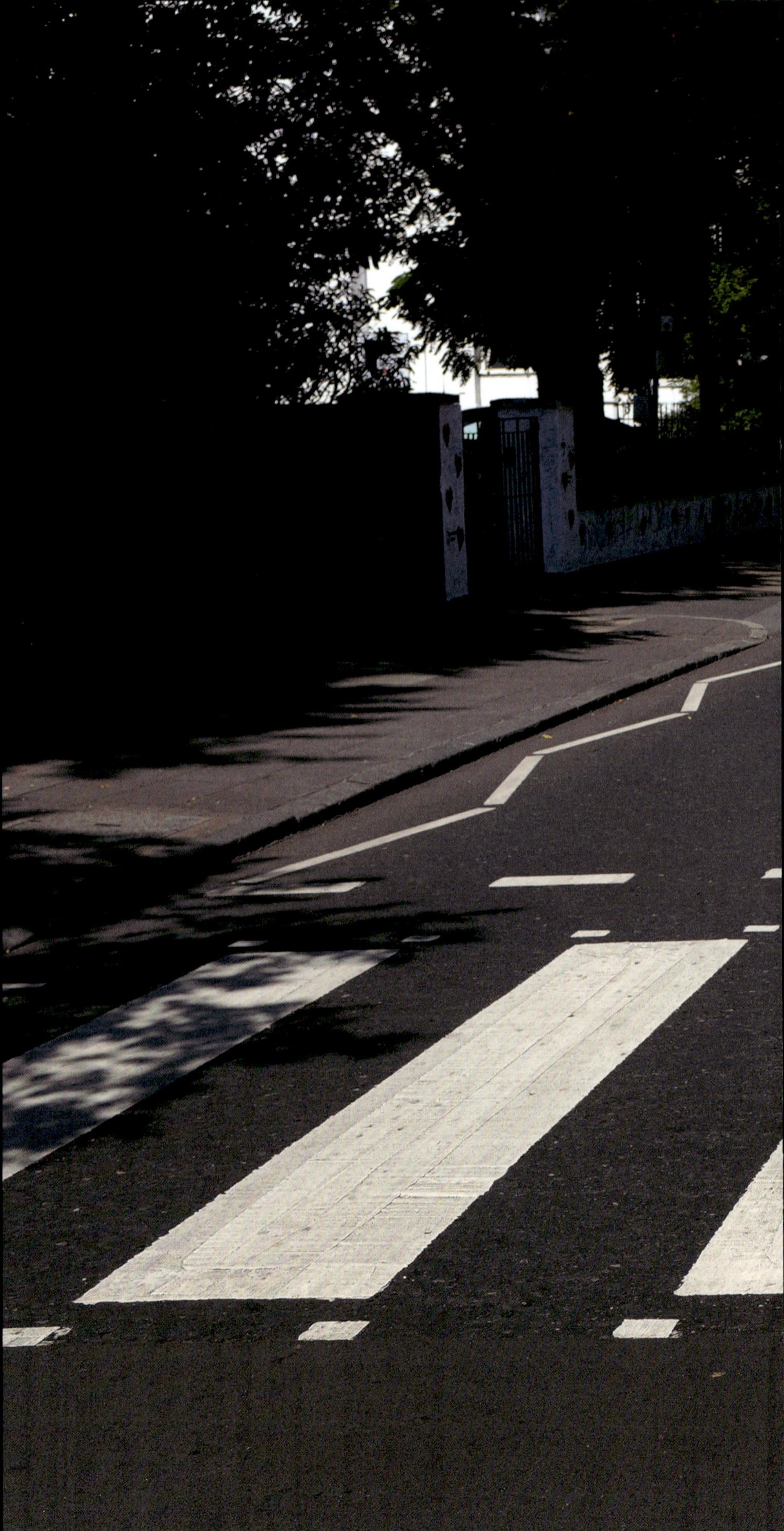

2020
London

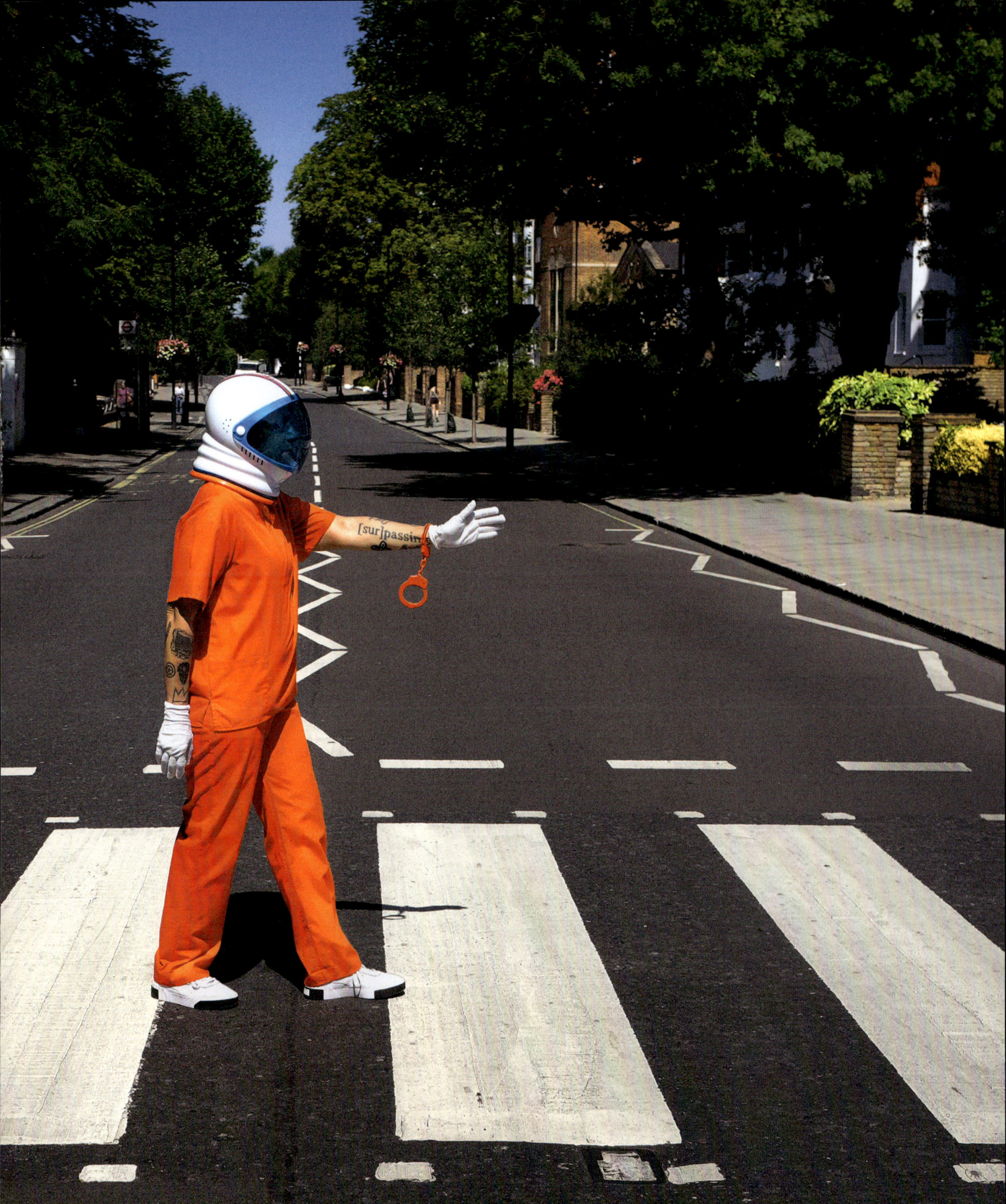

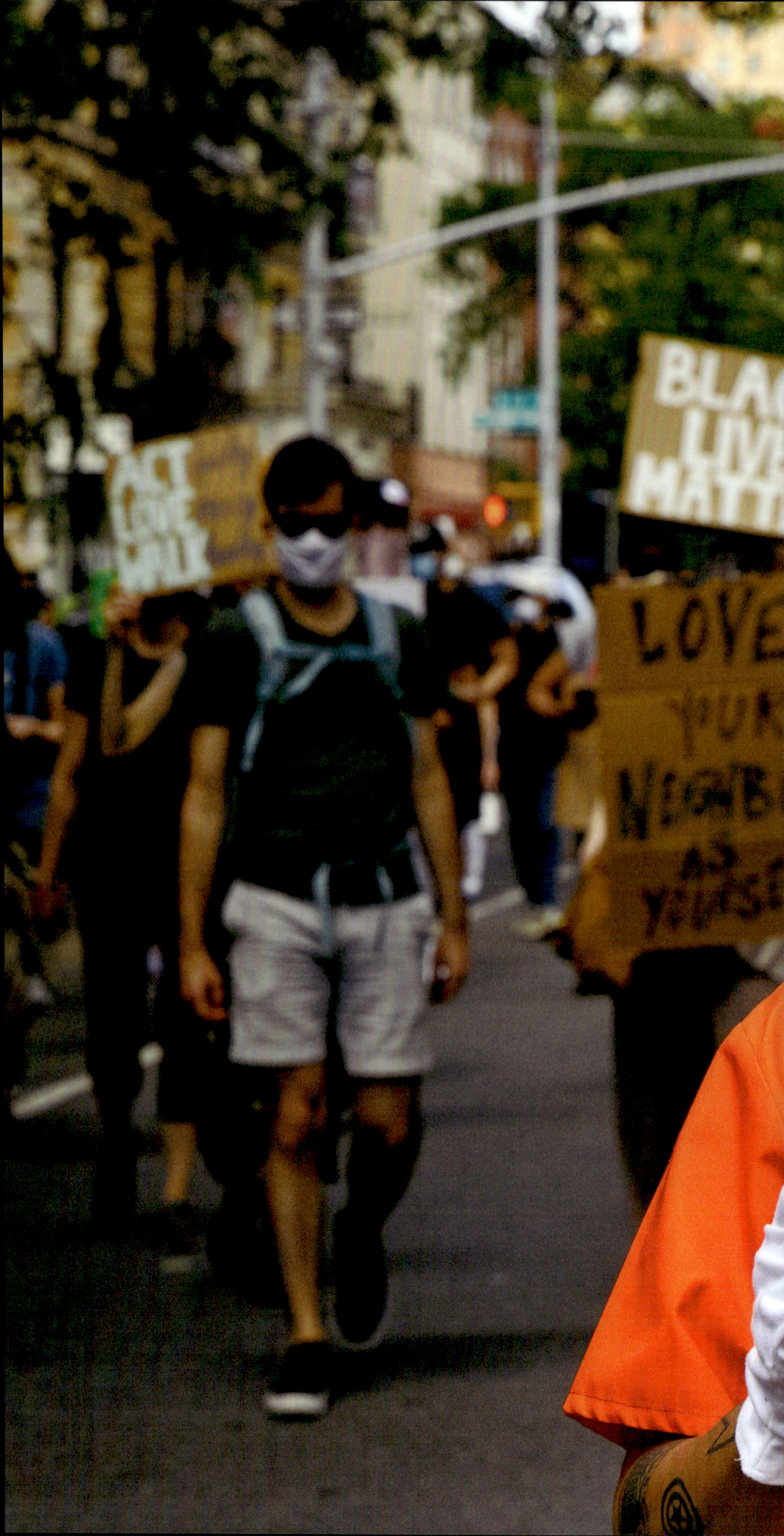

2020
New York

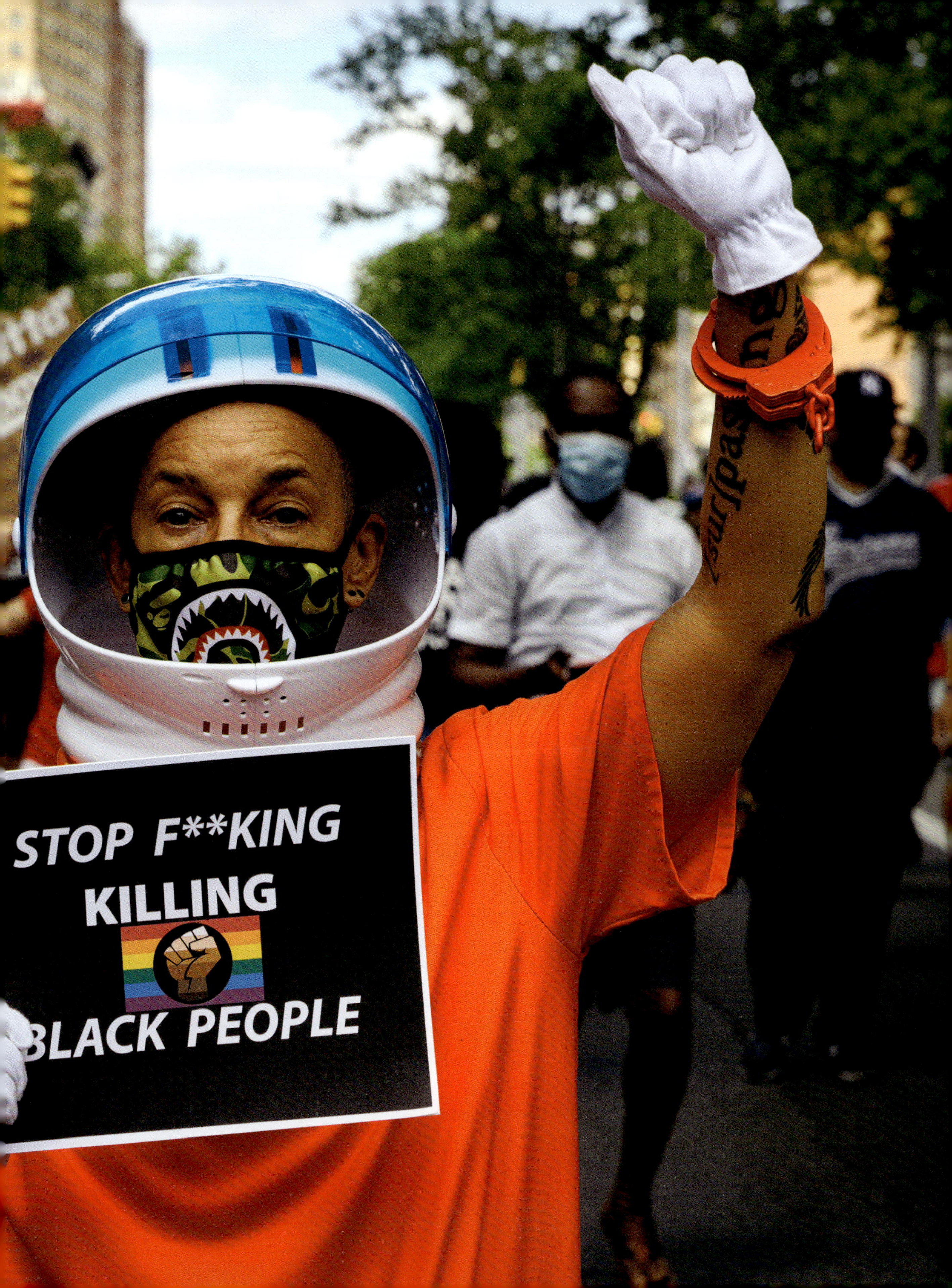
STOP F**KING
KILLING
BLACK PEOPLE

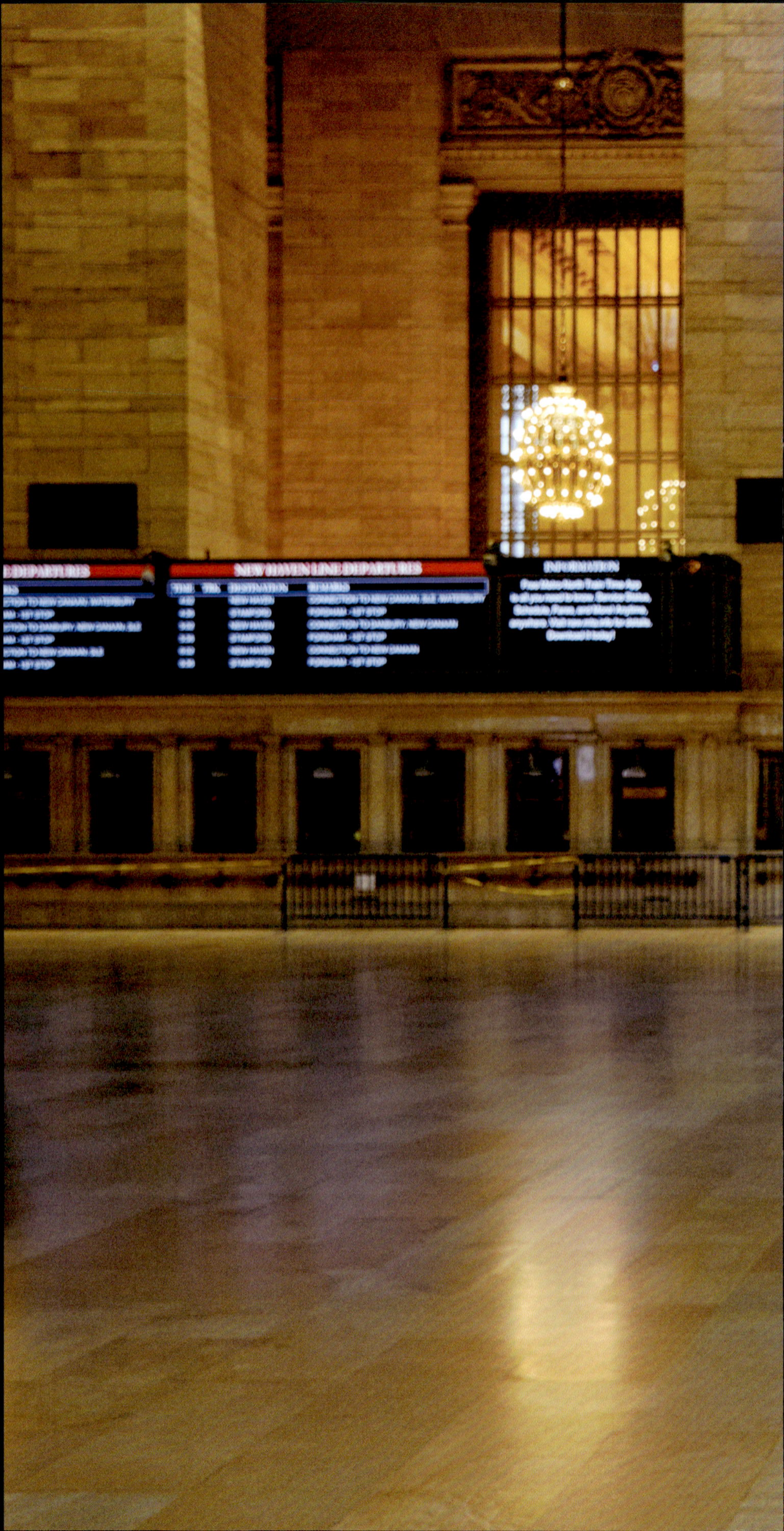

2020
New York

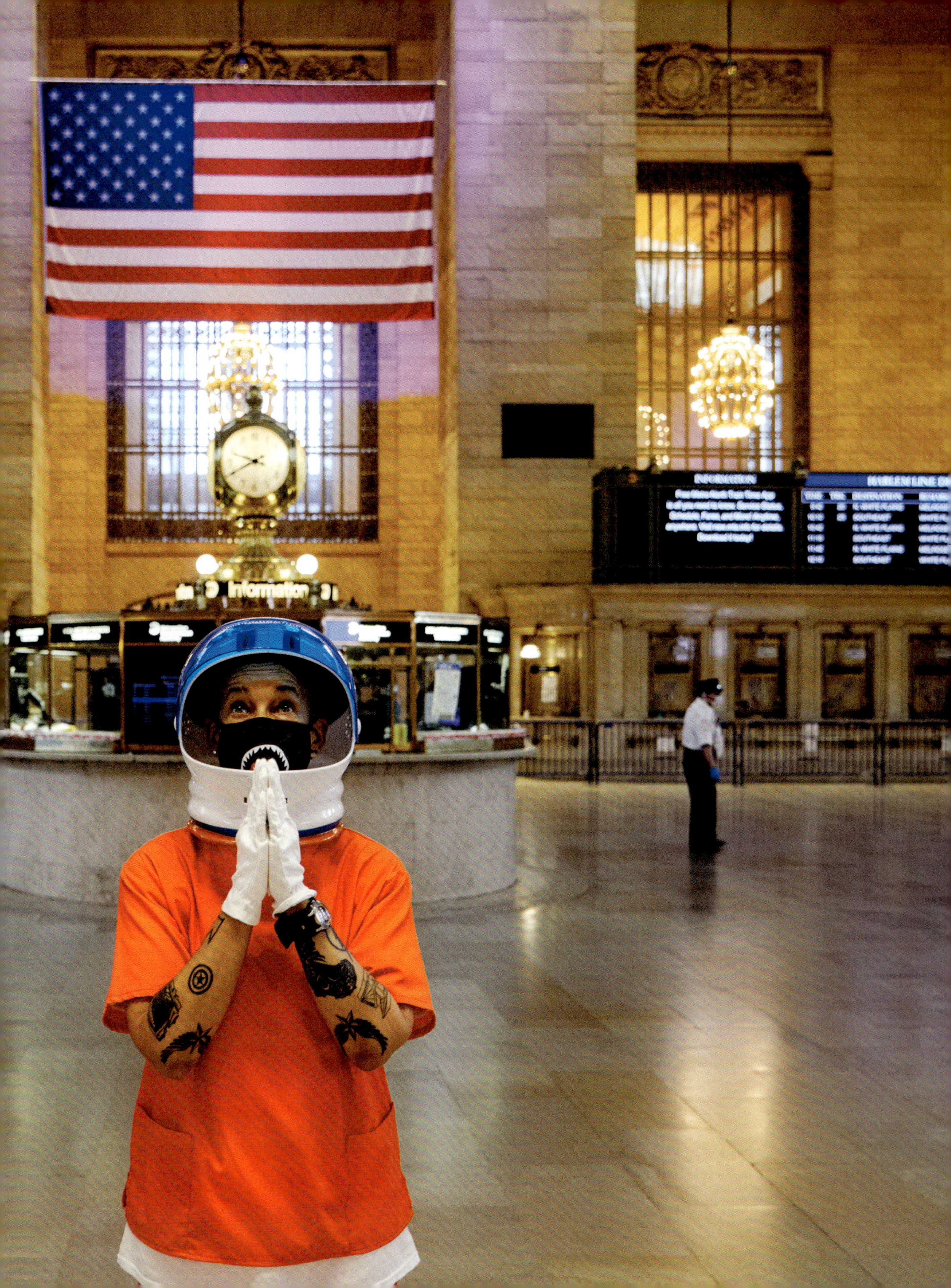
Information

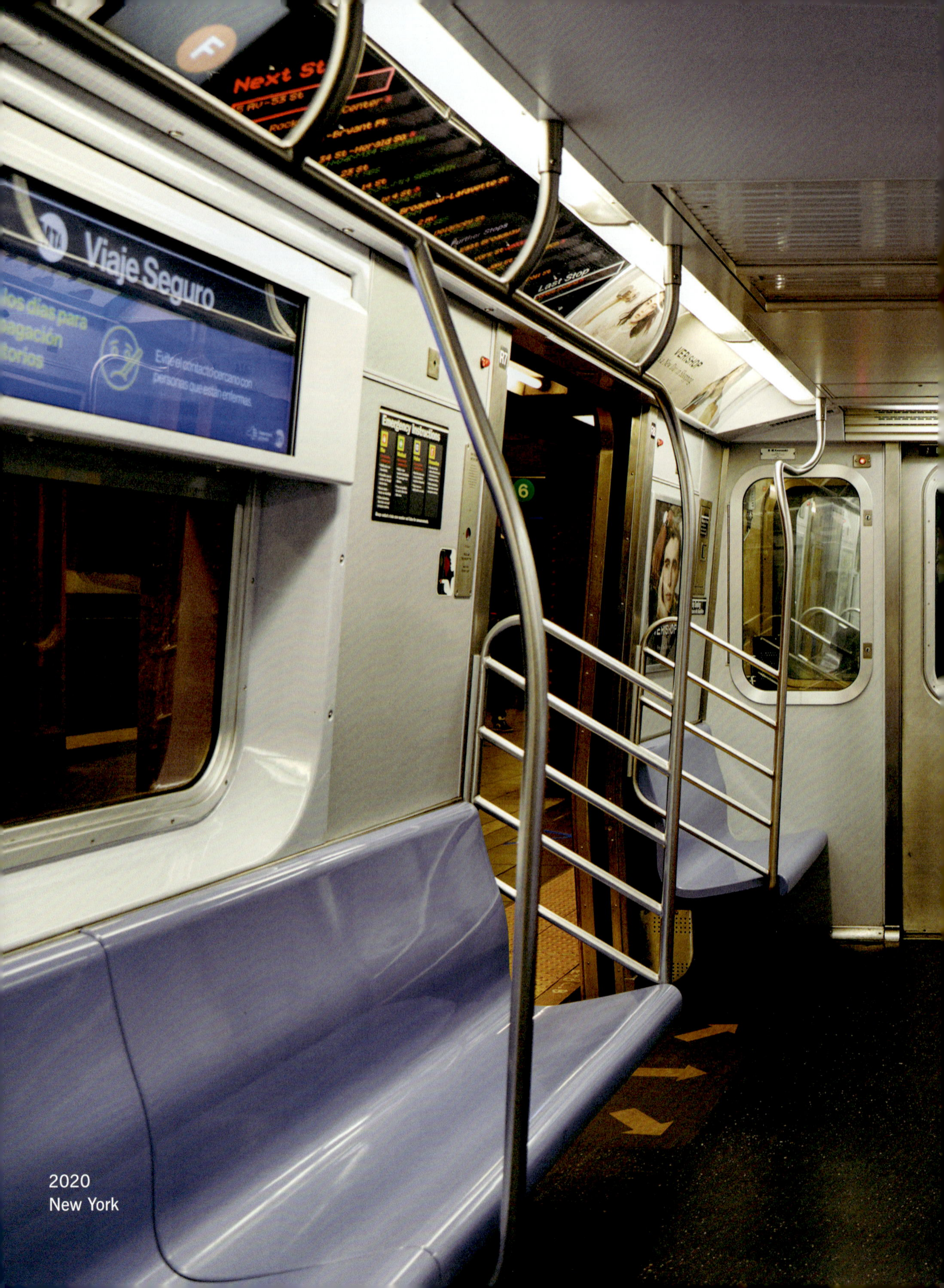

2020
New York

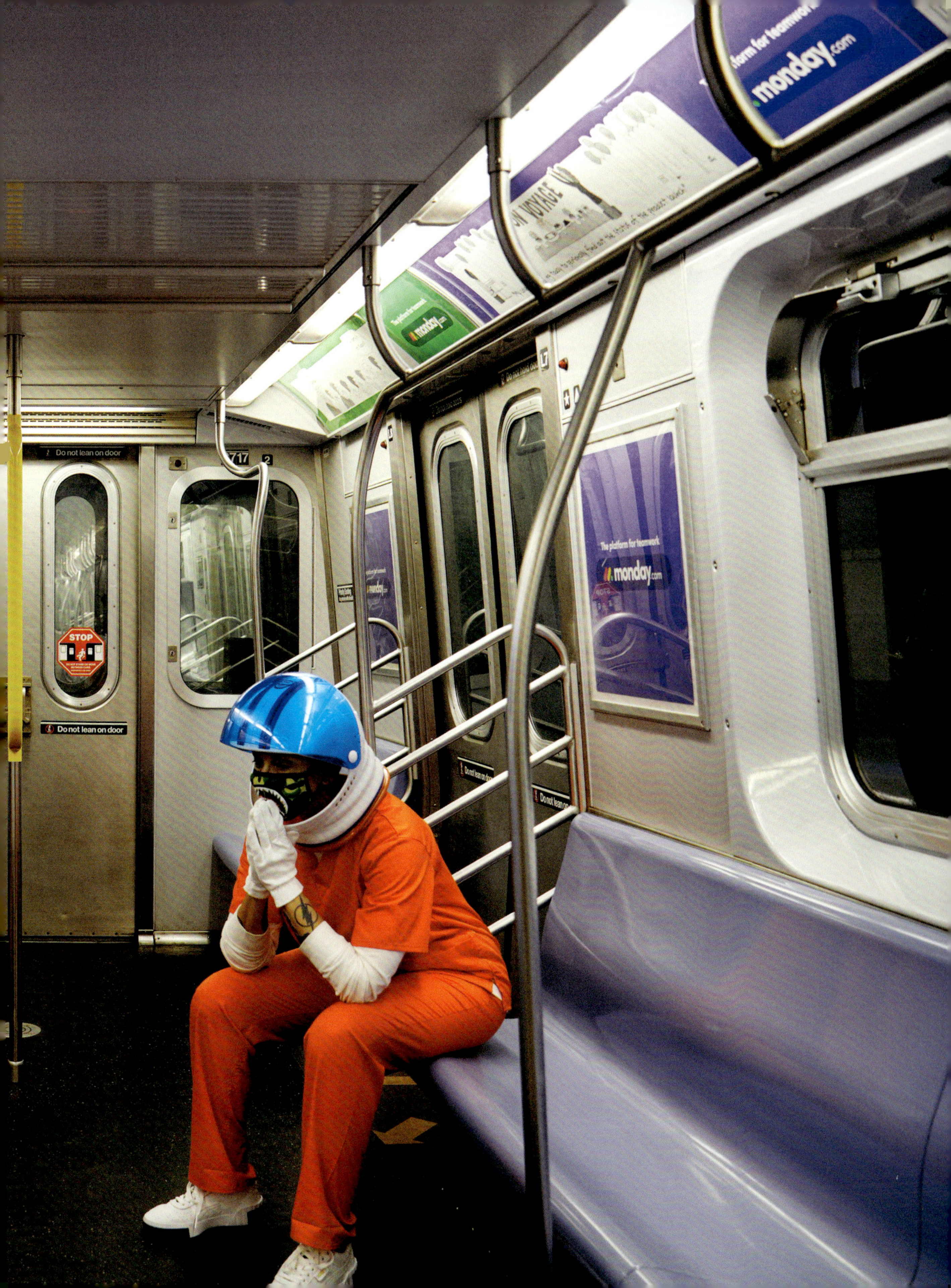
monday.com
The platform for teamwork
monday.com
Do not lean on door
STOP
Do not lean on door

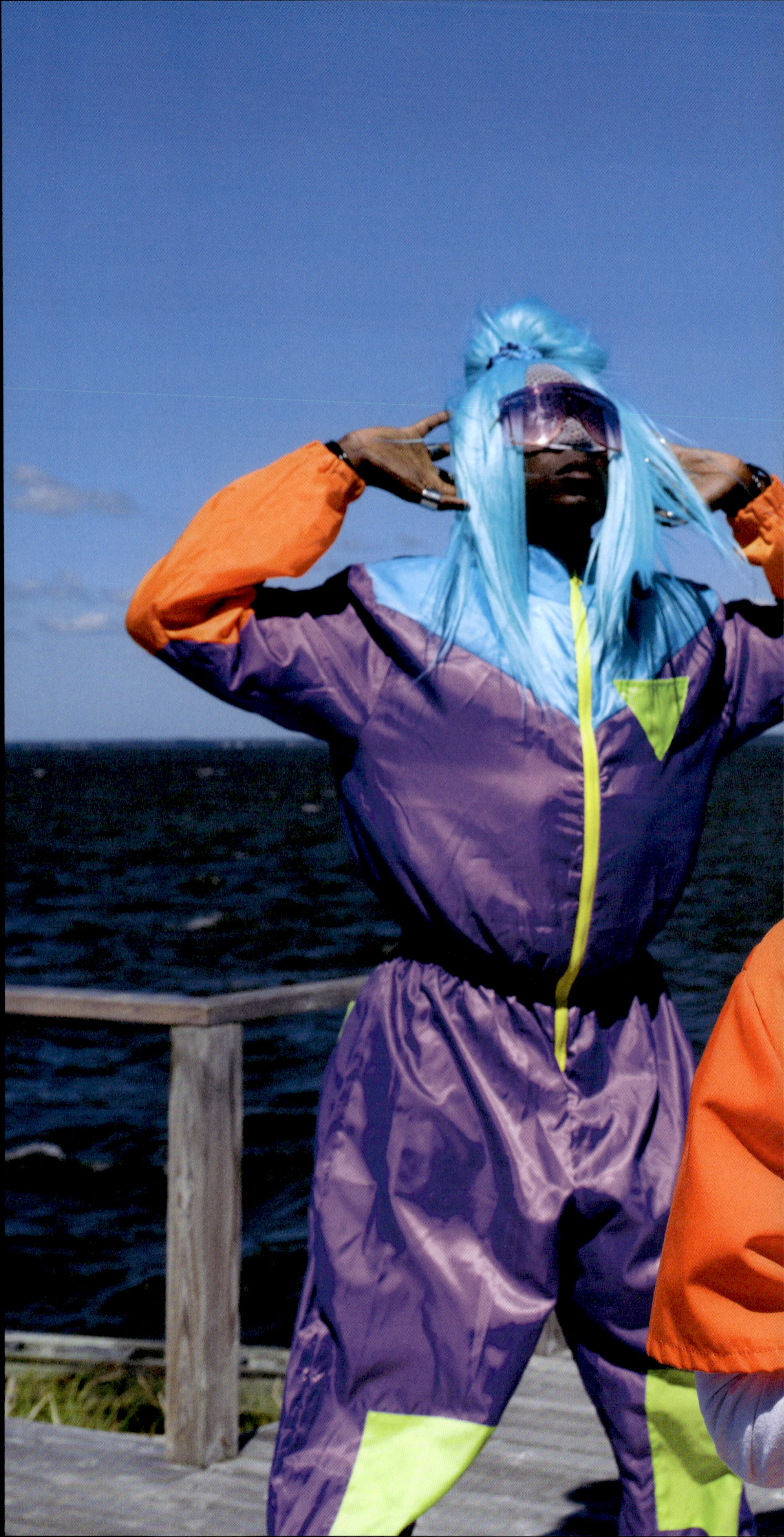

2021
Fire Island

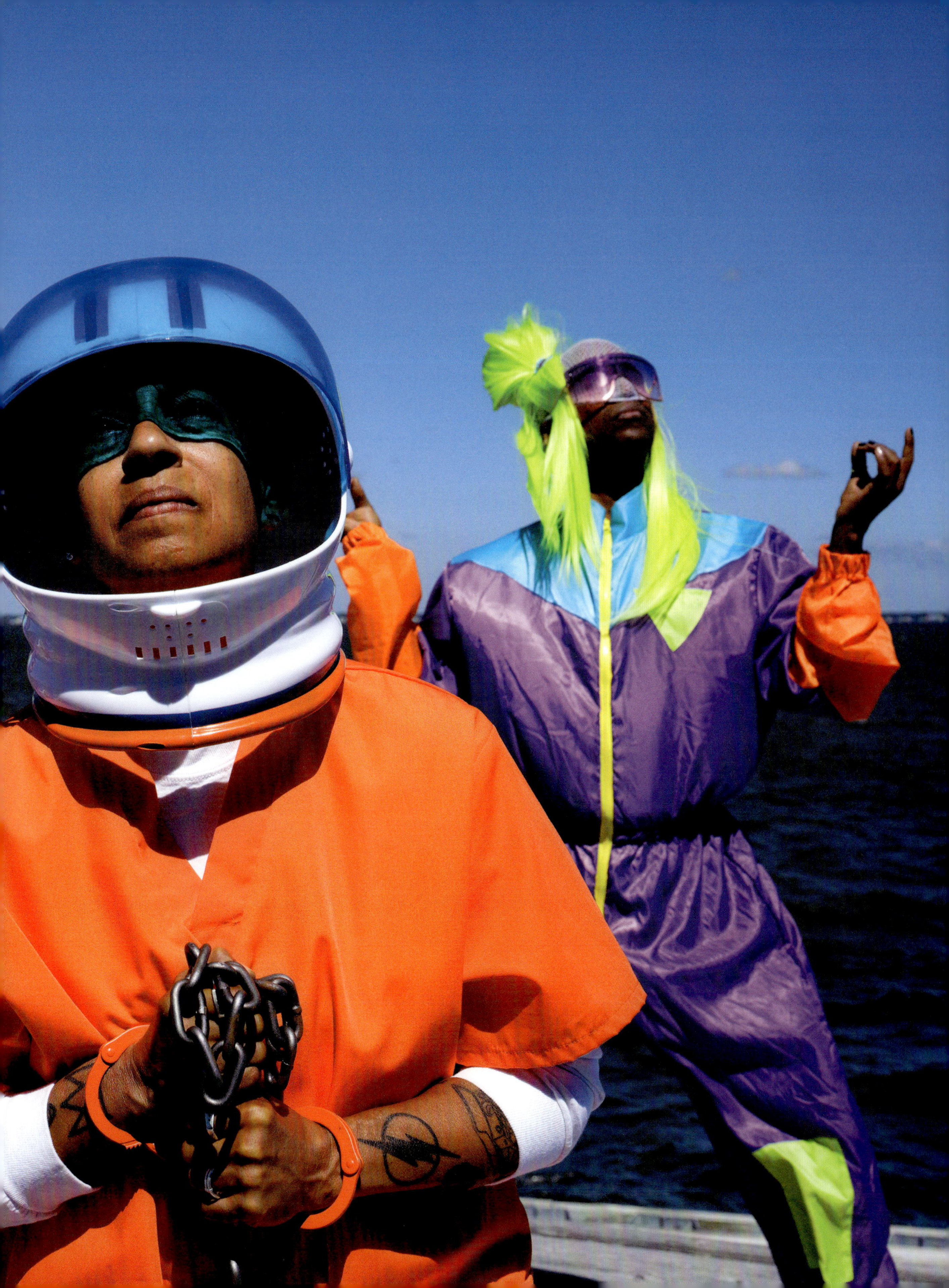

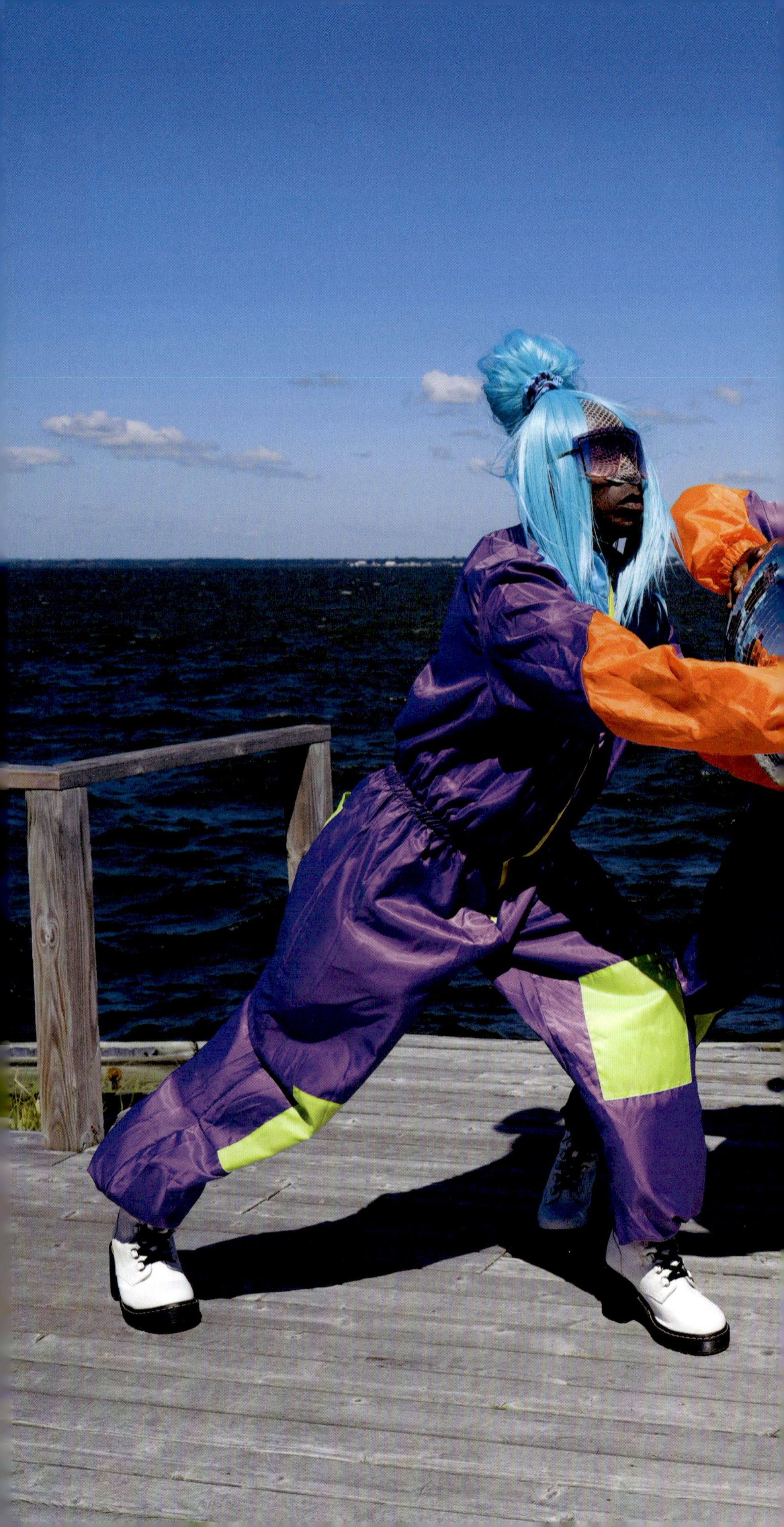

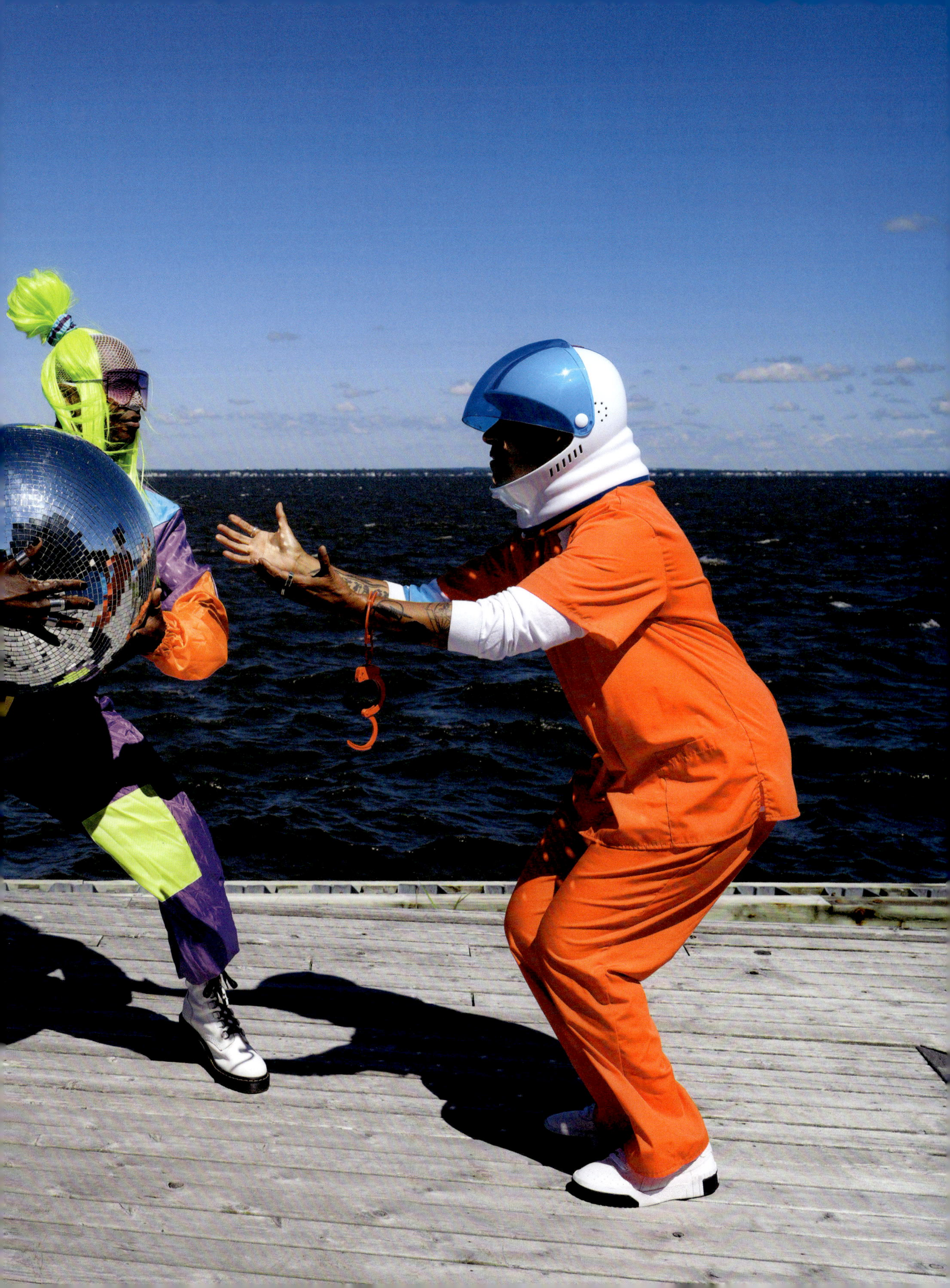

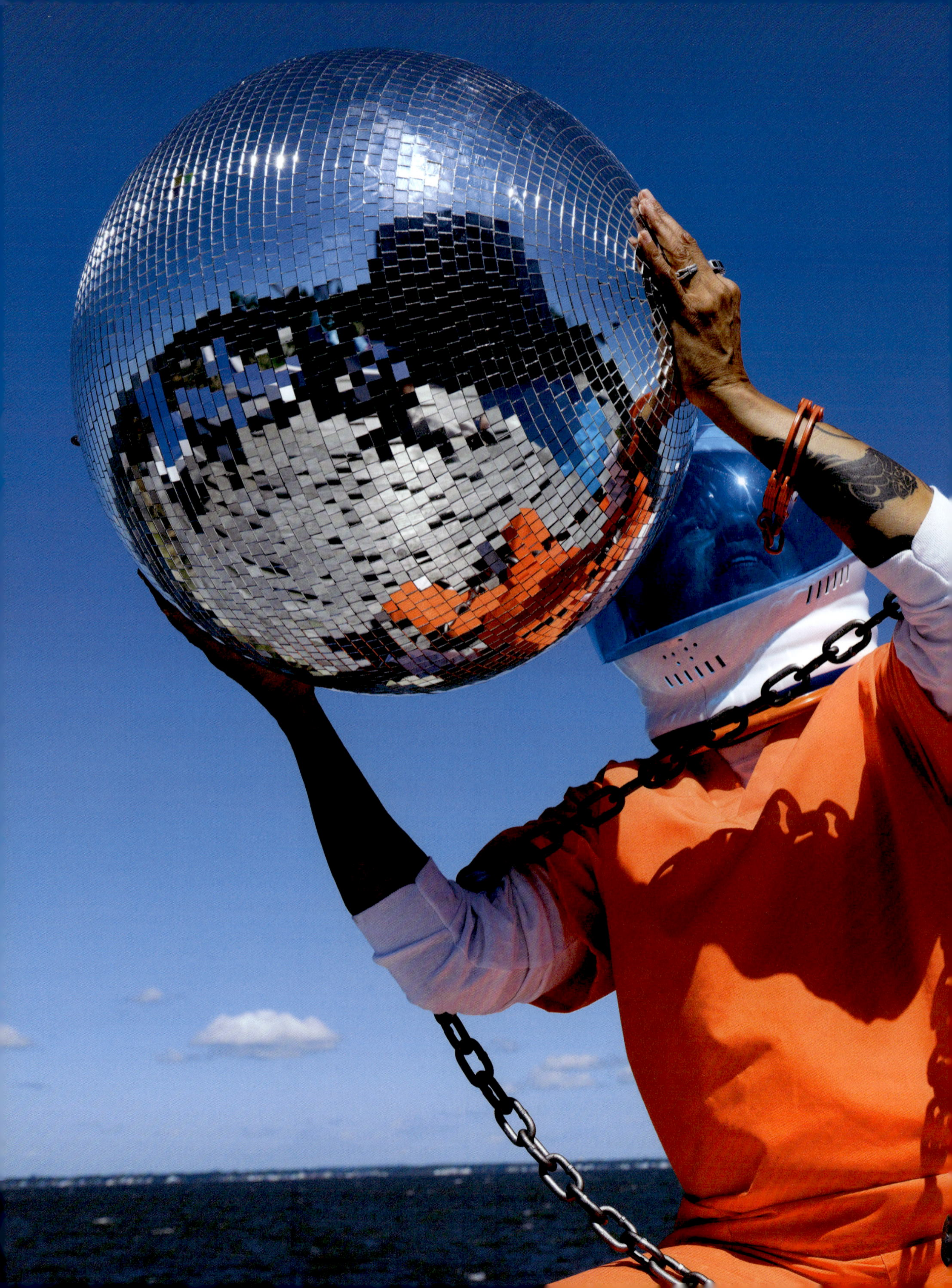

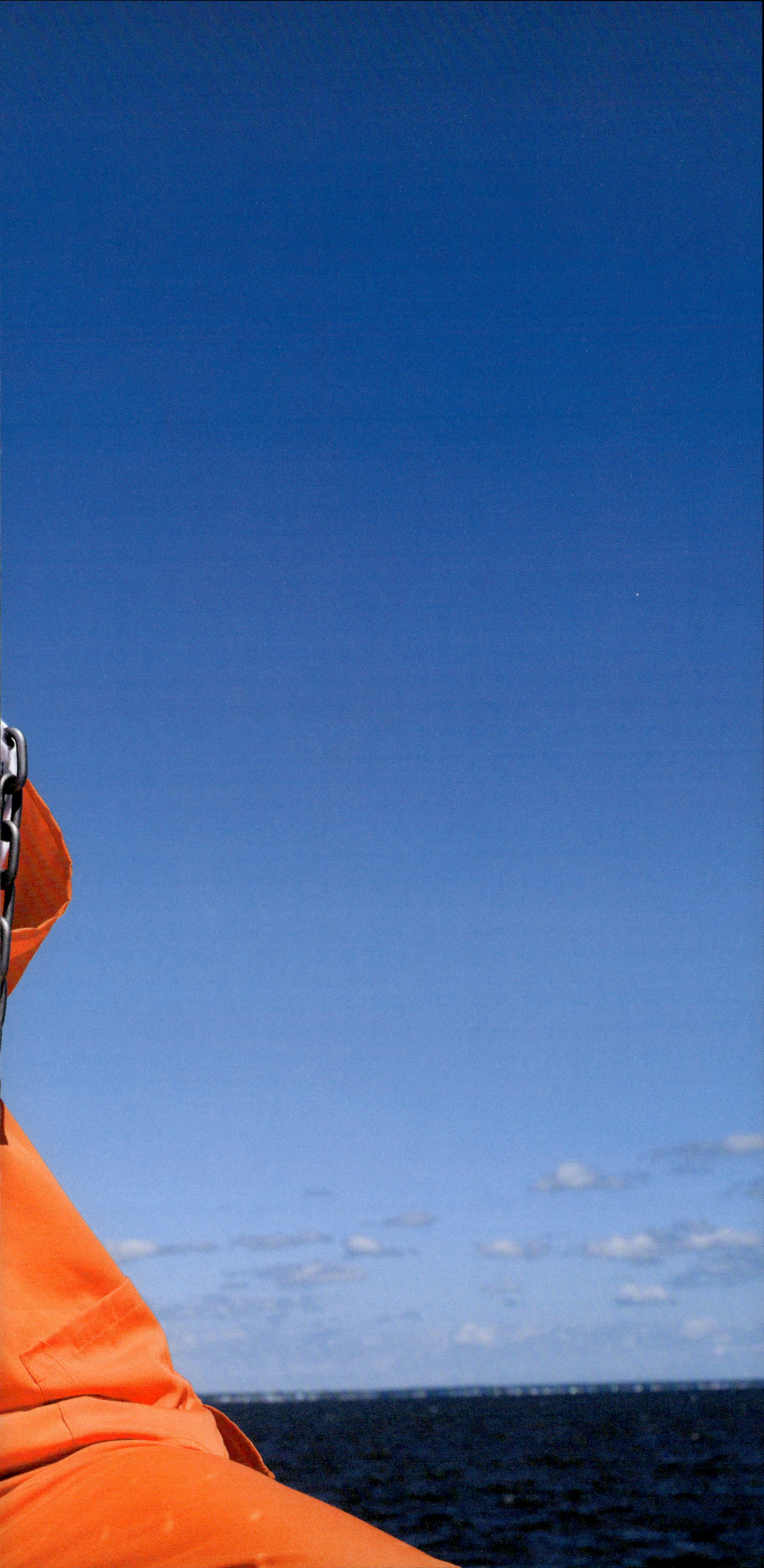

2021
Fire Island

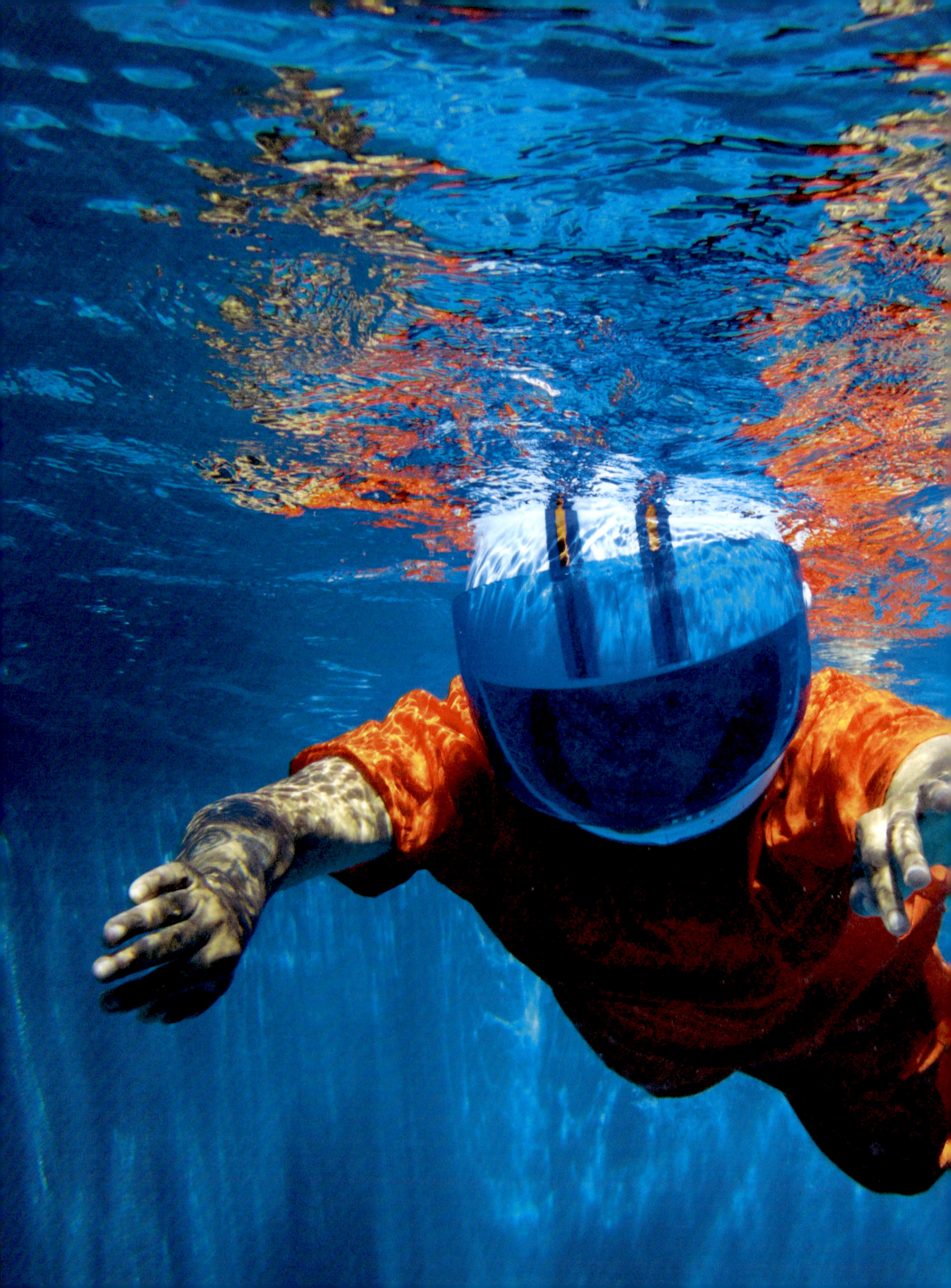

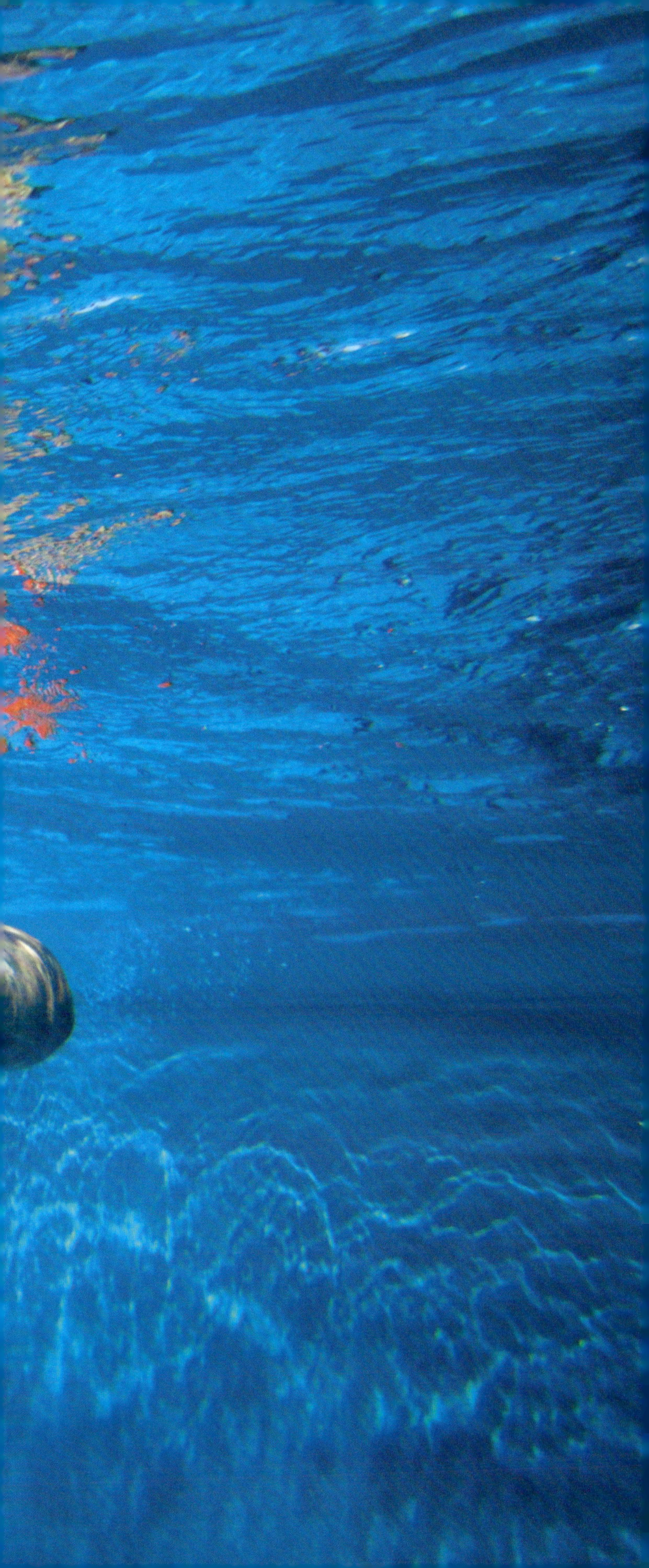

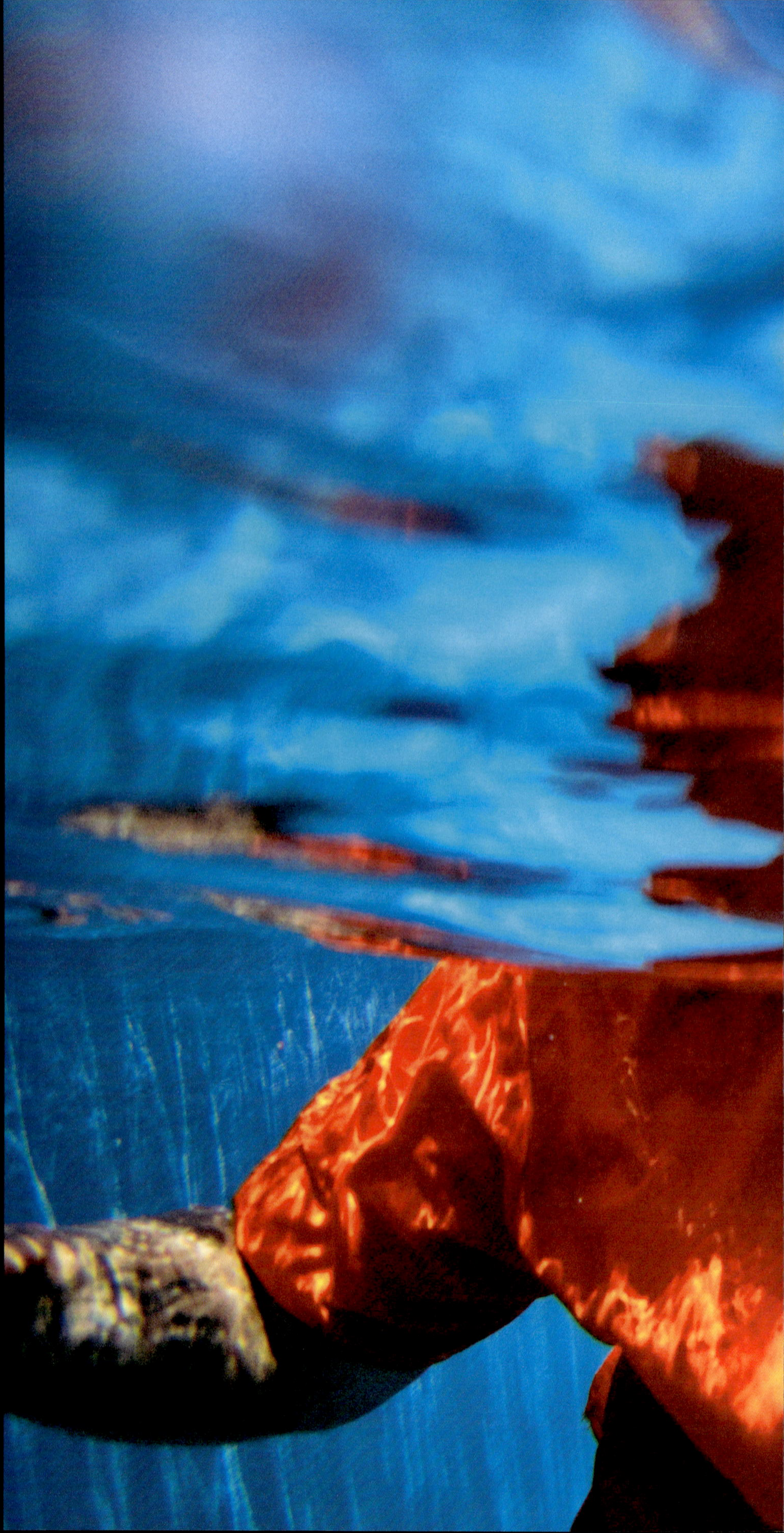

2021
Fire Island

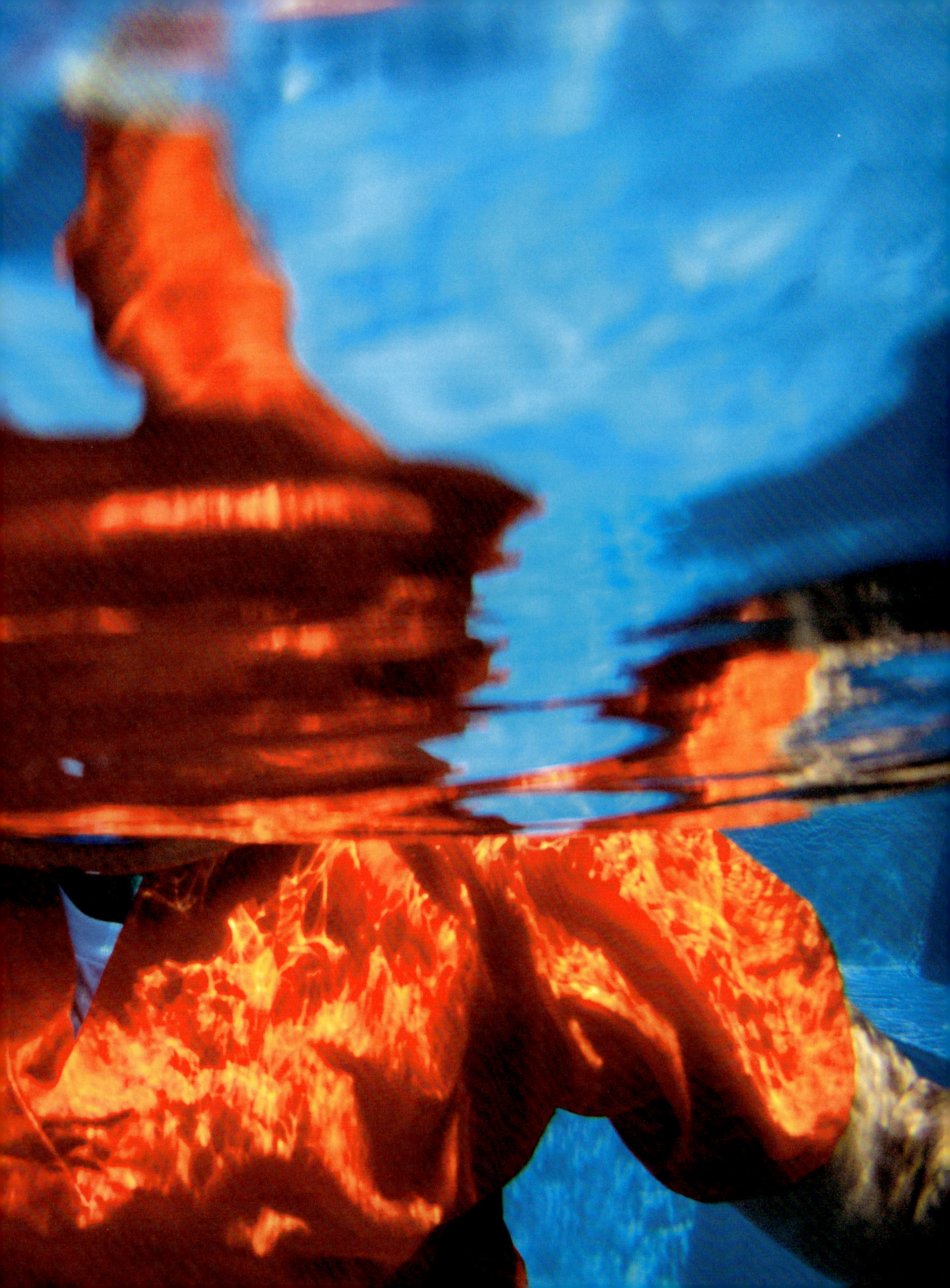

Acknowledgments

The photographs presented in this book were made possible by Jon Stryker: philanthropist, architect, and photography devotee.

This book was made possible in part by a grant from the arcus* FOUNDATION

We express our deepest gratitude to Jaishri Abichandani, Joan E. Biren, Jim Callahan, Clément Chéroux, Kate Conroy, Marty Correia, Parker Daley, Charles D. Dawson, Dawn Delikat, Sean and Barry Godfrey-Reives, Marcia Griffiths, Charles Guice, Aldo Hernandez, Afua Kafi-Akua, Soo Ok Kim, Lesly King-Hammond, Thomas (T) Lax, Bec Manson, Miriam Romais, Amy Sherald, Lowery Stokes, Halima Taha, Shawn Willson, and all the models.

I would like to thank my family and in addition to Jurek Wajdowicz, Lisa LaRochelle, Yoko Yoshida-Carrera, and everyone else at Emerson, Wajdowicz Studios for giving me this amazing opportunity.

Thank you Renée Mussai for the beautiful introduction for *Believable*. And thank you to Ben Woodward and everyone at The New Press for making this book a reality.

*The Arcus Foundation is a global foundation dedicated to the idea that people can live in harmony with one another and the natural world. The Foundation works to advance respect for diversity among peoples and in nature (www.ArcusFoundation.org).